International Political Economy Series

Series Editor: **Timothy M. Shaw**, Visiting Professor, University of Massachusetts Boston, USA and Emeritus Professor, University of London, UK

The global political economy is in flux as a series of cumulative crises impacts its organization and governance. The IPE series has tracked its development in both analysis and structure over the last three decades. It has always had a concentration on the global South. Now the South increasingly challenges the North as the centre of development, also reflected in a growing number of submissions and publications on indebted Eurozone economies in Southern Europe.

An indispensable resource for scholars and researchers, the series examines a variety of capitalisms and connections by focusing on emerging economies, companies and sectors, debates and policies. It informs diverse policy communities as the established trans-Atlantic North declines and 'the rest', especially the BRICS, rise.

Titles include:

Daniel Daianu, Carlo D'Adda, Giorgio Basevi and Rajeesh Kumar (*editors*)
THE EUROZONE CRISIS AND THE FUTURE OF EUROPE
The Political Economy of Further Integration and Governance

Karen E. Young
THE POLITICAL ECONOMY OF ENERGY, FINANCE AND SECURITY IN THE UNITED ARAB EMIRATES
Between the Majilis and the Market

Monique Taylor
THE CHINESE STATE, OIL AND ENERGY SECURITY

Benedicte Bull, Fulvio Castellacci and Yuri Kasahara
BUSINESS GROUPS AND TRANSNATIONAL CAPITALISM IN CENTRAL AMERICA
Economic and Political Strategies

Leila Simona Talani
THE ARAB SPRING IN THE GLOBAL POLITICAL ECONOMY

Andreas Nölke (*editor*)
MULTINATIONAL CORPORATIONS FROM EMERGING MARKETS
State Capitalism 3.0

Roshen Hendrickson
PROMOTING U.S. INVESTMENT IN SUB-SAHARAN AFRICA

Bhumitra Chakma
SOUTH ASIA IN TRANSITION
Democracy, Political Economy and Security

Greig Charnock, Thomas Purcell and Ramon Ribera-Fumaz
THE LIMITS TO CAPITAL IN SPAIN
Crisis and Revolt in the European South

Felipe Amin Filomeno
MONSANTO AND INTELLECTUAL PROPERTY IN SOUTH AMERICA

Eirikur Bergmann
ICELAND AND THE INTERNATIONAL FINANCIAL CRISIS
Boom, Bust and Recovery

Yildiz Atasoy (*editor*)
GLOBAL ECONOMIC CRISIS AND THE POLITICS OF DIVERSITY

Gabriel Siles-Brügge
CONSTRUCTING EUROPEAN UNION TRADE POLICY
A Global Idea of Europe

Jewellord Singh and France Bourgouin (*editors*)
RESOURCE GOVERNANCE AND DEVELOPMENTAL STATES IN THE GLOBAL SOUTH
Critical International Political Economy Perspectives

Tan Tai Yong and Md Mizanur Rahman (*editors*)
DIASPORA ENGAGEMENT AND DEVELOPMENT IN SOUTH ASIA

Leila Simona Talani, Alexander Clarkson and Ramon Pachedo Pardo (*editors*)
DIRTY CITIES
Towards a Political Economy of the Underground in Global Cities

Matthew Louis Bishop
THE POLITICAL ECONOMY OF CARIBBEAN DEVELOPMENT

Xiaoming Huang (*editor*)
MODERN ECONOMIC DEVELOPMENT IN JAPAN AND CHINA
Developmentalism, Capitalism and the World Economic System

Bonnie K. Campbell (*editor*)
MODES OF GOVERNANCE AND REVENUE FLOWS IN AFRICAN MINING

Gopinath Pillai (*editor*)
THE POLITICAL ECONOMY OF SOUTH ASIAN DIASPORA
Patterns of Socio-Economic Influence

Rachel K. Brickner (*editor*)
MIGRATION, GLOBALIZATION AND THE STATE

Juanita Elias and Samanthi Gunawardana (*editors*)
THE GLOBAL POLITICAL ECONOMY OF THE HOUSEHOLD IN ASIA

International Political Economy Series
Series Standing Order ISBN 978–0–333–71708–0 hardcover
Series Standing Order ISBN 978–0–333–71110–1 paperback

You can receive future titles in this series as they are published by placing a standing order. Please contact your bookseller or, in case of difficulty, write to us at the address below with your name and address, the title of the series and one of the ISBNs quoted above.

Customer Services Department, Macmillan Distribution Ltd, Houndmills, Basingstoke, Hampshire RG21 6XS, England

Multinational Corporations from Emerging Markets
State Capitalism 3.0

Edited by

Andreas Nölke
Professor of International Relations and International Political Economy, Goethe University, Frankfurt, Germany

Editorial matter, selection, introduction and conclusion © Andreas Nölke 2014
Individual chapters © Respective authors 2014
Foreword © Louis Brennan 2014

All rights reserved. No reproduction, copy or transmission of this publication may be made without written permission.

No portion of this publication may be reproduced, copied or transmitted save with written permission or in accordance with the provisions of the Copyright, Designs and Patents Act 1988, or under the terms of any licence permitting limited copying issued by the Copyright Licensing Agency, Saffron House, 6–10 Kirby Street, London EC1N 8TS.

Any person who does any unauthorized act in relation to this publication may be liable to criminal prosecution and civil claims for damages.

The authors have asserted their rights to be identified as the authors of this work in accordance with the Copyright, Designs and Patents Act 1988.

First published 2014 by
PALGRAVE MACMILLAN

Palgrave Macmillan in the UK is an imprint of Macmillan Publishers Limited, registered in England, company number 785998, of Houndmills, Basingstoke, Hampshire RG21 6XS.

Palgrave Macmillan in the US is a division of St Martin's Press LLC, 175 Fifth Avenue, New York, NY 10010.

Palgrave Macmillan is the global academic imprint of the above companies and has companies and representatives throughout the world.

Palgrave® and Macmillan® are registered trademarks in the United States, the United Kingdom, Europe and other countries

ISBN: 978–1–137–35949–0

This book is printed on paper suitable for recycling and made from fully managed and sustained forest sources. Logging, pulping and manufacturing processes are expected to conform to the environmental regulations of the country of origin.

A catalogue record for this book is available from the British Library.

A catalog record for this book is available from the Library of Congress.

Für Andrea

Contents

List of Illustrations	ix
Foreword by Louis Brennan	xi
Acknowledgments	xiii
Notes on Contributors	xv
List of Abbreviations	xvii

Introduction: Toward State Capitalism 3.0   1
Andreas Nölke

Part I   General Perspectives

1 (Multi?)national Corporations and the State in Established Economies   15
 John Mikler

2 Multinationals as an Instrument of Catch-up Industrialization: Understanding the Strategic Links between State and Industry in Emerging Markets   31
 Terutomo Ozawa

Part II   Country Studies

3 South Korean Multinationals after the Asian Financial Crisis: Toward Liberal Capitalism?   55
 Seung-il Jeong

4 Private Chinese Multinationals and the Long Shadow of the State   77
 Andreas Nölke

5 Russia's Multinationals: Network State Capitalism Goes Global   90
 Jonas Grätz

6 Sector Creation and Evolution: The Role of the State in Shaping the Rise of the Indian Pharmaceutical Sectoral Business System   109
 Heather L. Taylor

7 Financing the Expansion of Brazilian Multinationals into Europe: The Role of the Brazilian Development Bank (BNDES)   130
 Gilmar Masiero, Mario H. Ogasavara, Luiz Caseiro and Silas Ferreira

Part III International Institutions

8 How Policies Shape Foreign Direct Investment from
  Latin America to the European Union   155
  Judith Clifton, Daniel Diaz-Fuentes and Julio Revuelta

9 The Action-Reaction in the Global Trade: Comparing the
  Cases of the Brazilian Chicken and the Thai Tuna Industries 169
  Suthikorn Kingkaew

Conclusion: State Support for Emerging Market Multinationals   187
Andreas Nölke

Bibliography   199

Index   227

List of Illustrations

Figures

2.1	Stages of industrialization, state involvement, and homegrown MNCs in emerging economies: Generalized patterns and characteristics	46
3.1	Comparison of ratio of R&D to sales among chaebol groups, 1994–2006 (%)	67
4.1	FDI inward stock of GDP, 2011 (%)	80
7.1	Brazilian OFDI, annual average flows per historical period, 1970–2010	134
7.2	Brazilian OFDI stocks in selected regions, 2004–2010	142
8.1	FDI restrictiveness index, selected countries, 1997–2010	161

Tables

1.1	The nationality of corporations in the Fortune Global 500	17
1.2	LMEs versus CMEs	23
1.3	Measures of state intervention in corporate affairs, 1998, 2003, and 2008	27
3.1	Rates of net household saving, 1987–2011 (%)	61
3.2	Ratio of aggregate facility investment to GDP, 1990–2012 (%)	64
5.1	State instruments to support Russian MNCs	98
5.2	Largest Russian multinationals US$ million, 2011	100
6.1	Key policy implications, 1970–2005	119
7.1	BNDES participation in the ownership of BMNs (%)	139
7.2	Acquisitions by BMNs, 2007–2010	144
7.3	The internationalization of BMNs in Europe and BNDES support	146
8.1	Latin American FDI stock in the EU	164
8.2	EU IFDI stock regression analysis for selected control variables and FDI restrictions, 1997–2010	166
9.1	Import tariffs of major markets for chicken products	172

9.2	Import tariffs of major markets for tuna and canned tuna products	173
9.3	A global and local overview of the chicken and canned tuna industries	185
9.4	The different paths in becoming the largest exporters in chicken and canned tuna	186

Foreword

This book is to be welcomed as an important contribution to aiding our understanding of the growing phenomenon of emerging markets multinationals. In focusing on the role of the state in the development of such multinationals, the book offers a hitherto relatively unexplored perspective that greatly enhances our knowledge of this phenomenon.

The motivation of the volume is based on the premise that differences in the institutional and political backgrounds of the countries of origin of these multinationals relative to the established advanced economies can have an important influence on their transnational activities. Scholarly inquiry into these multinationals in cognate areas such as international business and political economy has not sufficiently taken account of these differences and their implications for this phenomenon.

The book is to be especially welcomed as it relies on the integration of approaches within a political economy perspective from economics, international business, and political economy – approaches that have traditionally operated within their disciplinary silos. In my own work on attempting to model the diverse and disjointed European responses to emerging markets multinationals, political economy colleagues have observed that my categorizing of such responses can be viewed as very aligned to the varieties of capitalism approach, thus demonstrating the intrinsic linkages between international business and political economy in addressing this phenomenon (Brennan 2013). The research presented in this volume recognizes that business, economic, and political systems are in reality deeply connected and hence should not be studied in separate domains.

This integration ensures a holistic understanding of the phenomenon of interest and also enables insights that reflect, and deepen our understanding of, the true machinations that help explain its development. As such the scholarly work presented in the book is a very worthy response to my earlier call for multidisciplinary inquiry into this phenomenon (Brennan 2011). The value of such an approach as so clearly demonstrated in this book should encourage colleagues to engage in similar forms of inquiry not only into this phenomenon but into the many challenges facing our deeply interconnected, highly integrated, and hence greatly interdependent world.

The implications of the major finding from the volume that emerging markets' governments support the expansion of 'their' multinationals in very comprehensive and important ways are many, not least for the established economies and international institutions. For Europe, it emphasizes the need for a common coordinated approach to the emergence of this phenomenon in the global economy. It also raises questions about the seemingly inwardly focused nature of competition policy in the European Union insofar as it relates to its 'own' multinationals. Rather than viewing competition considerations on a solely intra-European basis, competition policy in the EU needs to be informed by the realities of state capitalism 3.0 and of interregional competition, and to set policies accordingly that minimally do not hinder the performance of 'their' multinationals.

As chair of COST Action IS 0905 on the 'Emergence of Southern Multinationals and their Impact on Europe', I congratulate Andreas Nölke and the contributors to this fine volume on an outstanding piece of scholarship based on their integration of different disciplinary domains and on their invaluable contributions to our understanding of the development of emerging markets multinationals.

Louis Brennan
Trinity College Dublin

Acknowledgments

This book has been inspired and supported by the COST Action on 'The Emergence of Southern Multinationals and their Impact on Europe' (IS0905). I am very grateful to the Action and particularly its leader, Louis Brennan (Trinity College Dublin), for both intellectual and material assistance to this volume. Some of the papers for this volume were presented at a conference on 'The Role of Large Emerging Countries in the World Economy: Threats and Opportunities for European Firms?' in June 2012 at the University of Parma, sponsored by the COST Action. My thanks are due to Lucia Piscitello (Politecnico di Milano) and the other local organizers.

This volume is published in association with a sister edition, a special issue on 'Brazilian Corporations, the State and Transnational Activity' of the journal *Critical Perspectives on International Business* (Vol. 10, No. 4, 2014). The special issue follows a similar line of reasoning as this volume, but conducts an in-depth study of multinationals within a specific country, that is, Brazil. I am much obliged to the journal editors, Christoph Dörrenbächer and Joanne Roberts, and to the authors of this special issue, for highly valuable suggestions.

The idea for the specific theme of the volume, that is, state capitalism 3.0, stems from a research project on 'A "BICS" Variety of Capitalism: The Emergence of State-Permeated Market Economies in Large Emerging Countries' that is being funded by the German Research Foundation (GZ NO 855/3–1). I am deeply indebted to my associates in this project, Simone Claar, Christian May and Tobias ten Brink, for many highly inspiring discussions on the nature of state-permeated capitalism in large emerging markets. A special thank you is due to Tobias for jointly coining the term 'state capitalism 3.0', also used for our recent special issue of the German journal *Der Moderne Staat*. Very useful research assistance has been provided by Sabine Englert and Hauke Feil.

The book has also benefited from the support of our project on 'Parastatal Companies and Capitalist Development: The Interaction of South African and Chinese Enterprises in the Services Sector', funded by the German Federal Ministry of Education and Research in the context of the program on 'Africa's Asian Options' (AFRASO) at Goethe University. I am grateful to my collaborators in this project, Simone Claar, Nikolas Galbenis (both Goethe University), Boy Lüthje (Institute for Social

Research, Frankfurt), Daouda Cisse and Sven Grimm (both University of Stellenbosch), for highly useful input.

However, for all the material and ideational support provided by the various projects, the core contributions still stem from the authors of the subsequent chapters. I am very grateful to all the contributors for their very competent work and smooth cooperation. It was a real pleasure to be working with this global and multidisciplinary team. I am particularly indebted to Heather Taylor, who has helped me in shaping my thinking on multinational corporations from emerging markets since 2007.

Still, for all the excellent cooperation by the authors, the gestation of the book would have taken much longer (and the final version been much inferior), were it not for the excellent assistance by Johannes Petry. Johannes has supported me throughout the whole editing process in a most diligent and reliable manner. I am very grateful for the competent and patient language support by Jack Copley. My appreciation also goes to Paulina Nowak for relentless research assistance and to Brigitte Holden for her helpful secretarial support.

I should also mention that I would not have thought of editing this book without the suggestion by the Series Editor, Tim Shaw. I am very grateful to Tim and to Christina Brian at Palgrave, for all of their encouragement, and to Amanda McGrath and Ambra Finotello, for the competent cooperation throughout the publication process. Two anonymous reviewers have provided very helpful suggestions for improving the manuscript.

Last, but certainly not least, my gratitude goes to my family, Andrea, Antonia, and Anouk. You have suffered a lot from my (intellectual) absence throughout the production of this book. I am dedicating this book to Andrea, for all her unwavering support during the last 22 years.

Notes on Contributors

Louis Brennan is Professor of Business in the School of Business and Director of the Institute for International Integration Studies at Trinity College Dublin, Ireland.

Luiz Caseiro is Researcher at ProÁsia – Programa de Estudos Asiáticos, University of São Paulo, Brazil.

Judith Clifton is Professor of Economic Policy at the University of Cantabria, Santander, Spain, and Head Editor of *the Journal of Economic Policy Reform*.

Daniel Díaz-Fuentes is Professor of Economics at the University of Cantabria, Santander, Spain, and Secretary General of the World Economy Society.

Silas Ferreira Junior is a doctoral candidate at the Polytechnic School of the University of São Paulo, Brazil.

Jonas Grätz is a researcher at the Center for Security Studies at ETH Zurich, Switzerland.

Seungil Jeong is Lecturer of Economics at Kookmin University, Seoul, South Korea.

Suthikorn Kingkaew is Lecturer in International Business at Thammasat Business School, Bangkok, Thailand.

Gilmar Masiero is Professor of International Business at the University of São Paulo, Brazil.

John Mikler is Senior Lecturer in the Department of Government and International Relations at the University of Sydney, Australia.

Andreas Nölke is Professor of Political Science at Goethe University, Frankfurt am Main, Germany.

Mario H. Ogasavara is Professor of International Business at ESPM – Escola Superior de Propaganda e Marketing, São Paulo, Brazil.

Terutomo Ozawa is Professor Emeritus of Economics at Colorado State University and Research Associate at the Center on Japanese Economy and Business in the Graduate School of Business at Columbia University, United States.

Julio Revuelta is an assistant lecturer in Applied Economics at the University of Cantabria, Santander, Spain.

Heather L. Taylor is a research consultant and a PhD candidate specializing in International Political Economy at Goethe University, Frankfurt am Main, Germany.

List of Abbreviations

AMAD	Agricultural Market Access Database
APIs	Active Pharmaceutical Ingredients
BCG	Boston Consulting Group
BMN	Brazilian Multinationals
BNDES	Brazilian National Development Bank
BRIC	Brazil, Russia, India, China
CAP	Common Agricultural Policy
CEO	Chief Executive Officer
CIS	Commonwealth of Independent States
CME	Coordinated Market Economy
DME	Dependent Market Economies
ECLAC	United Nations Economic Commission for Latin America and the Caribbean
EU	European Union
EUROTHON	European Tropical Tuna Trade and Industry Committee
FDA	Food and Drug Administration
FDC	Fundação Dom Cabral
FDI	Foreign Direct Investment
FTA	Free Trade Agreement
GATS	General Agreement on Trade in Services
GATT	General Agreement on Trade and Tariff
GDP	Gross National Product
GRU	Glavnoye Razvedyvatel'noye Upravleniye (Russian Military Foreign Intelligence Service)
GT	Green Technology
IFDI	Inward Foreign Direct Investment
IMF	International Monetary Fund
IMNC	Indian Multinational Corporation
IPRs	Intellectual Property Rights
IT	Information Technology
LLL	Linkage, Leverage, and Learning
LME	Liberal Market Economy
M&As	Mergers and Acquisitions
MERCOSUR	Mercado Común del Sur/Southern Common Market
MITI	Japanese Ministry of International Trade and Industry
MNC	Multinational Corporation

NAFTA	North American Free Trade Agreement
NBS	National Business System
NCEs	New Chemical Entities
NGO	Nongovernmental Organization
NIE	Newly Industrialized Economy
OECD	Organization for Economic Cooperation and Development
OFDI	Outward Foreign Direct Investment
OIE	World Organization for Animal Health
OLI	Ownership, Location, Internalization
OPEC	Organization of the Petroleum Exporting Countries
R&D	Research and Development
SASAC	Assets Supervision and Administration Commission of the State Council
SME	Small and Medium-Sized Enterprises
SOE	state-owned enterprise
SVR	Sluzhba Vneshney Razvedki (Russian Foreign Intelligence Service)
SWF	Sovereign Wealth Fund
TNI	Transnationality Index
TRIMS	Trade-Related Investment Measures
TRIPS	Trade in Intellectual Property Rights
UNCTAD	United Nations Conference on Trade and Development
USDA	United States Department of Agriculture
USSR	Union of Soviet Socialist Republics
VEB	Vneshekonombank
VER	Voluntary Export Restraint
VoC	Varieties of Capitalism
WEF	World Economic Forum
WTO	World Trade Organization
WW2	World War Two

Introduction: Toward State Capitalism 3.0

Andreas Nölke

1 The rise of emerging markets multinationals

The rise of multinational corporations (MNCs) from emerging markets has been a major development during the last decade. Publications such as the United Nations Conference on Trade and Development (UNCTAD) Global Investment Report, the Fortune Global 500, and the FT Global 500 indicate the increasing share of these companies among the world's largest multinationals. This development not only relates to the BRICs (Brazil, Russia, India, and China; e.g., Petrobras, Gazprom, Tata, Sinopec) but also comprises companies from countries such as South Korea and Thailand (e.g., Samsung, PTT). Explaining the rather sudden rise of these companies has become somewhat of a growing industry over the last years (Brennan, 2011; Sauvant et al., 2010). Various international business scholars have developed or modified long-established analytical instruments in order to account for the rise of these companies. Theories such as the eclectic paradigm (Dunning, 1986) or the product cycle model (Wells, 1983) have been extended in order to account for the rise of these companies while others such as the Linking, Leverage, Learning-approach (Mathews, 2002b; 2006a) have been proposed to address this novel phenomenon.

However, most of these international business approaches do not fully take into account the fact that the institutional and political background in these companies' home states is quite different from that within most developed countries, and that this background may be very important for understanding the transnational activity of these corporations (Goldstein, 2007; Ramamurti and Singh, 2009; Ren et al., 2010). Moreover, the typical international business focus on internationalization motives and entry strategies neglects important issues, such as increasing tensions between established and emerging markets governments regarding takeover activities initiated by emerging market multinationals (Jiang, 2010; Jost, 2012). Similarly, literature in international political economy has only begun to address the implications of this specific MNC institutional background for the global economic order. The importance of MNCs in world politics, in particular of their relationships to host governments, was established many decades ago (Nye, 1974). Does the different institutional background of emerging market multinationals implicate new conflicts with host governments or even global business regulation (Nölke and Taylor, 2010; Nölke 2011b)?

This book is based on the assumption that a major feature of emerging market MNCs is their close relationship with their home states. To be sure, many Western MNCs cultivate close relationships with their home states as well (as, for instance, recently witnessed in the case of rescue operations for the financial sector), but this book investigates the special kind of relationship between the state and major corporations in countries outside of the (current) center of the world economy, as well as explores how this special relationship affects the cross-border activities of these corporations. In order to carry out this task, it opts for an integration of approaches traditionally kept separate because of the traditional disciplinary separation between international business and international political economy (cf. Konijn and van Tulder, forthcoming). This integration demonstrates that the development of emerging market multinationals heralds a 'rearticulation of the state-capital nexus' (van Apeldoorn et al., 2012), or, more simply, a new wave of state capitalism.

2 Three waves of state capitalism

Given the pertinence of a close relationship with the state, the recent rise of emerging market multinationals was named 'state capitalism' by an *Economist* special issue in 2012 (Wooldridge, 2012). This special issue is part of a broad popular debate on emerging markets' state capitalism that has been ongoing for a couple of years in the Western media, such as *TIME* (Schuman, 2011), *Businessweek* (Kurlantzick, 2013), Reuters (Bremmer, 2012), or the *Wall Street Journal* (Sharma, 2013). Usually, the term 'state capitalism' is meant in a pejorative way, but this is not necessarily appropriate (Rodrik, 2013). In any case, a more accurate label would be 'state capitalism 3.0' (ten Brink and Nölke, 2013), given that this is not only the third wave of state capitalism but also a distinct one, compared with the first two waves (and with some national variation, thereby making for 3.1, 3.2 etc.).

The first wave of state capitalism took place during the mid- to late 19th century and was associated with trade protectionism in countries such as the United States, Germany, parts of Scandinavia, and later Japan. Inspired by authors such as List (1841), the focus was on the development of domestic industry, in order to avoid colonization by the superior British economy. The main instruments of the first wave of state capitalism were tariffs, supported by the establishment of various infrastructures such as central banks. In the early 20th century, state capitalism went out of fashion, particularly during the liberal era of the 1920s.

The second wave of state capitalism designates the strongly increased role of the state in the economies of the United States, Europe, and the Soviet Union after the Great Depression, and also the rise of the East Asian developmental states after the Second World War. In contrast to the first wave of state capitalism, a much broader set of instruments was utilized, including most prominently a certain degree of central economic planning. State capitalism 2.0 took on various shapes, from the US New Deal, the Swedish model, fascism and Stalinism to the 1950s/1960s economic miracles in Japan and South Korea. In contrast to the first wave of state capitalism, state intervention was now far more comprehensive. It not only sought to protect domestic companies but also actively to steer business activity in various realms. As far as international regulation was concerned, national governments were allowed to pursue their national models, while agreeing to incremental trade liberalization ('embedded liberalism'). However, in spite of several decades of economic dynamism, the developmental state model lost its appeal during the 1980s and 1990s, also due to the rise of neoliberalism as propagated by the Reagan and Thatcher governments.

The third wave of state capitalism in countries such as China, India, or Brazil is again different, since emerging markets capitalism is neither based on prohibitive tariffs nor on one central command, but rather on a variety of formal and informal cooperative relationships between various public authorities and individual companies (ten Brink and Nölke, 2013, p. 26). East Asia provides for a particularly insightful empirical case regarding the juxtaposition of the second and third wave of state capitalism, given the proximity of the two waves both in time and in space: 'In short, China departs from the developmental state by embracing foreign competition and know-how, rather than protecting domestic private industry; pursuing sectoral reregulation based on a strategic value logic, rather than working closely with private industry to achieve national development goals; and privileging bureaucracies and state-owned companies over private actors when strategic assets are at stake' (Hsueh, 2011, p. 267; see also Ozawa in this volume). The strategic and selective use of both inward and outward foreign direct investment (FDI) for national economic development is a core pillar of this third wave. Correspondingly, this book will demonstrate that comprehensive state support is a major factor for explaining the emergence and behavior of emerging markets MNCs.

In a broader historical perspective, successful latecomers (such as Germany, Japan, South Korea, or China) have always initially protected their economies. However, this observation does not confirm a simple modernization theory. Depending on the timing of their integration into the global economic system, national socioeconomic systems may never completely converge on the model of the 'advanced' liberal model. Most importantly, we can observe a striking distinction between the economies of the liberal 'Lockean Heartland' comprising the white-majority English-speaking countries and the 'Hobbesian contender states', the latecomers of the industrialization process (van der Pijl, 1998). The latter tend toward a far more organized and coordinated version of capitalism (typically steered by banks, families, or the state), given the need to catch up with the advanced liberal economies (but to avoid colonization), as argued by observers such as List (1841) and Gerschenkron (1962). This finding is even more valid for the last round of successful latecomers – a striking aspect of the capitalist model developing in countries like Brazil, China, or India is a strong role for the state. Even if these (late-)latecomer economies will also be thoroughly affected by the liberalizing phases of global capitalism, they always remain more organized (or coordinated) than the United States.

In an even broader perspective, the evolution of different waves of state capitalism is linked to the timing of the insertion of a given economy into global capitalism. Latecomer economies always need a certain degree of catch-up process orchestrated by the state, in order not to be overwhelmed by those economies that are dominant within the world economy (Britain during the late 19th century, later the United States). The specific design of this state involvement, however, depends not only on the general size and level of economic development of the country under study but also on the timing of its integration into global capitalism (Hsueh, 2011, pp. 10–11). Thus, the German and Japanese coordinated economies were organized in the protectionist late 19th century, and South Korea was influenced by Fordism. Integrated into an intensively globalized economic system, state capitalism 3.0 is distinguished by making specific use of inward and outward FDI, designating the large emerging markets as 'third-generation late developers' (McNally, 2012, p.755).

3 Pinpointing state support for emerging market multinationals: structure of the book

In order to study the claim about the emergence of a new type of state capitalism, we first need to look at the general pattern of the development of business-government relations from a comparative perspective. Are emerging markets in this regard really different from established economies? Do emerging economies closely follow the pattern of the East Asian developmental states, or is their development different?

A second task is to look at the specific public policies and the more general structural issues that are closely linking state and multinationals in emerging markets. This obviously includes the role of (partial)state ownership among emerging markets multinationals, as well as direct financial support by (para-)state bodies, such as development banks or pension funds, or the regulation of specific sectors. But it can also relate to more structural issues such as the importance of close, formal, or informal interpersonal networks between major corporations and public officials in these countries, or the control of the costs of labor and other input factors, for instance, via monetary policy.

The third task pertains to exploring the cooperation between multinationals and governments, with regard to international relations. This not only includes the established topic of close relations between corporations and governments for gaining access to natural resources in other countries (in particular in the energy sector) but also negotiations about bi- and multilateral agreements on trade and FDI.

In order to address these issues, the book is divided into three major parts. In the first part, parallels and differences regarding state-business relationships in emerging economies such as China, in established economies, in East Asian developmental states, and during different stages of historical development will be addressed. The second part features country studies of BRIC's multinationals, and also of multinationals based in South Korea (the latter as a border case between the first and second part). The final part addresses the role of international institutions in the rise of these companies, in the two most important issue areas of FDI regulation and trade. Cross-cutting to the domestic/international and the country-specific selection is the sharing of tasks as regards specific measures, such as investment finance, corporate governance, trade policy, and so forth.

Taken together, the book not only provides the first systematic treatment of home government support for emerging market multinationals, but also carries a strong common message, that is, the emergence of a third, very particular wave of state capitalism with national variations.

The book is based on invited contributions from political scientists, economists, and business scholars, united by a political economy perspective that highlights that the economy and the political system are closely interwoven and should not be studied in separate domains. Analytical complementarities between contributions ensue not only via the sharing of tasks regarding specific subjects and countries but also through the combination of the more political, government-centric perspective of the political scientists and the business scholars' focus on company success, and by the combination of perspectives from within emerging markets such as Korea, Brazil, and Thailand, with those of academic observers from Australia, Europe, and the United States.

4 Content of individual contributions

John Mikler's chapter on '(Multi?)national Corporations and the State in Established Economies' argues that a single global model for corporate-state relations has never truly existed. Instead, great national diversity between states with advanced, industrialized economies has endured. In well-established economies, this diversity becomes deeply institutionalized over time in national structures of governance. States and corporations are bound by the institutional structures they have created and 'inhabit', and in which they become deeply embedded economically, socially, and politically. In the first section, the territorially grounded nature of MNCs is stressed (hence the question mark in the title). The locations of the world's largest corporations are like a map of power for the world, so that as the emerging market economies rise, so too do their corporations. The two are inseparable. However, the list of the world's largest corporations demonstrates that they still predominantly come from established economies. Furthermore, an analysis of their operations shows that their home bases remain crucial, and that the relationships they have with their home-state governments are therefore also crucial. In the second section, the nature of this relationship is considered on two levels. First, the variations from more liberal to more state-coordinated forms of national governance are considered. States tend to lie on a spectrum from more 'arms-length' to more integrated relations with their corporations. Second, it is demonstrated that these relations evolve over time, with the potential for this evolution both enabled and constrained in certain ways depending on the path dependence of existing institutions. For example, the post-World War II developmental states of East Asia have evolved into what are often termed 'coordinated market economies', while the earlier developing Anglo Saxon economies have tended toward more liberal forms of governance. The latter, in turn, may increasingly be conceived of as regulatory states. The chapter concludes by drawing out two key implications in the context of this book on multinationals based in emerging market economies. First, established economies are likely to work with their institutions of governance in the future, as in the past, in response to both global crises and the challenge they face from emerging market economies and their MNCs. Second, these emerging market economies and their MNCs have considerable 'room to move' as they develop new institutions of governance in the process of emerging, just as the established economies did before them.

Similarly, Terutomo Ozawa's chapter on 'Multinationals as an Instrument of Catch-up Industrialization: Understanding the Strategic Links between State and Industry in Emerging Markets' argues that a close relationship between state and industry in emerging economies – and the rise of MNCs from those economies – is the outcome of their national efforts (industrial policies and institutional setup) to promote catch-up industrialization. Moreover, Ozawa argues that this relationship necessarily evolves pari passu with the nation's economic development where the early stages of industrialization require their collaboration as joint inputs in catch-up strategies. A stages model is a useful tool in understanding and predicting the unfolding strategic relations between state and transnational operations of domestic firms in services, resources extraction, manufacturing, and finance. This stages perspective can be best illustrated in terms of a 'leading-sector' model, à la Joseph Schumpeter. Ozawa's model is built on a sequence of growth that is punctuated by stages, and in each stage a certain industrial sector can be identified as the main engine of structural transformation. So far the world economy has witnessed five tiers of leading-sector industry emerge in wave-like progression ever since the Industrial Revolution in England. The five tiers have been (i) endowment-driven industries (represented by textiles in labor-abundant economies), (ii) scale-driven, resource-processing industries (steel and basic chemicals), (iii) assembly-based industries (automobiles), (iv) research and development (R&D)-driven industries (microchips and computers), and (v) Internet-enabled industries (operating platforms, search engines, and social networking). Latecomers do not need to replicate the same sequence, but are free to jumble it, take shortcuts, or enter all stages from the low end even simultaneously – all depending on their catch-up strategies and capabilities.

Turning to specific country studies, the focus of the second part of the book, Seung-il Jeong's chapter on 'South Korean Multinationals after the Asian Financial Crisis: Toward liberal capitalism?' analyzes the many institutional changes regarding Korean multinationals in the last 15 years that have eroded a once-successful model of state capitalism. Seen as a highly effective model of industrial catch-up, South Korea's state-guided capitalism, which focused on export-oriented manufacturing sectors, was once praised as the hallmark of successful industrialization. But neoclassical critics argued that the 1997 Asian crisis revealed structural weaknesses in South Korea's economy and corporations. The market-friendly reforms driven by liberal and democratic governments (1998–2007) dismantled the growth engine behind South Korea's economic miracle. Large companies shifted their focus from long-term to short-term profitability, and therefore, long-term investments by large companies today tend to be polarized. Furthermore, under a regime of neoliberalism and shareholder value capitalism, many of South Korea's large companies strongly tend to diversify into sectors, where they can earn revenues in safe ways, through rent-seeking. Also, the Free Trade Agreements (FTAs) with the United States and the European Union (EU) will expand rent-seeking practices through privatization and deregulation. There still exist some heritages of industrial policy, and good examples are innovation policy and policy financing. However, in the overall circumstance of neoliberalism, industrial policy does not contribute to industrial growth as much as in previous periods. The successive liberal reforms driven by the two democratic governments and then by the conservative government have created a strong polarization in R&D and other long-term investments between a small number of large multinational companies and a majority of large companies. The passivity of a majority of large companies in long-term investment in manufacturing sectors is the key reason for sluggish growth in the South Korean economy since the 1997 Asian crisis.

China, in contrast, is still pursuing a developmental state strategy, as Andreas Nölke's contribution on 'Private Chinese Multinationals and the Long Shadow of the State' argues. While the prominent role of the Chinese state in regulating and supporting business is well known regarding its state-owned enterprises, much less known are the varied ways in which the Chinese state allies with private Chinese multinationals. The latter comprise about a third of Chinese outward foreign direct investment (OFDI) stock, mainly in manufacturing, but not including the largest Chinese multinationals, which partially explains why they are familiar to the Western public. Western observers are primarily worried by the existence of very large Chinese state-owned companies, potentially seen as a threat to Western interests. Still, even for companies such as Huwawei that are neither state-owned nor state-controlled, the state matters a lot. This includes various promotional measures in the context of the 'go global' policy, the close cooperation between provinces and local multinationals, for instance with regard to access to credit and – in a broader picture – the guarantee for continuing access to the most important country-specific advantage, that is, abundant and inexpensive labor. Based on *guanxi* (i.e., close and regular informal contacts between companies and government), private Chinese multinationals share many features of state-owned/controlled companies.

Nobody would dispute the importance of close relations with the state in the case of Russian multinationals, as demonstrated by Jonas Grätz in his chapter on 'Russia's Multinationals: Network State Capitalism Goes Global'. Russian multinationals have received some attention, as Russia has the largest OFDI stock of the emerging markets and of the notorious 'BRIC' countries in particular, despite having only a quarter of Chinese gross domestic product (GDP). In addition, Russian multinationals have been in the headlines due to their size and heavy-handed behavior in some host countries, as well as their connections to the state. The latter trend has been highlighted as the state contribution to Russian GDP is growing rather than shrinking. This chapter takes a closer look at private and state multinationals in the most important sector (energy), while also including some evidence from ferrous and nonferrous metal industries. It highlights in great detail how the domestic context, in particular the role of government policies and capacities, overrides other drivers of Russian OFDI, such as industry-specific variables.

As indicated by Grätz, state support for emerging market MNCs is usually sector specific. This consideration is further developed by Heather Taylor in her chapter on 'Sector Creation and Evolution: The Role of the State in Shaping the Rise of the Indian Pharmaceutical Sectoral Business System'. The chapter identifies the drivers of the internationalizing process of Indian MNCs in the pharmaceutical industries. Specifically, this chapter aims to understand both the direct and indirect role that the Indian state took in the internationalization process of this industry between 1990 and 2011. While much research has been devoted to emerging market multinationals' internationalization and resource-building processes and strategies, the particular structural characteristics of the industries in which these operate and the role of the state in dynamically shaping them have been neglected. As such this paper seeks to answer two specific questions related to this topic, namely: What are the national policy choices with regard to the respective sectors? What and how much has the Indian institutional and regulatory context done in order to influence the competitive capabilities of the sector? Main findings include the importance of the creation of a domestic sector with a strong set of skills before FDI liberalization, as well as the important role of competition regulation and patent laws more recently.

In the case of Brazil, state-sponsored financial support for outward FDI has been a crucial factor for the emergence of Brazilian multinationals, as argued by Gilmar Masiero, Mario H. Ogasavara, Luiz Caseiro, and Silas Ferreira in their chapter on 'Financing the Expansion of Brazilian Multinationals into Europe: The Role of the Brazilian Development Bank BNDES'. Brazil currently holds the sixth position in the ranking of the largest economies. In the past decade, Brazil has experienced an economic resurgence. As part of this boom, Brazilian multinational companies have emerged as leading economic players, including companies such as Vale, Petrobras, Embraer, Odebrecht, Camargo Correa, Gerdau, and Votorantim. In this chapter, Masiero et al. draw attention to how the Brazilian development bank (BNDES), the main state development financing agency, has supported the new wave of internationalization of Brazilian companies, specifically those operating in the EU. For decades, the EU has been one of Brazil's most important partners for trade, as well as for the international operations of its firms. Brazil is also the biggest BRIC investor in the EU market. Masiero et al. review the expansion of Brazilian MNCs and detail the types of financial support provided by BNDES for the overseas expansion of these companies, including both financing loans and becoming a shareholder (or both). They demonstrate that most of the Brazilian companies that have invested in the EU have benefitted from BNDES support, with about 60 percent having received loans and nearly 50 percent being affected by BNDES shareholding.

The expansion of emerging market multinationals is not only influenced by domestic state measures but also by state action on the international level, as demonstrated by the two chapters in the third part of the book. In their contribution on 'How Policies Shape Foreign Direct Investment: Examining Foreign Direct Investment from Latin America to the European Union', Judith Clifton, Daniel Diaz-Fuentes, and Julio Revuelta deal with Latin American OFDI to the EU. Increased investment from emerging markets to the EU represents something of a double-edged sword. On the one hand, this investment threatens to unsettle traditional investment privileges in the EU, and some interests may be tempted to resort to protectionist policies. On the other hand, the ongoing financial and economic crises mean that EU member states increasingly need FDI from emerging markets, and may therefore put into place liberalizing policies to make the EU a more attractive destination. Straddling these two 'extreme' policy tensions – toward liberalization and protectionism – are the complex and changing institutional arrangements guiding FDI policy in the EU. Traditionally, EU member states were responsible for FDI policy, but competence for FDI is being transferred, albeit partially, to the supranational level after the Treaty of Lisbon. It is in this context that this chapter answers two main questions. First, how has FDI policy as implemented by states across both regions evolved, vis-à-vis liberalization or protectionism, from the end of the 1990s to 2010? Second, did FDI policy shape investment patterns and to what extent? To do so, they analyze FDI policy by both home and host countries and contrast this with FDI stock levels during this period. Clifton, Diaz-Fuentes, and Revuelta uncover three main findings. First, overall, there has been a trend toward FDI liberalization by states in both Latin America and the EU. So, despite the crises, EU member states have generally resisted protectionist urges and maintained quite open FDI regimes until 2010 at least, in the countries and sectors analyzed. Second, FDI liberalization was indeed a determining factor in increased investment between the regions: greater liberalization is correlated with more investment. Third, where FDI policy did veer toward protectionism in the EU, FDI from Latin America was more negatively affected than FDI from the other sample countries.

Next to FDI regulation, trade policies are a major intergovernmental determinant of emerging markets' multinationals' behavior, as demonstrated by Suthikorn Kingkaew's chapter on 'The Action-Reaction in Global Trade: Comparing the Cases of the Brazilian Chicken and the Thai Tuna Industries'. This chapter examines the relationship between the support for MNCs by home state governments and the restrictions in international trade. It observes the different trends in international markets of two different food products, chicken and canned tuna. The global chicken market is highly restricted as the majority of demand is met by domestic supplies, with only 10 percent of global production being traded globally. In the trade-restricted chicken industry, the rise of the largest player, Brasil Foods, is the result of a deliberate plan of its home country's government. Through various governmental support measures such as loans for local and international mergers and acquisitions (M&A) activities as well as its ability to set the direction of the company through shareholding in the company by state pension funds, the Brazilian government has succeeded in driving this company to be the engine for the international market expansion for its agricultural products. In contrast, the Thai government never had a direct supporting role in the ascension of the largest canned tuna firm, TUF. This is because the global market is far less restrictive than the chicken market, with approximately 65 percent of global production being traded globally. Without such restriction, companies have successfully competed and expanded on their own, within the value chain. Based on this comparison, this article argues that the level of support by developing countries' governments is directly correlated with the level of restriction in international trade imposed by major importing markets, the United States, and the EU.

The conclusion to the volume summarizes the main findings as well as identifies a number of implications. It does so by elaborating a systematic overview of state support measures and locating the individual contributions in this overview. On the side of domestic support measures, it lists state subsidies, state ownership, provision of a low-cost work force, the selective protection of intellectual property rights, a competition policy geared toward the rise of national champions, and some sector-specific regulatory policies as well as OFDI support programs. As far as cooperation with regard to transnational activity is concerned, the most important issues include state-MNC collaboration for the access of natural resources, the negotiation of bilateral and regional trade and investment agreements, the representation of the preferences of emerging markets' MNCs in international institutions, and, finally, support via the less-than-stringent implementation of global norms that are detrimental to MNC strategies. All in all, the volume highlights the very comprehensive and important ways in which emerging markets' governments support the expansion of 'their' multinationals, thereby justifying the assessment of the emergence of a third wave of state capitalism.

Part I
General Perspectives

1
(Multi?)national Corporations and the State in Established Economies
John Mikler

1.1 Introduction

It is often claimed that corporations are increasingly multinational, and that they are therefore freed from the territorial 'shackles' of national governments. That liberal capitalism is writ large upon the global stage, with multinational corporations (MNCs) in the lead roles and states performing the supporting ones, was celebrated by the likes of Fukuyama (1992) with his much cited, although now modified, prediction of the 'end of history' with the end of the Cold War. There was the Washington Consensus of the 1980s and 1990s, through which the Bretton Woods institutions imposed such a neoliberal vision on developing countries. This is said to have since given way to a post-Washington Consensus, which is liberal rather than neoliberal – it is more a matter of principles to be made policies by states, rather than an inevitable 'blueprint' of measures to be adopted (see e.g., Headey, 2009). As such, a global vision, as opposed to an inevitable 'reality', is now more the case, but it is global nonetheless.

However, rather than taking a global perspective, this chapter focuses on corporate-state relations in distinct national, and to some extent regional, contexts in order to demonstrate the endurance of diversity between states with advanced, industrialized economies. This is because global capitalism is in many respects not as global as often claimed by those who stress the economic aspects of globalization.[1] MNCs' operations and locations remain more territorially defined than is often acknowledged, and in particular their home bases remain of great importance to them: many remain embedded in well-established economies where distinct national structures of governance have become institutionalized over time. While other chapters in this book analyze the way in which those MNCs that are emerging from the rapidly growing economies of Brazil, Russia, India, and China (the BRICs) are similarly embedding themselves in their home states, the central point made in this one is that the incumbent states and their MNCs are bound by the institutional structures they have created and in which they have become deeply embedded economically, socially, and politically over time.

In the first section, the territorially grounded nature of MNCs is considered. Contrary to the notion of the placeless, transnational corporation, the locations of the world's largest corporations are shown to be analogous to a map of world power – such corporations come from the world's dominant, established industrialized states. It is therefore the case that as market economies rise, so too in a similar fashion do their corporations. The two are inseparable. In the second section, the nature of this relationship is considered, particularly variations from more liberal to more state-coordinated varieties of capitalism, and in this respect the point is made that states lie on a spectrum from 'arms-length' liberal to integrated coordinated relations with their corporations. In the third section, it is demonstrated that these relations evolve over time, with the potential for this evolution both enabled and constrained depending on the path dependence of existing institutions. The implications for established market economies are that rather than convergence on a single variety of capitalism, or a single form of corporate-state relations, diversity is likely to persist on a national and regional basis even as the global economy becomes more interconnected. Similarly, the implications for emerging market economies are that their governments and MNCs potentially have considerable 'room to move' as they develop new institutions of governance in the process of emerging, just as the established economies did before them. The room they have – both the extent of it and what they have done with it – is the subject of the chapters to follow in this volume.

1.2 Reterritorializing multinational corporations

Corporations are increasingly multinational. However, this does not mean that a deterritorialized, or 'global', view of them is appropriate. While their economic interests and their operations increasingly transcend national boundaries, nevertheless they are based in some states and some regions from which they emerge to impact on others. Chang (2008, p. 32; see also Fuchs, 2007; Harrod, 2006) notes that the wealthy, industrialized countries account for 70 percent of international trade

Table 1.1 The nationality of corporations in the Fortune Global 500

	1996 (%)	2012 (%)
US	31	26
EU	31	27
Japan	28	14
BRICs (China)	1 (0)	19 (15)
Others	9	14

Source: Elaborated by author based on Fortune Global 500, at http://money.cnn.com. 1996 data is from Wilks (2013, p. 43).

and make 70–90 percent of global foreign direct investment (FDI). But more accurately, it is their corporations that do so. The FT Global 500 companies[2] are responsible for 70 percent of international trade and at least 80 percent of the world's stock of FDI (Rugman, 2000; Bryant and Bailey, 1997). The rather close correlation between the figures for rich, industrialized states' trade and FDI and those of these corporations is no accident. Their nationality – that is, where they are based – is like a map of global economic power. As this map of power has shifted, so too has their nationality. Table 1.1 demonstrates that as the emerging market economies of the BRICs have grown in global economic importance, so too have their corporations. Of the corporations in the Fortune Global 500,[3] the majority remain headquartered in the United States (US), the European Union (EU), and Japan. However, today they are also increasingly headquartered elsewhere, with new Chinese MNCs in particular now making up 15 percent of the world's largest corporations. As the center of the world economy has moved from the transatlantic closer to the Asian sphere, so has the location of the world's largest corporations. In fact, 36 percent of the Fortune Global 500 companies are now located in the Asian region.[4]

The implications of this go beyond merely their location, also raising questions as to their *control*. In particular, it has often been noted that national trade and investment figures are actually those of the corporations that produce them. By the 1990s, 60–70 percent of trade in manufactured goods between Organization for Economic Cooperation and Development (OECD) countries was intrafirm, rather than interstate (Bonturi and Fukasaku, 1993; see also Bardhan and Jaffee, 2005) – that is, the supply chains of the world's largest corporations are what produce the national figures. Rather than the data reflecting trade and investment on the basis of national comparative advantage, they reflect the corporate strategies of the world's largest corporations, headquartered in the world's largest economies. One response to this would be to say that these corporations are market actors being driven by market imperatives. As the market for goods and services is increasingly global, so are they, and they shift their operations accordingly. However, there are (at least) two points to make in respect of this.

First, casting MNCs in this manner 'underdraws' them as mechanisms of profit maximization, suggesting that they are purely the servants of market forces and market imperatives. Of course, they have to be profitable and successful in the markets for their goods and services, but I have previously argued that seeing corporations as 'market actors', and indeed 'the market' as a concept for understanding global economic relations, makes assumptions about the global economy that should be more widely challenged (Mikler, 2013, 2012). In particular, the reality is that the global economy is highly concentrated and oligopolistic. All of the world's major industrialized sectors are now controlled by five MNCs at most, and 28 percent have one corporation accounting for more than 40 percent of global sales (Harrod, 2006, p. 25; see also Fuchs, 2007). The world's largest MNCs, based in the world's largest economies, control trade and investment flows and do so because they control the markets for their products. They do not respond to market forces. They make them.

It is also the case that in making and controlling these markets, they do so from the states in which they are headquartered. Although they have global interests, their operations are much more territorially grounded than is often held to be the case. The United Nations Conference on Trade and Development's transnationality index (TNI) is a simple composite average of foreign assets, sales and employment to total assets, sales, and employment. Although 82 of the world's 100 largest corporations ranked by foreign assets have a TNI of over 50, and the average TNI of a corporation in this list is 63,[5] suggesting a high degree of independence from their home base, there are dangers in making generalizations. For example, the average TNIs of US, German, and Japanese firms in the top 100 MNCs are just 51, 55, and 52 respectively. On average, these well-established MNCs from the world's most well-established industrialized states retain half their sales, assets, and employment at home, although they have had the most time to 'go global' (UNCTAD, 2011a).

Furthermore, there is no reason to believe that there will be a future trend to a greater decoupling of these MNCs from their home states. Many of the seemingly most global MNCs are in fact more regional than global. There is a body of scholarship by Rugman with various co-authors (Rugman, 2005; Rugman et al., 2007; Rugman and Girod,

2003; Rugman and Collinson, 2004) that demonstrates that a very significant proportion of the Fortune Global 500 firms' assets and operations are located in their home region. As such, they use their headquarters in their home state as a base from which to control and dominate their region(s). Relatedly, some MNCs are more accurately seen as binational. For example, Voss (2013) notes that MNCs based in Taiwan and Hong Kong have very high TNIs simply because they locate factories in mainland China, but their headquarters remain at 'home'. As the opportunities for efficiencies/exploitation shrink with the rise of the BRICs and other emerging market economies, and as the cost of oil and carbon emissions ultimately must be factored into corporate strategic decision-making, enhanced national and regional, rather than global, strategies may become increasingly attractive to MNCs and an incentive for them to rationalize their supply chains (see, e.g., The Economist, 2011).

Clearly, the notion of the placeless MNC does not stand up to scrutiny. The reality is that all markets are highly oligopolistic, and therefore power is concentrated in the hands of a small number of corporations that dominate their industry sectors, and they are based in the world's dominant countries and regions. The relationships they have with their home state governments are therefore crucial. How they are institutionally embedded in their home states is considered in the following section, as well as the relationships they have with the governments of states in which they invest.

1.3 Varieties of capitalism, varieties of state-corporate relations

At the height of initial debates in the post-Cold War 1990s about what was then starting to be called globalization, the inevitability of an integrated global economy was seen as producing a tendency toward a neoliberal form of the state. Authors such as Fukuyama (1992), whose declaration that liberal capitalism writ large upon the world had delivered 'the end of history' were made as nothing less than a 'primeval scream of joy', as Bhagwati (2004, p. 13) colorfully put it, by someone standing astride the 'corpse' of the now-missing alternatives to the neoliberal policies of the Washington Consensus: minimal government in both size and scope; borders opened to trade and financial movements; national deregulation to let the market work; and the privatization and marketization of the provision of goods and services.

However, as these policies were imposed by the Bretton Woods institutions on developing countries in the form of loan conditions in the

1990s, it appeared that markets were the masters of governments not just because of a lack of alternatives, but actually by *design*. It was not so much the case that globalization meant that inevitably 'your economy grows and your politics shrinks' (Friedman, 2000, p. 105), resulting in Washington Consensus-style policies via convergence on a liberal and ultimately *neo*liberal form of the state. Instead, this policy 'choice' was imposed on countries that were comparatively less able to resist it. Indeed, those doing the imposing of the policies did not adhere to them themselves. In 2000, government expenditure in the world's major advanced economies (the G7) was 42 percent of gross domestic product (GDP) on average. By 2010, it had grown to 47 percent. This may be contrasted with the 25 to 30 percent average for Latin American, Caribbean, and Sub-Saharan African states (IMF, 2011). The consensus on the part of elites in the established economies still exists, even in the aftermath of the global financial crisis (according to Wade, 2010), but it does not seem to have produced a shrinking state in terms of size.

It also has not produced homogeneity in the role of the state. In reality, globalization remains very much 'what states make of it' (Clark, 1999, p. 55), although more accurately it is what *powerful* states make of it (see Drezner, 2007). A good starting point for understanding this is the consideration that the TNI of corporations may be seen to be related to the TNI of states. Similarly to the TNI of corporations, this measures the degree to which states' economies are internationalized, based on the average of the four indicators of FDI flows as a percentage of fixed capital formation; FDI inward stocks as a percentage of GDP; stock; foreign affiliate value added as a percentage of GDP; and employment by foreign affiliates as a percentage of total employment. It is only the smallest countries that have high TNIs. The highest are Belgium, Singapore, and Luxembourg with TNIs of 66, 65, and 65 respectively (UNCTAD, 2008). It is also the case that because they have very small domestic markets, the MNCs emanating from them also have very high TNIs. By comparison, not only do the MNCs from Germany, the US, and Japan have lower TNIs, but despite their huge role in the global economy, these states themselves have TNIs of just 11, 7, and 2 respectively. This is important because as Wilks (2013, p. 38) notes, 'indices of country economic transnationality are potentially also indicators of national influence within global governance'. Those states whose economies are more penetrated by corporations of other nationalities, are likely to find themselves pressured to conform to 'modes of behavior, styles of regulation and form(s) of political activism' (Wilks, 2013, p. 38) with which these corporations are familiar 'at home'. Putting it simply, states with a high TNI are more impacted by corporations from other states, while those with a low TNI's corporations do the impacting.

The manner in which this occurs is of course not straightforward. On the one hand, because MNCs' operations cross borders, they may be viewed as a bundle of organizational capabilities, one of which is their ability and flexibility to absorb and gain new knowledge in any context (e.g., Kogut, 2005). From this it follows that the learning ability of MNCs, and therefore their abilities to adapt and change in different national contexts, is crucial to their international performance. As they are international organizations as well as nationally and regionally embedded ones, they therefore can change and adapt according to their circumstances – thus they 'translate the relationship of globalization and regionalization into an organizational challenge' (Heidenreich, 2012, p. 557). However, a crucial point to make in this respect is that, as Whitley (2009) finds, because they are shaped by their national business systems, where possible they choose not to do so. Critics of globalization may find Wolf's (2004, p. 191) statement that 'multinational corporations would not dare operate plants in very different ways in different countries' odd, to put it mildly. Yet, in institutional terms, the statement rings true because in addition to being internationally active, as per the above discussion, MNCs should be seen as still very much nationally and regionally embedded organizations. As Heidenreich (2012, p. 567), puts it, 'the national embeddedness of companies contributes to the reduction of uncertainties and to the solution of organizational coordination problems', and as such there is little incentive for MNCs to 'fix' what they may not regard as 'broken'.

It follows that even if they have the capacity for adaptation, studies such as Kahancová (2007) show that rather than doing so unopposed in different national contexts, corporate organizational inertia means routines that have supported growth and legitimacy in an MNC's home country tend to be retained where possible. Having 'solved' their coordination problems, which shape the relationships they have with their employees, industry associations, unions, educational institutions, competitors, shareholders, banks, suppliers, customers, and other stakeholders, why would they be eager to change these arrangements unless forced to do so? Rather than some disembodied, transnational form of capitalism being spread by global companies of no nationality, in reality MNCs are still very much adapted to particular and differentiated national business systems. It follows that MNCs may be seen as effectively 'exporting' the national business systems to which they are adapted to other countries, particularly those states with highly internationalized economies. They find themselves having to adjust to the practices of MNCs from other states more than these MNCs feel the necessity to adapt to their new national circumstances.

What then are the institutional contexts within the powerful established states from which MNCs have historically come and, to a large extent, continue to do so: the EU, the US, and Japan? Although those authors who stressed the (neo-)liberalizing tendencies of globalization stressed the sameness of the structural relations underpinning capitalism, others have focused on the manner in which the institutional interpretation and expression of capitalism varies between states. They accept that a liberalizing agenda post-World War Two (WW2) coupled with the end of the Cold War has embedded liberal policies in international organizations, and created an increasingly liberal global trade and investment order. However, it does not follow that capitalism as practiced within national boundaries resembles a liberal 'institutional monoculture' (Watson, 2003, p. 227). Studies such as Dore et al. (1999) and Chang (2002), demonstrate that established economies have evolved distinct capitalist relations of production, with this evolution occurring over the course of the 20th century while having its historical roots considerably earlier than this.

A comparative capitalism literature has therefore burgeoned since the 1990s as various authors studying the national institutional variations of industrialized countries via multiple case studies (as well as the application of multiple categories that overlap but do not easily conform with one another) have sought to study the implications (see, e.g., Whitley, 2002). Some have focused on the social system of production, or the idea that national economies are socially constructed as a result of institutional complementarities that are largely socially determined (e.g., Hollingsworth and Boyer, 1997). Others have focused on national business systems, or 'systems of economic coordination and control' (Whitley, 1999, p. 34) as defined in terms of governance, collaboration, and employment relations (see also Doremus et al., 1999). The Varieties of Capitalism (VoC) approach of Hall and Soskice (2001a, 2001b) conceives of national economic systems as lying on a spectrum, at one end of which are liberal market economies (LMEs) and at the other coordinated market economies (CMEs). Corporations based in LMEs prefer to coordinate their activities via market competition, are more 'arms-length' in their interactions with the state, and are more focused on consumer demand and providing shareholder value. By comparison, CME-based firms prefer nonmarket, cooperative relationships to coordinate their activities, including with the state and society.

The VoC approach aims to locate firms centrally in the analysis of variations in the institutional basis of capitalist relations of production, which is what makes it especially relevant here. Hall and Soskice's (2001a, pp. 2, 6) desire 'to bring firms back into the center of the analysis of comparative capitalism', in recognition of the fact that firms are 'the crucial actors in a capitalist economy', means that their framework is useful for the study of corporate-state relations specifically, as opposed to states and markets, or national production systems. At the same time, while the desire is to focus on firms, the VoC approach inevitably 'take(s) the nation state seriously as a locus of economic regulation' (Howell, 2003, p. 110), on the basis of which 'in any national economy, firms will gravitate towards the mode of coordination for which there is institutional support' (Hall and Soskice, 2001a, pp. 8–9).

Table 1.2 summarizes the key differences, a central implication of which is that, while management autonomy to act on the basis of market demands and shareholder preferences is preferred in LMEs (hence the focus on competition, short-term financial returns, etc.), in CMEs there is a greater focus on cooperative relationships with stakeholders more broadly defined (see, e.g., Vitols, 2001). Focusing on the state specifically, it follows that its role in LMEs is in assuring management autonomy to set corporate strategy on the basis of market signals. Therefore, the state acts as a market regulator. By comparison, in CMEs, the state acts more

Table 1.2 LMEs versus CMEs

LMEs: US, UK, Australia, Canada, New Zealand, and Ireland	CMEs: Germany, Japan, Switzerland, the Netherlands, Belgium, Sweden, Norway, Denmark, Finland, and Austria
Short-term company finance (i.e., equity finance)	Long-term industrial finance (i.e., debt finance)
Deregulated labor markets	Cooperative industrial relations
General education	High levels of vocational and firm-specific training,
Strong intercompany competition	Cooperation in technology and standard-setting across companies
Production and market strategies that seek to exploit easily transferred assets	Production and market strategies that seek to exploit the advantages of nontransferable or specific assets
Competitive advantage through radical forms of innovation	Competitive advantage through incremental forms of innovation

Source: Hall and Soskice (2001b) based on the summary in Jackson and Deeg (2008).

as a market shaper, working with corporations and industry associations to further national objectives, and helping to strategically coordinate economic activities. Rather than an arms-length relationship between the state and corporations, it is more the case that they operate hand in glove. While LME-based corporations desire deregulation and hands-off laissez faire market operations, CME-based corporations operate more on the basis of consensus-oriented negotiation and cooperation with the state. While business 'cooperation' with government has as its goal the capture of regulatory agencies, or reducing their capacity to intervene in markets, in CMEs it is more readily accepted that the state's role is that of an agenda setter, coordinating firms or informally suggesting strategies. Rather than what may be characterized as a more lobbying-conflict model between the state and corporations in LMEs, in CMEs corporations operate within a collaborative-consensus environment through which business and government develop regulations, agree on targets to be met, and establish priorities and goals to be achieved in the national interest.

As such, there appears to be a tension between the observation that the world economy is increasingly more interconnected, while the MNCs and states that underpin it retain national and regional preferences for their operations. But is there a tension? Rather than it being the case that all states are increasingly 'merely the handmaidens of firms' (Strange, 1997, p. 184), the *relationship* between states and corporations remains important (see, for instance, the contributions in Mikler, 2011). Therefore, a more accurate way to understand the greater interconnectedness of the world economy is to consider the way in which these states and their corporations respond *together* to the challenges that arise – that is, the different ways in which they are enabled or constrained in their responses (Weiss, 2003). States and their corporations are not 'blank canvases' on which policy choices for addressing economic challenges are drawn. These choices are substantially institutionally determined. If institutions are 'a set of rules, formal or informal, that actors generally follow, whether for normative, cognitive, or material reasons' (Hall and Soskice, 2001a, p. 9), it follows that there is a path dependence in how states employ their methods and systems of governance. This is because institutions establish the 'rules of the game ... that structure political, economic and social interaction' (North, 1990, p. 97), and for addressing the challenges states and their corporations face. This is considered in the following section.

1.4 The evolution of state-corporate relations

The above discussion is of course something of a caricature of variations in corporate-state relations. The LME and CME categories are more ideal types than congruent representations of reality.[6] They are heuristically useful, however, especially if seen as representing two ends of a *spectrum* of propensities that states and their corporations tend toward to one degree or another. Several studies have borne this out, such as Hall and Gingerich (2009), who demonstrate that the VoC approach does not just study ideal types that have been inflated to categories. They show that states may indeed be grouped into LMEs and CMEs, and that there are subnational institutional complementarities within them that reinforce this tendency. Furthermore, Hall and Thelen (2009) argue that despite forces for institutional change, such change occurs in a path-dependent manner, due to preexisting national institutional complementarities. States and their corporations are more likely to work *within* established institutions of governance to which they are accustomed, rather than abandoning them through what would have to be thought of as a quite dramatic paradigm shift.[7] They do not so much abandon the institutional basis for their relations (indeed, it stands to reason that they cannot easily do so) as find new ways to re-embed these relations.

There is not the space to go into this in great detail here, although I have previously demonstrated that measures of the size and nature of state intervention are remarkably stable over time, and that there are indeed variations between states that are categorized as more LME-like versus more CME-like (Mikler, 2012).[8] Even if a 'slide' toward more liberal capitalism worldwide over the last two decades is observable, it follows that if anything the *gap* between states has widened, along with a clustering around the two categories proposed by the VoC approach. This is because it is easier for LMEs to become more LME-like than it is for CMEs, and it is preferable for institutional complementarities that have served states well to be reinforced in the face of international challenges rather than abandoned (as discussed in Thelen, 2001; Hall and Soskice, 2003; Hall, 2007; Hall and Thelen, 2009; Hall and Gingerich, 2009).

The evolution of LMEs since the 1990s serves to illustrate the point. Despite the initial severity of the impact of the global financial crisis in the US and UK, and the seemingly chronic economic malaise it has produced, Kang and Moon (2012, p. 96) find that 'shareholder-value-driven corporate governance has not been sufficiently discredited to warrant a path-shifting change'. This may seem a surprising finding, yet it seems to be the case that a process of evolution through a stronger regulatory role for the state in these countries is taking place, as Weiss (2010) suggests. Furthermore, this predates the crisis. Prior to it, authors such as Braithwaite (2008) and Jordana and Levi-Faur (2004) pointed out that the increasing concentration evident within industrial sectors, and the growth in size and influence of the corporations in them, and in their states and regions, has led not to the demise of the state but a reorientation of its role. Rather than what Braithwaite (2008) dubs 'the neoliberal fairytale' of the demise of the state, in the face of industry sectors dominated by a visible handful of megacorporations, it is more efficient for states to reach agreement on rules for their operations rather than seeking to curtail these. As Vogel (1996) observed even earlier in *Freer Markets More Rules*, privatization and what was initially seen as deregulation was actually more accurately reregulation as LMEs became 'regulatory states' embracing what might be thought of as a form of 'regulatory capitalism'. As Braithwaite (2008, p. 4) puts it,

> In the era of regulatory capitalism, more of the governance that shapes the daily lives of most citizens is corporate governance than state governance. The corporatization of the world is both a product of regulation and the key driver of regulatory growth, indeed of state growth more generally... The reciprocal relationship between corporatization and regulation creates a world in which there is more governance of all kinds.

Even as they have come to rival states, or perform roles over which states were once more unilaterally in control, corporations are increasingly regulated by states in how they perform such roles, even if such regulation is chiefly conducted through the market and market-based mechanisms.

The evolution of LMEs therefore exhibits considerable institutional continuity rather than flux, as the smooth functioning of the market through effective state regulation is the aim. Authors such as Streeck (2009) and Aoki et al. (2007) are cited in Kang and Moon (2012) for their analysis of the manner in which German and Japanese CME capitalism has been resistant to pressures for change. This is similar to the way that authors like Dore (2000a, 2000b) and Vogel (2001) found nearly a decade earlier at the height of debates around the inevitability of a neoliberal form of the state that nonliberal capitalist states seemed to be 'stalled on the road to the liberal market model'. Indeed, OECD data in Table 1.3 on the extent to which the state intervenes to ensure employment protection, regulates markets, exerts control over business enterprises; imposes legal and administrative barriers to entrepreneurship; and has barriers to international trade and investment in the largest OECD LME and CME states, demonstrates this to be the case.[9] Although overall a trend toward liberalization is exhibited across all states, a gap between the major LME versus CME states remains in all cases, as well

Table 1.3 Measures of state intervention in corporate affairs, 1998, 2003, and 2008

	1998	2003	2008
Strictness of employment protection[a]			
LMEs			
US	0.21	0.21	0.21
UK	0.60	0.75	0.75
CMEs			
Germany	2.34	2.09	2.12
Japan	1.62	1.43	1.43
Product market regulation[b]			
LMEs			
US	1.283	1.007	0.841
UK	1.070	0.824	0.842
CMEs			
Germany	2.062	1.598	1.328
Japan	2.188	1.409	1.112
State control of business enterprises[c]			
LMEs			
US	1.406	1.193	1.102
UK	1.51	1.278	1.504
CMEs			
Germany	3.18	2.131	1.958
Japan	3.149	2.589	1.432
Legal and administrative barriers to entrepreneurship[c]			
LMEs			
US	1.406	1.193	1.102
UK	1.451	0.954	0.824
CMEs			
Germany	2.307	1.835	1.315
Japan	2.965	1.378	1.368
Barriers to international trade and investment[c]			
LMEs			
US	0.421	0.198	0.185
UK	0.249	0.241	0.199
CMEs			
Germany	0.698	0.827	0.712
Japan	0.838	0.736	0.717

Sources: Elaborated by author based on OECD (2010a, 2010c).

[a] This is based on 'indicators of the strictness of regulation on dismissals and the use of temporary contracts', derived from 'the procedures and costs involved in dismissing individuals or groups of workers and the procedures involved in hiring workers on fixed-term or temporary work agency contracts' (OECD n.d. a). Higher scores denote stricter protection.

[b] These are 'a comprehensive and internationally-comparable set of indicators that measure the degree to which policies promote or inhibit competition in areas of the product market where competition is viable. They measure the economy-wide regulatory and market environments in OECD countries in (or around) 1998, 2003 and 2008' (OECD n.d. b).

[c] A subset of the product market regulation index.

as some interesting variations. For example, the UK appears to have increased employment protection since 1998 and control of business enterprises since 2003, while Germany's barriers to international trade and investment are higher in 2008 than they were in 1998, although lower than 2003 levels.

As such, states have the capacity to choose how they regulate and interact with market actors as variations in state-corporate relations evolve over time. Whether states have historically embraced greater state coordination of economic affairs, or a more arms-length relationship with markets and corporations, they tend to build on the institutional frameworks they have rather than invent new ones. This is because agents 'cannot simply "make up" their realities in ways that are disconnected from the environments they inhabit at any given point in time' (Bell, 2011, p. 906; see also Mahoney and Thelen, 2010; Olsen, 2009). The material realities and the historical legacies of previous decisions that underpin their institutional bases for coordinating economic activity both enable and constrain their interpretations and responses to the challenges they face. Rather than fixed *in* time as LMEs or CMEs, or whatever other categories one may apply to states' varieties of capitalism, states are fixed *over* time in adjusting and modifying the institutional basis for capitalist relations of production given their established LME or CME characteristics. Their 'strategies of adjustment to globalization are influenced by comparative advantages – of CMEs *vis a vis* LMEs – and by these economies' desire to maintain such advantages' (Marzinotto, 2002, p. 632; see also Howell, 2003). There is no reason why this should not also be the case for the BRICs and their corporations.

1.5 Conclusion

The purpose of this chapter has primarily been to make the point that the places where economic activity occurs and where corporations are based, as well as where they invest, still matter a great deal. Globalization means that the global economy is indeed increasingly interconnected, and characterized by complex interdependence between states and nonstate actors such as MNCs. However, the latter are actually not as global as much of the conventional wisdom would have it. They remain located in the world's economically dominant states and regions, the markets of which they in turn dominate. As the new market economies emerge, it therefore follows that they are emerging *together* with their new MNCs. As the established states evolve and adapt in the face of both national and global challenges, they do so together with their established corporations.

Therefore, a comparative perspective on state-corporate relations remains important, and perhaps more so than ever given that states and their corporations must face global as well as regional and national challenges, yet do so in distinct national contexts. Specifically, comparative capitalism perspective, such as the VoC approach, is appropriate. While a good deal of abstraction from reality has been involved in the above analysis, as it is in the VoC approach itself, and criticism on this basis would be valid as indeed is the case in the debates surrounding it (see Hancke, 2009), nonetheless I would contend that considerably less abstraction has been the case than if a global analysis of state-corporate relations had been undertaken. Such abstractions have produced erroneous predictions in the past about the inevitability of a convergence on a liberal form of the state and economic relations, and in the post-2008 economic crisis environment afflicting the major developed economies, particularly those of Europe and the US, a global consensus seems more elusive than ever. There has never been a global convergence of corporate-state relations, and the more it is asserted as inevitable, the more it seems to perpetually shift 'over the horizon' as a state of affairs predicted in the near future but never realized.

Notes

1. Here I particularly have in mind both liberal and Marxist scholars who stress the underlying similarity in the structural basis of capitalist relations of production, this being either a good or a bad thing depending on whether they fall into the former (e.g., Bhagwati, 2004) or the latter (e.g., Bruff, 2011) camp.
2. The world's top 500 companies on the basis of their stock-market capitalization.
3. The world's top 500 companies on the basis of their global revenue.
4. Specifically, they are located in China (15 percent); Japan (14 percent); South Korea (3 percent); Australia (2 percent); India (2 percent); Taiwan (1 percent); and one corporation each from Malaysia and Thailand. See http://money.cnn.com.
5. This is the simple average of their TNIs. If the top 100 corporations are treated as a group, calculating their transnationality in total based on the sum of their assets, sales, and employment yields an average TNI of 59 – that is, slightly less.
6. The same may be said of other categories employed in the broader comparative capitalism literature.
7. Even if this is what Hall (2013) says is necessary in the aftermath of the global financial crisis.

8. This was on the basis of comparing the size of government expenditure (larger in CMEs versus smaller in LMEs); the size of the welfare sector (larger in CMEs versus smaller in LMEs); the extent to which the state provides general public services and social protection (more in CMEs versus LMEs); the extent to which business is autonomous and 'free' to act on the basis of market forces (in LMEs) or is constrained by the state (in CMEs); and the extent to which the state regulates and controls markets (higher in CMEs versus lower in LMEs).
9. These are also often seen as the most established and archetypal examples of the two categories, or the states that most clearly exhibit a shareholder versus stakeholder model of capitalism.

2
Multinationals as an Instrument of Catch-up Industrialization: Understanding the Strategic Links between State and Industry in Emerging Markets*

Terutomo Ozawa

2.1 Justifications for state involvement in catch-up growth

Emerging-market multinational corporations (MNCs) rise from rapidly catching-up economies, *not* from any so-called emerging ones. Their appearance on the world stage is concomitant with their success in initiating and sustaining industrial modernization in their home countries. And a successful catch-up can be planned, promoted, and achieved by a proactive government in an emerging economy that has a strong national determination for economic development. Market forces alone are not enough to spark an industrial takeoff. State involvement is practically a necessity, since market failures and externalities (notably negative ones) are rampant, both prior to, and in the early stages of, industrialization.

In this regard, even market-supremacy neoclassical economists allow for state intervention in such circumstances, albeit only as a temporary corrective measure. In contrast, however, so-called 'structural economists' (as opposed to neoclassicists) actually go even further and argue that emerging economies are plagued by obstacles, bottlenecks, and constraints, both internally and externally, that inhibit the structural changes and flexibilities needed for economic development. In other words, the market (or price) mechanism, if it exists, remains dysfunctional, and the only way to remedy the situation is state involvement. As Ian M. D. Little (1982) explains,

[T]he production structure of developing countries [is] very different from that of developed countries. To achieve development, this structure [must] be changed rapidly. The direction of the structural change required could be discerned by cross-country studies of the structure of production and trade. *As development proceeds, these structures must approximate more closely to those of the [more developed countries].* The structuralist view of the world provides a reason for distrusting the price mechanism and for trying to bring about change in other ways...it primarily seeks to provide *a reason for managing change by administrative action* (emphasis added, pp. 20–21).

In other words, the goal of catch-up is to attain a 'structure of production and trade' at the same level as advanced economies – that is, to close the existing gap in industrial structures. However, many emerging economies are stuck at the lower levels and are simply unable to move up. Some are caught in a vicious downward spiral, becoming bogged down in a morass of poverty. Structural rigidity is a critical obstacle that the market mechanism alone cannot clear away. Hence, a decisive administrative action on the part of government is called for.

Moreover, the market forces operating across borders under global capitalism are distorted by the monopolistic / anticompetitive holds of large, dominant MNCs. Not only are many advanced-market MNCs so large that they control the market, but also their business expansion abroad is often orchestrated by their home governments as a tool of foreign economic diplomacy – and also motivated by macroeconomic (i.e., fiscal, monetary, and foreign exchange) policy measures. MNCs' risk-taking behaviors may even reflect the moral hazard of 'too-big-to-fail' bailouts by their home governments. In general, states themselves are involved, either directly or indirectly, in international commercial activities in pursuit of national interests. The Organization of Petroleum Exporting Countries' (OPEC) market-influencing decisions are a good example of how such a huge global oil market comes under the influence of international cartelization (peculiarly with perfect impunity under global capitalism – but perhaps rationalized as a necessary tool to secure a 'fair' share of profits from the Western oil majors).

Consequently, market distortions, market failures, negative externalities, and structural rigidities are necessarily all the more pervasive and prevalent in global markets, hampering national industrialization and growth. Government is thus expected to play the key role of directing, coordinating, and facilitating the course of catch-up development. In other words, a 'facilitating state' is indispensable, as stressed by Justin

Lin (2012) in his advocacy of 'new structural economics' for economic development, a hybrid between free-market and structural economics. In this approach, then, emerging-market governments need to be capable of effectively formulating and implementing a national development strategy.

According to Bresser-Pereira's development strategy called 'new developmentalism', such a state capability is the key to the question of 'why some emergent countries succeed while others fall behind' (2010). 'Old developmentalism' was focused on import substitution under infant-industry protection, forced promotion of savings through the state, and complacency about public deficits and inflation – namely a development model once widely adopted across Latin America, but that ultimately failed. New developmentalism is also an alternative to the Washington Consensus or 'conventional orthodoxy'. The latter places full trust in the market mechanism through deregulation, privatization, and liberalization. But this too has turned out to be a disappointment. New developmentalism is built on export-led growth, disciplined fiscal and monetary management, an indirect promotion of savings and corporate investment, and an outward-focused, strong, and competent administration.

Here, new developmentalism chimes with Joseph Stiglitz's (2003) formulation of what he calls 'a new paradigm of development', a paradigm that is an amended version of the Washington Consensus, in which the market mechanism is lubricated, directed, and reinforced by government involvement. His new paradigm draws on the East Asian growth experiences in which 'these countries did not follow the standard [neo-liberal] prescriptions, [but in] most cases, national governments played a large role' (p. 81). Stiglitz also stresses the problems of bounded rationality and imperfect information flows (i.e., types of market failure) and advocates a proactive developmental role for government: 'government not only has a restraining role: it has a constructive and catalytic role – in promoting entrepreneurship, providing the social and physical infrastructure, ensuring access to education and finance, and supporting technology and innovation' (2012, p. 57).

In this respect, it should be kept in mind that even if the market is perfectly functional, the market per se is merely a resource-allocative mechanism and does not automatically achieve the social / public goal of catch-up growth all by itself. As pithily said by the Cambridge school of economics, 'Like fire, the market is a good servant, but a poor master' (Eatwell, 1982). Put differently, the market is basically neither goal setting nor goal pursuing; it is goal neutral at best, and sometimes even goal hindering (Ozawa, 1996). What is needed, then, is *a good master,* namely a goal-focused government that can make the best use of the market for industrialization purposes. After all, catch-up growth itself is a public good, so to speak. And when it comes to public goods, the market is known for ineptitude.

In addition to market failures, emerging economies in particular face serious government failures (e.g., corruption and bureaucratic inefficiency). And not only may government failures be even worse than market failures, but also the former often *aggravates* the latter. The most debilitating case is, therefore, a *simultaneous* occurrence of market and government failures, in which many emerging markets are ensnared despite all sorts of economic aid from the advanced world. This dire situation occurs, especially in what Gunnar Myrdal called 'a soft state' in his seminal work, *Asian Drama* (1968). In contrast, however, a 'hard state' can minimize and overcome government failures through reforms, self-discipline, and a concerted devotion to national interests. On the other hand, a centrally planned economy without the market mechanism creates the worst-case scenario of government failure in which the economy is rendered totally inefficient.

In sum, what really matters in a market-based economy, then, boils down to the culture, traditions, mores, ethos, and other intangible institutional factors that can be mobilized by a strong political leadership in such a way to minimize government failures and remedy market failures and structural rigidities. A foresighted and unswerving political and / or bureaucratic-elite leadership that can carry out a national development strategy is no doubt what is needed for industrial takeoff (although for higher stages of growth in which entrepreneurship and innovation play a pivotal role in growth, state dominance is a shackle, as will be discussed below).

2.2 Developmental states and state capitalism

National development strategies have been most ardently pursued by successful East Asian economies – first, Japan, then, the NIEs (Singapore, Taiwan, and South Korea)[1], and most recently, China. There are good reasons why Japan and the NIEs, in particular, were once called 'developmental states', the concept introduced by Chalmers Johnson (1982) in connection with his study on 'the Japanese miracle' – and also known as 'hard states' in the discipline of international political economy. In essence, this development model is basically a bureaucratic / technocratic elite-led *industrial structural policy* for catch-up by capitalizing on the market forces of global capitalism. In the words of Johnson,

[Industrial structural policy] concerns the proportions of agriculture, mining, manufacturing, and services in the nation's total production; and within manufacturing it concerns the percentages of light and heavy and of labor-intensive and knowledge-intensive industries. The application of the policy comes in *the government's attempts to change these proportions in ways it deems advantageous to the nation.* Industrial structure policy is based on such standards as income elasticity of demand, comparative costs of production, labor absorptive power, environmental concerns, investment effects on related industries, and export prospects. The heart of the policy is the *selection of the strategic industries* to be developed or converted to other lines of work (1982, p. 28, emphasis added).

This approach is in line with a structuralist's perspective on the process of catch-up growth previously mentioned: government must guide the economy to change its present proportions of different industrial sectors at home in such a way as to 'approximate more closely to those of the [more developed countries]'(Little, 1982, p. 20) – namely, the very aim of catch-up industrialization.

In essence, the developmental state takes on 'developmental functions' (Johnson, 1982, p. 19) in addition to performing 'regulatory functions' that every government does. It thus gets closely involved in promoting and coordinating *market-based* economic activities in such a way as to achieve the national goal of catch-up. Despite active government involvement, the private sector or the market serves as the main engine of catch-up growth, and 'self-control' and 'cooperation' – rather than 'state control' – are the standard modus operandi. 'Self-control means that the state *licenses* private enterprises to achieve developmental goals' (Johnson, 1982, p. 310, emphasis added). In the Japanese model, the state licensed cartels for a specified period of time and allowed these cartels to administer themselves. Cooperation took (and still takes) the form of 'deliberation councils' and 'discussion groups' that were comprised of government officials, industry representatives, and scholars. State control was thus shunned, at least in principle, in respect for free enterprise and democracy. Government corporations were, however, often set up for a specified period in 'such high-risk areas as petroleum exploration, atomic power development, the phasing out of the mining industry, and computer software development [in the 1950s and 1960s]' (Johnson, 1982, p. 315). What Johnson calls 'situational imperatives' or 'situational nationalism' compelled the Japanese government to directly take up those activities / projects, on a temporary basis, that were too risky for the private sector to undertake. The end result is that Japan emerged as a market-capitalist economy. Taiwan, South Korea, and Singapore followed, on the whole, in Japan's footsteps and similarly have grown into market-driven capitalist economies, although their situational imperatives were necessarily different and led them down divergent paths (for an analysis of how recent market reforms in South Korea have impacted its corporate sector and Korean multinationals, see Jeong in this volume).

By contrast, although China's catch-up strategy was clearly influenced by the success of its neighbors, its growth model is distinct from that of a developmental state – in that the role of government is meant to be enduring, pervasive, and motivated primarily for political purposes. In fact, it is classified separately as 'state capitalism'. According to Ian Bremmer's definition, state capitalism is 'a system in which the state functions as the leading economic actor and *uses markets primarily for political gain*' (2009, p. 41, emphasis added). Here, although not pointed out by Bremmer, two types of political gain need to be distinguished: one type is an internal political gain from rapid economic growth to legitimize the political monopoly of the Chinese Communist Party, and the other is an external political gain from China's rise as a major geopolitical – and potentially military – power (in a sense, China pursues its own version of the 'rich country, strong army' strategy once adopted by Japan with a calamitous result). No doubt, China has skillfully blended the authoritarian power of the state (controlled by one party) with the wealth-creating power of capitalism to drive catch-up growth and boost its geopolitical power – while quelling the countervailing power of democracy against autocracy at home.

Bremmer (2009) also observes that four primary actors represent state capitalism: national resource (especially oil) corporations, state-owned enterprises (SOEs), privately owned, but government-favored national champions, and sovereign wealth funds (SWFs). They all operate as MNCs and serve as a critical instrument of their home countries' growth. China has all four of these primary actors, although its national champions (such as Huawei and Lenovo) were only recently birthed. It does not mean, however, that all four actors have to exist simultaneously to be identified as state capitalism. Nor does the mere presence of one of the four actors in a country alone necessarily make state capitalism. For instance, SWFs are now set up even in market-capitalist economies (e.g., Norway, Singapore, and South Korea). They are similar in functions and purposes to large-scale domestic pension funds (such as the California Public Employees' Retirement System).

As is well expected, China's approach is strongly oriented to state control – instead of self-control and cooperation that is pivoted on the private sector. This modality presents the major difference from developmental states. Despite its touted privatization in the recent past, China's economy is still dominated by state-backed companies, which account for 80 percent of the value of China's stock market (The Economist, 2012a). Even the private sector is still closely linked with the Chinese state, especially at the provincial level (see Nölke in this volume). Thus, the market remains as a captive servant for its sole master, China's Communist Party. In other words, China's model goes beyond a regulatory state and a developmental state – and forms an authoritarian state. Nevertheless, it has so far turned out to be quite efficacious in producing nationally planned economic results. One obvious advantage of China's state capitalism is that the state needs no decentralized democratic decision-making, which is often time-consuming, cumbersome, nearsighted, and parochial, namely – the inherent failings (or 'negative externalities' that hinder rapid economic development) of electoral democracy. For example, where else can a state bulldoze away a vast number of old farming communities in order to build modern urban communities with high-rise apartments, schools, clinics, shopping malls, and so forth so that it can move 250 million rural citizens into cities – whether they like it or not – just for the sake of making the economy more consumption-driven rather than investment- and export-driven? On the other hand, one big disadvantage is that Chinese MNCs, especially state-owned ones, are often suspected of harboring hidden political motives in the host countries.

Be that as it may, state capitalism has recently emerged as an alternative to free-market capitalism, challenging the existing world order built on the Western ideology of free enterprise and democracy. Undoubtedly, China cleverly seized the 'Nixon and Kissinger' diplomacy intended then to remake China as a capitalist ally against the USSR, a miscalculation that has resulted in exactly the opposite outcome. The United States is now confronted with a China-Russia alliance over an array of intractable and potentially explosive issues in world affairs. China's state capitalism is a textbook-perfect fusion of state and industry in pursuit of economic and political gains. Vietnam's communist regime is the same type of state capitalism, although on a much smaller scale and with less efficiency. Also, Cuba has taken its first steps toward state capitalism by partially freeing farmers and shopkeepers from state control, while remaining communist in polity. And the four major actors of state capitalism are active, if not all at once, in other BRIC (Brazil, Russia, India, and China) countries, too, although these countries (all with electoral democracy) are less efficient at and less capable of achieving industrial modernization than China is.

Given the current rise of state capitalism, state-owned or -backed enterprises are being increasingly established across the emerging world. For instance, state-owned enterprises dominate in resources-abundant emerging countries in the Middle East, Latin America, and Africa, where the private sector is incapable of organizing large-sale enterprises on its own for resource extraction and export. Also, resources in emerging markets are regarded as national assets that need to be shared by the public – hence the state ownership of mining and oil companies is justified. The upshot is that '[g]overnments, not private shareholders, already own the world's largest oil companies and control three-quarters of the world's energy reserves' (Bremmer, 2009, p. 40).

Also, state-owned businesses persist in the former centrally planned emerging economies (e.g., China, Vietnam, Russia, and other former USSR countries) that adopted a capitalist mode of industrialization. These economies, despite their initial move to privatization, still retain state-owned enterprises in large numbers, especially in what they regard as strategic industries. Consequently, many emerging-market MNCs are state-owned or -backed. Furthermore, those SOEs that operate as multinationals are clearly on the rise. '[SOEs] are serious players in the world FDI market. UNCTAD identified more than 650 SOEs that are multinational enterprises [in 2011]' (Sauvant and Strauss, 2012, p. 1). These MNCs are mostly diversified conglomerates that have grown in underdeveloped home markets where small fragmented pieces of different local markets for goods and services need to be stitched together to form a viable size of sales. And SWFs are, in fact, state-owned financial MNCs.

It should be noted that state ownership necessarily signifies state control. But state control may be motivated either for purely economic or for political/ideological reasons. Even in the United States, the citadel of free-market capitalism, major banks and automakers were temporarily 'state owned' for the bailout in the aftermath of the 2008 financial debacle. As mentioned above, SOEs may be the only viable enterprises in emerging markets where the underdeveloped private sector is unable to undertake high-risk, large-scale ventures. When Japan embarked on industrial modernization in the mid-19th century, SOEs were deliberately set up in strategic industries, but soon privatized as the private sector developed. These expedient measures were still consistent with free-market capitalism, since they were intended to foster or safeguard the free enterprise system. By contrast, SOEs may be designed to achieve political / ideological goals (e.g., income redistribution, a direct source of state revenue, and socialist, nationalist, or any other nonmarket ideological ideals) – hence, intended to exist on a permanent basis. After all, government ownership under state capitalism is meant essentially for political purposes, not for the sake of economic expediency and efficiency. Economic growth and prosperity is not the ultimate goal of state capitalism, but a mere means to fulfill political purposes.

2.3 Nurturing national enterprises as multinationals

A catch-up development strategy taken up by an emerging economy with strong national determination and leadership is accompanied by an equally strong nationalism that evokes a public devotion to – and even self-sacrifice for – national interests in order to attain a respectable degree of economic sovereignty. Many emerging economies are likely to adopt a policy to create their own *national / indigenous* companies, if not state owned or -run, – but, most desirably, national champions. True, in this age of globalization, government may pragmatically permit – or in fact, even *proactively* encourage in many instances – foreign MNCs to participate as a critical *joint input* in industrial modernization, especially in the early stages. Their investments in the host economies are expected to create industrial knowledge spillovers to local industry. Such dependence on foreign interests, however, will (or may be policy guided to) decline once a particular new industry is initiated and gets well on track to sustained development. Hence, it becomes imperative to promote national companies, which, although they may initially serve as junior partners in joint ventures with foreign MNCs at home, will eventually grow into their nations' *own* MNCs to compete in the global market.

As is expected, national companies can better serve national economic interests. For example, they can spawn innovations at home and spin off new local businesses, thereby contributing directly to more autonomous development. In cases where overseas-trained expatriates are encouraged to return home as one important conduit for knowledge inflows, national companies also can serve as a desirable receptacle for reverse brain drain (or what is popularly called 'sea turtles' in China). Most importantly, they can eventually engage in overseas business activities in the capacity of homegrown MNCs in such a way as to serve their national economic – and often political – interests. In other words, depending on whether business enterprises are nationally or foreign owned, the direction and outcomes of industrialization will be vastly different. Therefore, as Alice Amsden emphasized,

[n]ational firms must be nursed and nurtured to fulfill the functions that foreign affiliates are less likely to undertake. There is little substitution. For this reason, specific institutions must be built to promote national assets. Good models in Asia are the Republic of Korea and China, and in the Middle East, many OPEC members (2012, p. 3).

Similarly, Michael Porter advises that emerging economies should not become dependent on foreign MNCs that invest on the basis of factor cost considerations (e.g., low wages). Instead, '[g]overnment should encourage the formation and upgrading of indigenous companies in related and supporting industries to those in which multinationals operate, not solely with an eye toward import substitution but ultimately as international competitors' (1990, p. 679). In other words nurturing and developing indigenous companies into a nation's own competitive multinationals is another critical role assigned to government.

In addition, it is worth noting that inward foreign direct investment (IFDI), in particular, creates two opposing effects on local industries: 'knowledge spillovers' and 'crowding out' (Pathak, et al., 2012). Which effect will be more dominant and prevailing than the other hinges largely on each host economy's capacity to maximize the positive, while minimizing the negative, effect. These two effects, however, clearly presuppose the existence of indigenous firms as beneficiaries of knowledge spillovers and as victims of crowding out. Hence, the net outcome is determined by how strongly and adequately the national firms have been fostered and have grown to absorb knowledge spillovers and stand up to crowding-out competition.

Also, in this regard, Seev Hirsch raises an interesting related question of 'whether, *ceteris paribus*, nation states have an economic interest in becoming home countries to [MNCs]' (2012, p. 1). His answer is 'yes', basically because '[t]his enables home countries to increase the benefits they derive from the international division of labor, exploitation of economies of scale and the ownership advantages of their MNCs' despite the costs of cross-border activities of national firms such as 'tax losses and the diminution of sovereignty implied by outward FDI' (Hirsch, 2012, p. 1). Although not touched upon in Hirsch's short essay, the social benefits and costs involved also depend on the stage of catch-up growth. Tax losses and sovereignty diminution do not necessarily occur. In fact, outward FDI may complement and strengthen MNCs' home operations and profits, thereby enabling them to pay more taxes at home. Indeed, sovereignty may be enhanced as MNCs acquire some strategically significant foreign assets, real and financial alike, thereby projecting their national power.

In short, nation-states as the gatekeepers for foreign MNCs' entry into home markets must formulate appropriate policies to harness and maximize the benefits of inward FDI and simultaneously nurture national firms as their own MNCs that will bring home gains from overseas business operations. Consequently, if national firms' activities are impeded by overseas markets' restrictions on trade and investment, their government may be all the more proactively compelled to assist and promote them to overcome such restrictions (On this point and for a specific example, see Kingkaew in this volume). Therefore, there necessarily arise close links and interplays between state and industry in their national efforts to industrialize by bringing up indigenous enterprises during the course of catch-up growth.

In sum, state-industry relations in those emerging economies that initiate a catch-up drive are closely collaborative, although unequal. The state often fosters, governs, and even controls the growth of domestic enterprises and industries in hopes of creating national champions that can serve as their own MNCs. It is expected, however, that as the economy succeeds in economic development, such a close-knit relationship will become loosened – as a general trend (For a contextual example of how Latin America's state-business relations evolve, see Clifton et al. in this volume). This is because the economy becomes increasingly integrated with the outside world, and the private sector grows and pursues its own interests by expanding businesses abroad. Eventually, once the economy reaches advanced status, state-business relations become more 'arms-length' in nature. The private business sector in pursuit of its own commercial gains may even grow insensitive and unresponsive to national interests and needs, as evidenced in many advanced economies. All this said, nevertheless, the evolving scenario sketched out above assumes the world economy continues to exist under global free-enterprise capitalism. State capitalism (China's model in particular) with its recently emerged MNCs may write and play out its own unique scenario for state and industry linkages.

2.4 Catch-up growth and the role of MNCs

Economic development is fundamentally a *derived* phenomenon – 'derived' in the sense that the process and pace of development are basically determined by how effectively an emerging economy can *emulate, and learn from,* more advanced economies through interactions (via trade and investment) with the outside world. In other words, catch-up growth is the process of absorbing and assimilating industrial knowledge from the advanced world so as to attain the higher levels of industrial structure. Hence, the speed and scope of catch-up itself is determined by the *size* of the existing stock of advanced knowledge that can be tapped into and by *how quickly and efficiently* an emerging economy can absorb such knowledge from abroad. As Alexander Gerschenkron nicely summed up,

> [i]ndustrialization always seemed the more promising the greater the backlog of technological innovations which the backward country could take over from the more advanced country. Borrowed technology, so much and so rightly stressed by Veblen, was one of the primary factors assuring a high speed of development in a backward country entering the stage of industrialization (1962, p. 213).

Also, industrialization necessarily involves a succession of structural change and upgrading, exhibiting different stages for catch-up – that is, to climb the ladder of economic development (a nebulous notion heretofore widely used in development economics, but to be defined below). This process requires, and is driven by, technological progress. It is, moreover, in this context that national companies emerge as MNCs – as outcomes of such technological and structural transformation at home. They build up their firm-specific advantages inherent in the different stages of growth, advantages they can exploit by going overseas. In other words, disparate types of MNCs are spawned pari passu with structural changes and growth (that is, up the ladder of economic development). The above perspective poses two key questions:

- If the emergence of MNCs is inherent in growth stages, what really are the stages of economic development? In other words, we must specify the hitherto casually used, nebulous notion of 'the ladder of economic development' – in terms of different levels of industrial structure.
- In what way can the homegrown MNCs serve as an instrument of catch-up by engaging in overseas business activities? In other words, how does the state get involved in promoting overseas business activities for national interests? Are there any stage-specific justifications for this? These questions will be addressed below.

2.5 The ladder of economic development specified

The essence of economic development is a series of structural changes brought about by innovation. MNCs are a creature of such structural changes. This is because new enterprises come into existence as they succeed in innovating, and eventually advance abroad as multinationals to exploit their firm-specific advantages. This proposition can be explained in terms of the 'leading-sector' stages model, à la Schumpeter (Schumpeter, 1934; Ozawa, 2005; 2009). The model is built on a *historical sequence of growth that is punctuated by stages (that can be captured as 'structural breaks' in econometrics), and in each stage a certain industrial sector and technological thrust is identifiable as the main driver of structural transformation*. The perspective here is in line with what Schumpeter (1934) called 'the perennial gale of creative destruction' that drives the process of industrial upgrading under capitalism. The same idea was emphasized by Rostow (1960) in his view of 'economic history *as a sequence of stages rather than merely as a continuum*, within which nature never makes a jump' (p. 16, emphasis added). It is out of such structural changes (hence, stages) brought about by innovations that *stage-specific* MNCs are homegrown.

Thus far, the world economy has witnessed five tiers of leading-sector industry emerge in wave-like progression since the Industrial Revolution (see column A, in Figure 2.1 below) – and a sixth tier looms in the making. The five tiers have been (I) endowment-driven industries (represented by textiles and other light industry goods in labor-abundant countries and by extraction of minerals and fossil fuels in resource-endowed countries), (II) resource-processing industries (steel and basic chemicals), (III) assembly-based industries (mass-produced automobiles), (IV) research and development (R&D)-driven industries (computers and pharmaceuticals), and (V) information technology (IT)-enabled industries (digital telecoms, operating platforms, search engines, and social media) – and (VI) a new emerging tier of green technology (GT)-based industries (energy-saving and pollution-abating devices, new cleaner energies [solar, wind, geothermal, etc.] that foster a healthier living environment [augmented by both public and personal health and medical sciences]) – all in an effort to create a 'green economy' and 'sustainable growth' (Ozawa, 2011).

The above series of tiers simply traces out the broad *historical* sequence in which different leading sectors have transformed the industrial structure in current advanced economies. This model clearly indicates the different levels of industrial structure, namely the rungs of the ladder of economic development, which emerging economies aspire to climb.

2.6 A caveat to stages theory

The above stages model is a road map, so to speak, for a progression of structural changes and industrial upgrading for catch-up industrialization.

In other words, this road map shows the concrete structural changes expected and required of catching-up economies. It is worth repeating Little's observation quoted earlier: 'As development proceeds, [their] structures must approach more closely to those of the [more developed countries]' (1982, pp. 20–21). This does *not* mean, however, that late industrializers need to replicate exactly the same sequence of growth trail-blazes by earlier industrializers. On the contrary, latecomers are totally free to jumble it, take shortcuts by leapfrogging, or enter all stages even simultaneously – although normally from the *low* end (i.e., the labor-intensive segment) – depending on their catch-up strategies, capabilities, and circumstances. In fact, this flexibility constitutes a latecomer advantage. Thus, they can emulate advanced countries' growth patterns in a *broad* manner, but always *customize their own catch-up processes in adaptation to their country-specific circumstances*. As Gerschenkron puts it, '[i]n every instance of industrialization, *imitation* of the evolution in advanced countries appears in combination with *different, indigenously determined* elements' (1962, p. 20, emphasis added; indeed, this pattern of indigenous distinction applies to state-corporate relations, as emphasized by Mikler in this volume).

It should be noted that, although the development of these stages in earlier industrializers required a series of breakthrough innovations, such 'wheels' no longer need to be reinvented. Many are readily available for presently emerging economies. For example, the technologies for tier-I (e.g., textiles and garments) and -II industries (e.g., steel, chemicals, and cement) are practically so standardized that any aspiring economy can set up those industries by simply importing industrial knowledge – in a variety of ways, from licensing to plant imports, to build-operate-transfer (BOT) contracts, to inward FDI.

2.7 The 'double-helix' ladder of growth: Side ladders added

In addition to the *inter*industry ladder of structural upgrading, each stage has produced a *vertical* concatenation of multiprocess *intra*industry subsectors, the upper end of which is highly capital intensive and technologically sophisticated, while the lower end is labor intensive and technologically standardized (Ozawa, 2009). This *intra*industry (often *intra*firm or *intra*product) vertical division of labor is also known as 'production process fragmentation' (Jones, 2000). This side ladder, as it were, has been built mostly by MNCs since the end of WWII, but especially in recent years. Consequently, the progression of industrial upgrading (of the *inter*industry type) and the vertical chains of value added (of the *intra*industry type) have opened up opportunities for firms in *both* advanced and emerging markets to pursue a *new* division of labor by establishing cross-border supply chains of production and marketing within each tier. Supply chains can be established within a *multilayered hierarchy of economies* operating at different stages of growth – hence, different levels of technology, skills, and wages to be used as inputs in a complementary manner.

Also, the side ladder is a focus of technological innovation in, and for, emerging markets. Local companies are now striving to 'innovate on the cheap', while foreign MNEs similarly try to introduce the low-end lines of products suitable for local consumers' pockets in emerging markets. The low-priced Nano minicars produced by Tata Motor, India's recently innovated stripped-down medical devices, its generic drugs manufacturing, and its low-end outsourcing services (e.g., call centers and back-office work) are some representative examples of the former, and Nissan's latest plan to dust off and reintroduce its once-discarded old Datsun brand at as low a price as US$ 3,000 illustrates the latter. Some are taking a different tack. For example, China FAW Group introduced a luxury sedan, Hongqi H7 (priced at US$ 49,000), to rival BMW and Audi, at the 2013 Shanghai auto show. Although the Chinese government is promoting this automobile under the national rejuvenation slogan of 'the Chinese Dream', its market is still limited to government procurement. All these examples are meant to illustrate how global corporations are active in product development on the intraindustry side ladders.

2.8 Stage-specific types of multinationals and government involvement

As emphasized above, different types of MNCs come into existence at different growth stages, for example, apparel MNCs from tier I, mining MNCs from tier II, automobile MNCs from tier III, electronics MNCs from tier IV, and social media MNCs from tier V. In other words, no country will have its own automobile MNCs when the home country is still in the tier-I stage or only in the tier-II stage of industrialization. Likewise, no MNCs in electronics or other R&D-based goods would emerge from a country that is still in the tier-II stage. The stage-determined patterns of the rise of homegrown MNCs and their government involvement are illustrated in Figure 2.1.

Here, postwar Japanese experiences (as one prototype of the developmental state) can highlight those patterns. Despite war devastation,

A) Growth stages	B) Internal forces for outward push	C) State involvement in: i) Growth	C) State involvement in: ii) Overseas business	D) Types of home MNEs' activity by motive
• Tier I: Labor-driven (textiles, sundries, & assembling)	Labor shortages & rising wages (towards the end of tier-I stage)	High, direct	Low, indirect	Labor-seeking Export-substituting
• Tier II: Scale-driven, capital/resources-intensive (metals, chemicals)	Needs for resources Space & environmental constraints	High, direct		Resources-seeking Space-seeking
• Tier III: Assembly-driven, parts-intensive (automobiles)	Needs for technology, brands, & export markets	Medium, indirect		Market-seeking Brands-seeking Protection-skirting
• Tier IV: R&D-driven, high-tech (computers and pharmaceuticals)	Needs for technology & brands	High, indirect	Low, indirect	Knowledge-seeking Brands-seeking
• Tier V: IT-enabled, telecom/Internet-driven	Needs for latest technology	High, direct	Low, indirect	Alliance-seeking

Figure 2.1 Stages of industrialization, state involvement, and homegrown MNCs in emerging economies: Generalized patterns and characteristics

Note: These stage-related patterns and characteristics vary in intensity, depending on the efficacy of the catch-up strategy, the 'lateness' and rapidity of catch-up industrialization, and the nature of political economy on both sides of a catching-up country and more advanced countries.

Japan, having already developed tier-I and -II industries in prewar days, swiftly modernized its surviving (but severely damaged) heavy and chemical industries and further climbed the ladder of industrialization. The country quickly succeeded in catching up with the West and joining the ranks of advanced countries – against the backdrop of close state-industry collaboration (dubbed as 'Japan, Inc.'), and thanks mostly to a then-still-existing stock of human capital in the early stages of catch-up. The first wave of Japan's postwar overseas investment (which turned its national enterprises into contemporary MNCs for the first time[2]) swelled in the 1960s and 1970s, involving tier-I and -II industries. Having already been competitive in prewar days but now confronted by rising wages at home, starting in the late 1960s, companies (mostly small and medium-sized) in labor-intensive tier-I industries (such as textiles, toys, and other sundries) shifted production to neighboring countries such as Taiwan, Singapore, Hong Kong, Taiwan, and South Korea. Lacking the necessary capacity to go overseas on their own, they were normally assisted by Japan's general trading companies as co-investors (Ozawa, 1979). The government was not much involved – except for indirect support given by way of providing some financial assistance and overseas market information. This period marked an era of 'labor-seeking' investment abroad.

At the same time, the reconstruction and expansion of resource-intensive tier-II industries compelled resource-indigent Japan to hunt for minerals and fuels overseas. Japan's *keiretsu* groups (corporate conglomerates) each aggressively modernized its scale-based tier-II industries (such as steel, shipbuilding, metals, and chemicals) within itself under the so-called 'one-set principle'.[3] They also eagerly competed in entering new petroleum-based industries (e.g., petrochemicals and synthetics). All these efforts required advanced technology. Since Japan's catch-up policy at that time was to avoid, as much as practically possible, inward FDI in fear of foreign domination over domestic industry, licensing became the main conduit of technology acquisition from the advanced West (Ozawa, 1974).

As expected of a resource-poor country, Japan's buildup of tier-II industries led to a sharp rise in demand for oil and other natural resources, compelling the *keiretsu* soon to organize resource-seeking MNCs in groups. Their search for overseas resources was proactively supported by the government in both financial and diplomatic terms. Special loans were arranged via such state agencies as the Overseas Economic Cooperation Fund, the Ex-Im Bank, and the Japan International Cooperation Agency.[4] This period thus witnessed the most active government involvement in overseas investment and the use of its own homebred MNCs as a strategic vehicle for securing resources abroad to feed Japan's rapidly growing heavy and chemical industries. Moreover, such an expansion of tier-II industries in space-limited and energy-indigent Japan soon hit the limits of location and the environment, making it desirable to relocate some resource-processing production (such as smelting, sintering, refining, and so forth) to resource-rich emerging economies. This second wave of Japan's overseas investment was thus both of the resources-seeking and the industrial space-seeking type from tier-II industries.

Entering and building up higher-tier (III and above) industries required further technological progress. Here, Japanese companies continued to rely on licensing, but focused more on seed technologies that they could commercialize through adaptive R&D. Also, many of Japan's manufacturers in tier-III industries strove to improve and refine assembly operations – not only by use of advanced robotics that could relieve factory workers from what they called '3-D' ['dirty', 'dangerous', and 'demanding'] tasks but also by treating workers as 'brains' (instead of 'brawn') so that they would become an invaluable source of information and ideas for further technological and organizational improvements. At the vanguard of this unique approach was the automobile industry (tier III) led by Toyota Motor that introduced a new assembly innovation, the 'Toyota production system' (Ohno, 1978), which soon afterward came to be more popularly known overseas as 'flexible (or lean) production' (Womack et al., 1990). This resulted in both higher productivity and higher product quality. With this newly acquired technological and managerial advantage, Japan's carmakers became competitive MNCs, setting up overseas shops across the world in the 1980s and onward – mostly to skirt rising protectionism in their export markets, especially in response to the 'voluntary' export restraints (VERs) imposed by the United States in the early 1980s. For these overseas investments, however, the government's involvement remained indirect by way of special loans provided by Japan's Ex-Im Bank (Ozawa, 2009), although it had to administer the VERs.

This fourth wave of overseas investment (of the 'protection-skirting' type), which was soon joined in the 1990s by Japan's electronics makers, similarly sparked adaptive product innovations at home for color televisions, cathode ray tubes (CRTs), DRAM (dynamic random access memory), video recorders, and so on. They began actively to invest in Western markets, where Japan's explosive exports met local clamors for protection. And there was little direct involvement of the state in the electronics companies' advance overseas. Their technological advantages at that time were so strong that they hardly needed any support from the government.

Indeed, the above-described basic characteristics of the stage-inherent emergence of multinationals have been replicated across the rest of East Asia. South Korea and Taiwan in particular, which are similarly as land space-constrained and lacking in resources as Japan, closely followed suit. They have displayed similar features in accordance with their stages of growth. Nevertheless, their catch-up strategies and their MNCs' behaviors as late industrializers are necessarily differentiated in detail from Japan's due to their different time (history)- and space (geography)-specific circumstances. For example, South Korea and Taiwan relied on foreign MNCs' investments in tier-I industries by setting up export-processing zones. And their compatriot scientists and engineers, who had been educated and job-trained in the United States, returned home to build higher-tier, high-tech industries, especially electronics. Here, their governments played an active role in luring back those skilled compatriots (and expatriates) from abroad. Also, Taiwan, Singapore, and Hong Kong had ethnic and cultural advantages in advancing into China's markets.

China is also a good illustrative case for comparison. At present, for instance, MNCs from China exhibit four investment features. They are investing most actively in (i) resource extraction (i.e., minerals and fuels) and accompanying infrastructure projects (such as pipelines, port facilities, rails, and highways) (FDI feature #1); (ii) low-end manufacturing like textiles in other emerging economies (such as Vietnam, Cambodia, Bangladesh, and even faraway countries in sub-Saharan Africa) (FDI feature #2); (iii) state-sponsored, trade-supportive facilities abroad (FDI feature #3); and (iv) corporate mergers and acquisitions (M&As) in the advanced world to obtain advanced technology, business know-how, and globally known brands (FDI feature #4).

These features clearly reveal that China, despite its meteoric rise to the world's second-largest country in terms of gross domestic product (GDP), has just been graduating from the tier-I stage and is still in the midst of modernizing tier-II industries, although it is trying to build tier-III and -IV industries simultaneously from the low end of each industry. An exception is tier-V (IT-enabled) industries, which China has succeeded entering without any gap to close simply because this new tier has only recently originated in the United States. Furthermore, China's overseas investment pattern reflects how far up the ladder of development its economy has climbed. FDI feature #1 reflects the height of tier-II resource-intensive growth; FDI feature #2 signals the end of tier-I growth with the sudden appearance of labor shortages and wage hikes at home; FDI feature #3 shows China's still export-driven, import-dependent growth despite its effort to shift toward a new phase of domestic consumption-led growth and away from the past export-cum-investment-led growth; and FDI feature #4 mirrors its drive to acquire badly needed technologies and brands in order to further climb onto higher-end manufacturing.

Now, the Chinese government is heavily involved in promoting its 'go global' policy by supporting the overseas advance of Chinese enterprises, notably state-owned or -backed ones. As pointed out earlier, China is the paragon of state capitalism that is bent on challenging the world order of free-market capitalism. Here exists a source of political friction in the wake of China's success in tier-V (IT-enabled) industries that evokes suspicions of cyberattacks, cyber espionage, computer hacking, and online theft of technology – and suspicions about China's IT multinationals like Huawei and ZTE as an arm of its military establishment. Moreover, China has successfully gone through the relatively easy initial phase of catch-up (i.e., tier-I and -II stages), which corresponds to what Paul Krugman (1997) characterizes as 'perspiration (or input)-driven'. However, it now has to upgrade knowledge-intensive, higher-tier (III through IV) industries, which matches what Krugman calls 'inspiration (or efficiency)-driven'. Free-market capitalism is more likely inspiration conducive than the Chinese brand of state capitalism that represses freedom of speech in political affairs (thereby constricting freewheeling thinking and information flows in general) in the name of 'social harmony and stability'.

In sum, despite some distinctive undertones of its political economy, China is an excellent example, attesting to the relevancy of our stages model that can shed light on the stage-determined trend of industrial structural upgrading, the stage-specific debut of homegrown MNCs on the global scene, and the role of state-industry relations in growth and overseas business activity.

2.9 Concluding remarks

This chapter has explored the state-industry linkage, the stage-specific rise of homegrown MNCs, and their role as an instrument of catch-up industrialization in emerging economies (excluding the resource-abundant economies, which require another separate study) by drawing on the experiences of East Asia.

Government involvement in catch-up growth is the norm, since the market and its supporting institutions are necessarily underdeveloped prior to industrialization. The market, even if developed, remains dysfunctional with rampant market failures, disruptive externalities – and most of all, structural rigidities. Government is thus compelled to play the role of the kick-starter of catch-up growth. Yet, government failures are equally prevalent. As is often the case, furthermore, government failures themselves worsen market failures. Such an adverse situation is pronounced in 'soft states', creating a deadly trap of market-cum-government failures, in which many emerging economies are bogged down. As demonstrated by East Asia's successfully industrialized economies, however, a 'developmental state' or a 'hard state', even if not totally free from government failures, can overcome market failures and structural rigidities, igniting and sustaining an industrial takeoff. Also, China's state capitalism has so far proved quite effectual for industrial takeoff and catch-up, although its future may not be so spectacular and promising because higher tiers of the industrial structure require freer and more transparent sociopolitical environments for new ideas and information flows.

In essence, economic development is nothing but a sequence of structural changes driven by innovations, entailing different stages of growth. It is out of such a sequence that diverse types of enterprises come into existence in a stage-inherent manner – and rise and fall by the logic of 'creative destruction'. Since different stages open up new business opportunities overseas, indigenous enterprises have to go multinational to exploit those opportunities abroad in pursuit of profits. In this sense, MNCs are basically a creature of structural changes at home. And at the same time, their overseas operations can be used by their home governments as an instrument to facilitate structural change and economic growth – and as a tool of international economic and political policy. To this end, however, the state needs to nurture domestic enterprises in the first place so that some, if not all, will grow into competitive MNCs. All of these developments related to the evolving state-industry links in emerging economies and the stage-specific rise of their homegrown MNCs can be best examined in terms of the 'leading-sector' stages model, à la Schumpeter, of growth (that specifies 'the ladder of economic development'). After all, the essence of development is a progression of structural upgrading (i.e., a climb on the ladder), and the goal of catch-up is the attainment by an emerging economy of the higher level of industrial structure that prevails in the advanced world.

Notes

* This chapter is based on a book manuscript (in progress), *The Evolution of the World Economy: The 'Flying-Geese' Theory of Multinational Corporations and Structural Transformation*, Edward Elgar (copyright © T. Ozawa: forthcoming).
1. This excludes Hong Kong, which is a free-market economy with minimum government intervention. Yet under its policy of 'positive noninterventionism', the government has been skillfully supporting private businesses in terms of providing up-to-date infrastructure and information to facilitate economic growth.
2. In prewar days, Japan's enterprises did make FDI in several key locations abroad, mainly Manchuria, as part of its colonial policies.
3. Under this principle, each major *keiretsu* group established a set of key strategic industries, such as steel, metals, petrochemicals, and shipbuilding, bringing about dynamic oligopolistic rivalries.
4. In a similar fashion, Brazil's MNCs are financially supported by its development bank (BNDES), as examined by Masiero et al. in this volume.

Part II
Country Studies

3
South Korean Multinationals after the Asian Financial Crisis: Toward Liberal Capitalism?

Seung-il Jeong

3.1 Introduction

Known as the 'Miracle of East Asia', South Korea remains a successful case of late industrialization. South Korea's rapid economic growth since the 1960s transformed it from one of the world's poorest countries into an economic powerhouse with per capita income of US$ 23,000 as of 2012. Seen as a highly effective model of industrial catch-up, South Korea's state-guided capitalism focused on export-oriented manufacturing sectors and was once praised as the hallmark of successful industrialization (see also Ozawa in this volume). Now it is the twelfth-largest economy in gross domestic product (GDP) terms, and its global companies are leading in electronics, car manufacturing, and shipbuilding. At the same time, due to its strong emphasis on exports, it has coped with the global financial crisis of late 2008 better than most developed economies.

But 15 years ago, when the Asian crisis hit the country in late 1997, GDP growth fell sharply. Then it started to rise steadily, but only reached half of the pre-1997 figure. More seriously, even though its GDP has nearly tripled in the last two decades, this growth has become decoupled from the lives of ordinary people, whose real incomes have grown by less than half that rate in the same period (Statistics Korea, 2012). Incredibly, South Korea's household saving has plummeted from the highest to the lowest among the Organization for Economic Cooperation and Development (OECD) nations, while its corporate saving has soared from the lowest to the highest (OECD, 2013). While the large multinational companies have become more productive and efficient, they have hired fewer workers at home – growth has been jobless. Their share of domestic employment has fallen by one-third, from 18 percent to

12 percent, even as they have expanded rapidly overseas (Bank of Korea, 2012).

What is the cause of these dramatic changes? The purpose of this paper is to investigate the deep structural changes that have occurred in the South Korean economy and its multinational companies in the last two decades. The plan of the paper is as follows: Section two explains briefly why such changes occurred, by analyzing the East Asian crisis at the end of 1997 and the liberal structural reforms that followed. Sections three and four will deal with how South Korea's banks and multinational firms changed as a result of those reforms. And section five will deal with the role of the free trade agreements (FTAs) with America and Europe, concluded in 2010 and 2011 respectively, in recent changes.

3.2 The Asian crisis and structural reforms

The period from the mid-1980s to the mid-1990s was truly East Asia's decade. Many Western researchers praised Japanese business (see, for instance, Clark and Fujimoto, 1991), and some others found praiseworthy characteristics in firms and markets in Japan, South Korea, and Taiwan, relating these to their particular social, historical, and economic institutions (Whitley, 1992; Fallows, 1995). In its report on the 'Asian Miracle' (1993), the World Bank also praised the East Asian economies.

Belief in the invincibility of East Asia was, however, shattered by the Asian financial crisis that occurred in late 1997. Beginning at that time, a large body of research appeared, explaining the unfolding of the crisis and its causes. Some argued that the crisis was homegrown, the product of crony Asian capitalism (see, for instance, Corsetti et al., 1998a; 1998b; Greenspan, 1998). In this view, the crisis was caused by institutional and structural distortions in East Asian capitalism, which produced moral hazard. Others, however, emphasized the role of the financial panic arising from the embedded instability of liberalized financial markets (Furman and Stiglitz, 1998; Chang, 1998; 2000).

Such divergent interpretations implied different policy prescriptions for the crisis. If the crisis was primarily one of panic, then the policy goal should be to control unstable financial markets by creating reassuring regulatory rules. But if East Asia's crash was essentially an inevitable result of the specific features of its variant of capitalism, then structural reforms were necessary to dismantle that kind of capitalism. The International Monetary Fund (IMF) and World Bank adopted the latter view and urged the crisis countries to introduce radical reforms (Fischer, 1998; Claessens et al., 1998; 2000). Making East Asia's corporate system resemble the Anglo-American one was one of the most important goals of the structural reform policy. This particular line of reform related only to South Korea's large companies, since Japan and Taiwan had not been affected by the 1997 crash and the other crisis countries had no such large industrial companies.

The chaebol, South Korea's family-controlled business groups with large multinational companies, had been praised as the engine of Korea's rapid economic growth prior to 1997 (Amsden, 1997). Chaebol companies such as Samsung Electronics and Hyundai Motors had developed to the point where they competed with US, Japanese, and European firms in world markets. Extensive studies praised South Korea's idiosyncratic institutions such as state interventionism, bank-based finance, and big business groups. 'Korea Inc.' was the term that resumed this close cooperation between state, banks, and business (Amsden, 1989; Chang, 1994; Shin and Chang, 2003).

But the East Asian crisis dramatically changed the research landscape. Neoclassical critics argued that the crisis revealed structural weaknesses in South Korea's economic institutions. Its large companies, including chaebol firms, were criticized for their structural features such as moral hazard, a too-big-to-fail mentality, low transparency, low profitability, and high debt (Claessens et al., 1998; Hahm and Mishkin, 2000; Dornbush, 1997). Shareholder value advocates emerged who maintained that these features resulted from fundamental distortions in corporate governance and financing (Black et al., 2001; Jang, 2001; Yoo, 1999). They argued that strengthening the principle of shareholder value was essential in order to enhance the efficiency of the South Korean corporate and economic system.

In November 1997, the Kim Young-sam government signed onto an IMF bailout program in order to overcome mounting foreign exchange problems. The reliance on an IMF bailout was widely regarded as a national shame, and this effectively contributed to the first change in ruling party since the start of industrialization in 1961; the democratic Kim Dae-jung government came to power in February 1998.

However, neoclassical views predominated among politicians and policymakers in the new democratic government; a program of structural reform was introduced whose goal was to transform Korea's corporate, financial, public, and labor market systems into new ones resembling free market models (Cho et al., 2007; Shin, 2000; Chang, 2006). This program tried to change the financial system into one similar to Wall Street, while the governance and capital structures of large companies were reorganized to be consistent with shareholder value capitalism.

Market and profitability principles were introduced into the management of the public sector, and many public companies were privatized. Labor markets were made flexible by breaking the practice of lifetime employment, expanding irregular employment, and introducing layoffs. Furthermore, entry barriers for foreign capital were lowered, and regulations against real estate speculation were eased.

South Korea successfully removed the immediate causes of the 1997 financial crisis: huge amounts of foreign short-term borrowings exceeding foreign exchange reserves. Short-term foreign borrowings were transformed into long-term ones, and various regulatory limitations imposed on new short-term foreign borrowings. At the same time, between 1998 and 2012, Korea built up US$ 327 billion of foreign exchange reserves to deal with the danger of sudden outflow of short-term international capital. This amounts to the seventh-largest foreign exchange reserve in the world.

Two factors contributed to the growth in foreign exchange reserves. The first is an increase in exports and the current account surplus every year from 1998 up to now, and the second is an increase in foreign capital inflow in the form of portfolio investment and direct investment (mostly, the acquisition of Korean firms). The first factor is not an achievement of liberal reforms, but is instead due to the strength of Korea's existing export industries that had been nurtured by the developmental state before 1997. The second, however, can be attributed to the liberal structural reforms.

Until the early 1990s, foreign investors were not allowed to enter Korea's stock and bond market. In 1993, however, the Kim Young-sam government, which sought Korea's entry into the OECD, allowed foreign investment in the stock market. But the scope of this reform was limited: foreigners were only allowed to own a maximum of 20 percent of outstanding shares of a listed company. In 1998, the IMF demanded a complete opening for foreign investors, which the Kim Dae-jung government accepted. As a result, foreign shareholding grew from 14.6 percent in the pre-1997 era to 30.1 percent in 2000, and peaked at 43 percent in 2004. The 2008 global financial crisis resulted in foreign capital outflow, but the current figure is still high – around 32 percent.

But far more significant is the fact that, while foreigners hold more than 30 percent of the total market capitalization in the South Korean stock market today, they effectively control over 50 percent of the whole outstanding value of the market because shares owned by controlling shareholders, amounting to some 20 percent of the total market capitalization, are not traded in the market.

Furthermore, among around 700 companies listed in the South Korean stock market, foreign portfolio investors focus on some 40 blue-chip companies. This is because fund managers based in Wall Street, the City of London, or Hong Kong, strongly tend to invest only in such companies that are suitable to their investment standard – the so-called global standard.

The blue-chip companies they prefer are mostly either chaebol subsidiaries or privatized companies and privatized banks. As regards chaebol firms in general, foreign funds own 30 to 80 percent of market capitalization. Therefore, including domestic portfolio investors, portfolio investors own considerably more shares than chaebol families, which, as controlling minority shareholders, hold just 1 to 4 percent of market capitalization of the chaebol subsidiaries.

Shareholding by subsidiaries of a chaebol group, a kind of indirect cross shareholding, can complement the small number of shares owned by chaebol families. But the two successive democratic governments from 1998–2007, the Kim Dae-jung and Roh Moo-hyun governments, strictly limited this practice in order to enhance the position of portfolio investors (Haggard et al., 2003). As portfolio investors own far more shares than chaebol families and group subsidiaries combined, chaebol groups are now sensitive to the demands of these investors.

Portfolio investors are also the biggest beneficiaries of the privatization of public companies. With privatization, restrictions against foreign investment in the public sector were also eased. For example, foreign investors hold 65 percent of shares in POSCO, South Korea's biggest steelmaker, previously under public ownership. Now, as there are nearly no controlling shareholders, portfolio investors (domestic and foreign investors combined) dominate the company's decision-making. A similar situation prevails at KT&G (previously a monopoly manufacturer of cigarettes under public ownership) and at KT (the second-largest mobile service company, formerly under public ownership). The privatized companies are naturally managed according to shareholder value principles. Since the privatization, dividend payout, and stock buyback have greatly increased, while research and development (R&D) and facility investment, compared to sales, have dropped.

Furthermore, as the democratic governments facilitated hostile mergers and acquisitions (M&A), many listed companies, including chaebol subsidiaries and privatized companies, came to fear a possible hostile M&A. Calpers, a prominent US pension fund, which campaigns worldwide against institutions that prohibit hostile M&A, supports some South Korean nongovernmental organizations (NGOs) that lobby for minority shareholder rights and the transparency of chaebol companies (Kim and Park, 2008).

3.3 Privatization of banks and increasing role of policy financing

From the start of industrialization and throughout the 1980s up to the Asian crisis, most South Korean banks had been either publicly owned or under public control; they had been one of the most important policy instruments used by the developmental state even though some of them were partly privatized from the 1980s. The partly privatized banks were renationalized during the Asian financial crisis due to their increasing bad assets, and then reprivatized extensively as part of the structural reform program (Cho and Kalinowski, 2010). The privatization of banks during 1998–2004 was so hasty that American buyout funds such as Carlyle, Lone Star, and New Bridge Capital came to acquire controlling shares of Hanmi Bank, Korea Exchange Bank, and Cheil Bank respectively (Kwon, 2004). Also South Korea's other commercial banks came under the strong influence of portfolio investment funds, with the exception of Woori Bank, which is still publicly owned, as South Korean governments have failed to privatize it in spite of their repeated efforts. By the end of 2004, when bank privatization had nearly been completed, foreign investment funds were holding 65 percent of market capitalization of all commercial banks, and as of the end of 2012, they still held 60 percent.

The restructuring of South Korea's banking sector – privatization of state-owned banks, bank mergers, and the foreign sale of some banks – resulted in drastic change in banking operations (Kim S-J, 2002). Shareholder value has become the guiding principle of banks' operations, and bank loans are largely directed to the housing sector, which is regarded as safer than the corporate sector. Large corporations and small and medium-sized enterprises (SMEs) are only considered for loans if they have a high credit rating and reliable collateral. The statistics tell the story: the ratio of household lending to corporate lending was 10:90 in 1991 and 35:65 in 1997, but developed to 54:46 in 2002. This was the first reversal since the beginning of industrialization in the 1960s.

One reason for this reversal was the new attention paid to the soundness of assets in the banking sector demanded by regulatory authorities (Kim S-J, 2002; Kim and Shin, 2006). But yet another reason for the change seems to have been the new orientation toward the interests of portfolio investors. This is shown in the fact that the increase in household lending was more dramatic in banks that had come under direct control of foreign capital, such as Hanmi Bank, which was sold to Citi Bank, Cheil Bank to Standard Chartered, and Korea Exchange Bank to Lone Star. Also, such banks reduced lending to SMEs more than others. Changes in the business of commercial banks brought about macroeconomic change. First, the decrease in corporate lending led to the reduction of facility and other long-term investment, and this in turn, together with the short-term orientation of the corporate sector, resulted in stagnating economic growth. GDP growth of the economy has fallen by half, from over 8 percent before 1997 to under 4 percent after 1998. Second, the increase in household lending, especially housing mortgage loans, has generated speculative bubbles in the housing sector.

The increase in household lending, together with labor market reforms that resulted in employment instability and income reduction, accompanied a drastic fall in household saving. The rate of net household saving had been more than 20 percent from the end of 1980s up to the early and mid-1990s. However, as both household lending and household debt increased, it plunged to almost 0 percent in 2002. Now it remains at 3 percent, which is half the average level of OECD member countries (OECD, 2013).

The democratic governments from 1998 to 2007 emphasized economic growth driven by SMEs and venture business, rather than by large companies and the chaebol. Furthermore, they reoriented industry policy toward SMEs and venture business. However, as a result of liberal reforms, banks decreased lending to SMEs and venture companies. Inevitably, the governments, even though they declared themselves to be liberal, had to expand the role of policy financing institutions, the frame of which had been established by the developmental state.[1] Consequently, SMEs and venture companies still borrow from banks because the government supports borrowing through various means of policy financing.

Before 1997, the role of policy financing in lending to SMEs and venture business was limited because the developmental state obligated the commercial banks to give more than a certain percentage of total corporate loans to SMEs (45 percent for commercial banks, 80 percent

Table 3.1 Rates of net household saving, 1987–2011 (%)

1987	1990	1993	1996	1999	2002	2005	2008	2011
22.9	22.2	21.7	17	15	0.4	6.5	2.6	3.1

Source: Bank of Korea, *Online Services of Statistics*, at http://ecos.bok.or.kr/

for regional banks). This regulation, however, was eased by the liberal reforms after 1998, and commercial banks subsequently greatly reduced loans to SMEs and venture companies. Thus, the three liberal governments from 1998 to 2012 had no choice but to expand policy financing for SMEs and venture companies.

Industrial policy, the most prominent component of the developmental state in East Asia, has not been discarded; it has just changed its form and style. Today, it is called *innovation policy*: the government defines some key technologies such as IT, BT and nanotechnology (NT), and helps the companies operating in these areas. In addition, the government still selects some key industries such as parts and materials, pharmaceuticals, and telecommunications, and nurtures them in various ways. An important policy tool for this new form of industrial policy is still the diverse policy financing institutions.

Following the global financial crisis of late 2008, the role of South Korea's policy financing institutions became even more important in preventing a credit crunch in the corporate sector. In addition, they are still the leading financial institutions capable of providing bailout loans for insolvent large companies and SMEs. All South Korean businesses, from start-ups to chaebol companies, acknowledge the importance of policy financing; that is why government officials and policymakers insisted (successfully) on excluding policy financing institutes from FTA negotiations with the United States and the European Union (EU).[2]

3.4 Korean multinationals under shareholder value

Structural reform after the 1998 crisis radically changed the landscape of South Korean multinationals. One-third of the 30 largest chaebol groups collapsed and were completely dismantled; Daewoo, Ssangyong, and Haetae were among the largest in this category. Another third lost assets in radical ways; Halla Group is a typical case. Only the remaining third, including Samsung, Hyundai Motors, LG, and SK Group, proved strong enough to recover from the crisis without such asset curtailments; they were, however, required to significantly reorganize their governance, finance, and business structures (see, for instance, Jwa and Lee, 2000). Their corporate structure today is a mixture of the old system and the new shareholder value-oriented system (Jwa and Lee, 2000; Lee and Lim, 2000; Shin and Chang, 2003).

Most South Korean multinationals today fall into three categories. The first is formerly state-owned companies that were privatized in the 1990s, particularly after the Asian crisis of 1997. The most prominent case is POSCO, a steelmaker, which had been established in the late 1960s and was then completely privatized after 1998. The second is firms that remain subsidiaries of chaebol groups such as Samsung, LG, and Hyundai. And the third consists of firms that once belonged to a chaebol group, but which were separated from it by the structural reforms. Daewoo Motors, now renamed GM-Korea, is a typical case (Jeong, 2004).

Irrespective of the differences between them, however, it is fair to say that all Korean multinationals have undergone radical restructuring. First, their capital structure changed radically; they reduced debt and increased equity capital in dramatic ways. Second, there was a shift in focus from long-term to short-term profitability measured by return on assets and return on equity. Now they have an explicit commitment to shareholder value, and actively communicate with portfolio investors and security analysts (Cho et al., 2007).

The third major change concerns corporate organization. Prior to the reforms, the departments in charge of strategic planning and future growth had been the most powerful; after the reform, however, organizations in charge of investor relationship and finance began to dominate. These departments review existing business operations from the viewpoint of quarterly and yearly gain and cash flow, and they often put a brake on new long-term investments. Risk-averse business behaviors spread throughout large companies, including chaebol firms. The structural reforms dismantled the risk-sharing mechanism that had linked chaebol, banks, and the government, because neoclassical policymakers considered this link to be the culprit of the 1997 financial crisis. Therefore, even chaebol companies became much more cautious in long-term investment, as they must take risks all alone.

Changes in the corporate governance of large companies are closely linked with the changed business of banks; these transformations have resulted in a dramatic shift in investment financing. Even when companies are willing to invest, it has become more difficult to attract investment funds from banks or the securities market. Thus they have come to depend more on internal reserves for investment financing.

Today, South Korean companies finance long-term investment from internal reserves rather than from bank loans or bond issuance. This has apparently emerged as a way of financing facility investment in manufacturing sectors (Jeong, 2005). Before 1997, only one-fourth of facility investment was financed from internal reserves; the rest came from external sources, especially from bank loans. By the year 2000, however, the figures show that more than 80 percent of facility investment was

Table 3.2 Ratio of aggregate facility investment to GDP, 1990–2012 (%)

1990	1994	1996	2000	2002	2004	2010	2011	2012
14.7	13.5	14.1	12.8	10.4	9.3	10	9.9	9.5

Source: Bank of Korea, *Online Services of Statistics*, at the home page, http://ecos.bok.or.kr/

financed from internal reserves, and only 20 percent from bank loans or bond issuance. Financing from stock issuance had declined to the level of 0.1–0.3 percent, much lower than before 1998. This pattern continues today. Changes in corporate governance and investment financing resulted in an overall stagnation in facility investment. This can be seen in the ratio of aggregate facility investment to GDP; the ratio had been around 14 percent until the mid-1990s, but fell to below 10 percent after 2001.

Long-term investment by South Korea's large companies today tends to be polarized. This is because internal reserves, the main source of funds for long-term investment, depend on net profits, which today are strongly polarized. That is, some companies show excellent profitability and therefore have abundant internal reserves, but many others do not. There are two types of companies with excellent profitability and abundant internal reserves: one type consists of companies belonging to the ten largest chaebol groups, especially the four biggest ones; the other consists of privatized public companies. As of 2012, sales of 80 listed companies belonging to the ten largest chaebol groups made up 54 percent of total sales of all 700 listed firms. Sales of companies belonging to Samsung Group accounted for 16.8 percent; sales of Samsung Electronics alone amounted to 11.4 percent of the total sales of all listed companies. That of listed companies belonging to Hyundai Motors Group accounted for 11.1 percent, LG Group for 8.1 percent, POSCO for 4.8 percent, and SK Group for 4.7 percent.

Furthermore, the share of the ten largest chaebol companies in the total corporate profit of all 700 listed firms is bigger than their share of sales. The operating income of the listed companies belonging to the ten largest chaebol groups amounted to 74.5 percent of that of all 700 listed companies, and in the case of net profit, it was 78.1 percent. Samsung Group and Hyundai Motors Group in particular take up a dominant proportion of profitability; the combined net profits of three companies, Samsung Electronics, Hyundai Motors, and Kia Motors (a subsidiary of the Hyundai Motors Group) are increasing – they made up 51 percent of the total net profit of the top 100 listed companies in 2012, whereas it was 19 percent in 2007, but the total net profits of the top 100 listed companies, including the three companies, was higher in 2012 than in 2007.

A small number of large companies, with abundant profits and internal reserves, are leading long-term investment. This is clearly shown in facility investment. In 2005, facility investment by the top 30 companies, ranked in terms of sales, accounted for 87.2 percent of all 200 large companies. In other words, the other 170 companies were responsible for just 12.8 percent of total facility investment. Furthermore, the share of facility investment by the top five companies, Samsung Electronics, Hyundai Motors, Kia Motors, LG Electronics, and POSCO, was even more striking – it accounted for 55.7 percent of that of all 200 companies (Jeong, 2005). This polarization can still be seen today. The passivity of many large companies in the area of long-term investment is the key reason for sluggish facility investment in the South Korean economy, a new phenomenon that first appeared in the 2000s.

In spite of stagnating facility investment among many large companies in South Korea, mainstream economists maintain, following the endogenous growth theory (Lucas, 1988; Romer, 1994), that innovation is more important than facility investment. It is also argued that South Korea's past rapid growth was not sustainable because an input-driven growth relying on facility investment inevitably reaches its limit (see, for example, Krugman, 1994). The economists and policymakers who had driven the free market-oriented reforms suggested an alternative model of economic growth for South Korea – one that relies more on productivity growth, in particular total factor productivity growth (see, for instance, Kim W-K, 2004).

Then, do South Korean companies that lead technological innovation today fit the model of free market-driven economic growth? Not at all. The 15 leading companies in R&D investment today are mostly either chaebol companies or companies previously under public ownership.[3] In other words, they are the product of developmental state interventionism. Furthermore, the industrial sectors in which those ten leading companies are engaged, are those that had been designated by the developmental state as strategically key ones. With the help of industrial policy, the companies in these sectors had succeeded in accumulating technological capabilities, and in catching up to multinational companies from developed economies.

Throughout the 2000s and up to the present day, South Korea's large companies have increased R&D investment. Therefore, it looks as if corporate R&D is growing due to the structural reform. But this is an illusion. Only a small number of large companies have been increasing

R&D spending; most have not. As a result, the share of R&D investment by a small number of large companies in the total R&D investment of the corporate sector has increased over the past years (Jeong, 2005; Kim S-H, 2012). R&D investment by a majority of large companies, however, has stagnated. First, privatized companies do not increase R&D. For example, the ratio of R&D spending to sales at POSCO and KT has decreased, while they have greatly increased dividend payout and stock buyout. The management of POSCO and KT declared that they would distribute half of their net profits to shareholders, and they have kept their promise for the past ten years. Second, R&D investment in large companies acquired by foreign transnational companies has also declined. The best examples are Daewoo Motors, acquired by General Motors, and Samsung Motors acquired by Renault-Nissan. Their ratio of R&D investment to sales today is lower than in the past. Third, companies that had previously belonged to chaebol groups and then were bought by American or European private equity funds have also reduced R&D and facility investment. In some cases, private equity funds have intentionally driven target companies into a breakup, and this has led to mass layoffs and the abandonment of long-term investment plans.[4]

In sum, throughout the 2000s and up to the present day, the ratio of R&D investment to sales in the majority of large companies has remained the same. Liberal reform has resulted in the stagnating R&D investment in these companies; this contrasts strongly with the expectations of Lucas and other mainstream economists. Two hundred large companies, ranked in terms of R&D investment, account for two-thirds of the total corporate R&D investment in South Korea. Their strategic decision-making regarding technological innovation has a huge influence on that of the whole corporate sector and eventually of the economy. Therefore, it is a significant obstacle to innovation-driven growth that R&D investment among a majority of large companies has stagnated.

There are many chaebol groups that have not increased R&D and facility investment. As a result, the gap between the four largest chaebol groups and smaller groups in R&D investment is growing. Let us look at this in more detail. The ratio of R&D investment to sales among the four largest chaebol groups was 2 percent in 1994 and had increased to over 3.5 percent by 2004. Samsung Electronics, LG Electronics, Hyundai Motors, and Kia Motors were responsible for much of this increase. Now it is more than 4 percent. In fact, the four largest chaebol groups are engaged in industries that require intensive R&D and other technological innovation to ensure that they remain competitive – electronics and electricity, automobiles, and telecommunications.

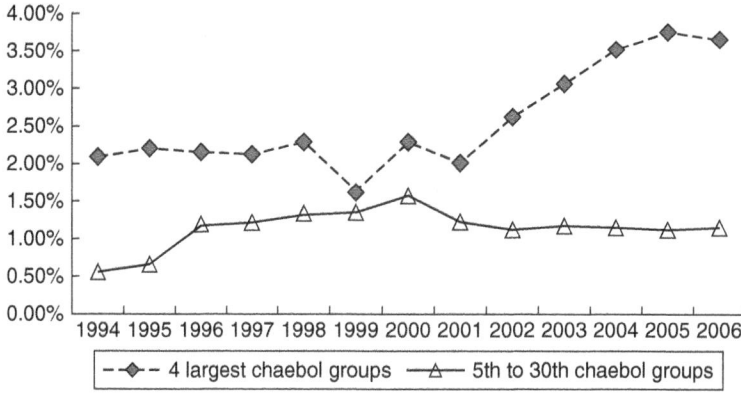

Figure 3.1 Comparison of ratio of R&D to sales among chaebol groups, 1994–2006 (%)
Source: Jeong (2007), p. 121.

It is true that the four chaebol groups also have service-sector subsidiaries in insurance, credit cards, and logistics. Naturally, these service-sector subsidiaries focus on domestic markets. But in all four groups, the share of sales and profits made by subsidiaries engaging in export-oriented manufacturing is overwhelming. And these companies earn high profits and therefore have abundant internal reserves, so that they are able to invest heavily in R&D and facility expansion.

But the landscape of the smaller chaebol groups – the fifth- to the thirtieth-largest chaebol groups in sales size – is quite different. It is noteworthy that the ratio of their R&D investment to sales jumped from 0.5 percent in 1994 to 1.2 percent in 1996. This shows that they had diversified into industries that needed more technological investment. In fact, in the mid-1990s, the Kim Young-sam government partly abolished industrial policy that had limited industrial entrance. This led to a boom of industrial entry by smaller chaebol groups into electronics (including semiconductors), automobiles, shipbuilding, and other manufacturing sectors. This shows also that, in spite of the Kim Young-sam government's neoliberal reforms, the risk-sharing mechanism based on mutual support between subsidiaries of a chaebol group still functioned against risky investment.

However, increases in the ratio of R&D investment to sales among smaller chaebol groups stopped after 1998. The ratio *did* increase to 1.3 percent in the period between 1998 and 2000, but only because of decreased sales. The ratio among companies of the fifth- to the thirtieth-largest chaebol groups in sales size stagnated at 1.1 percent between 2001 and 2006, and this trend has continued to the present day (Kim S-H, 2012). This shows that the smaller chaebol groups reached a certain limit in corporate growth based on technological innovation in the 2000s. In spite of stagnating R&D, the sales figures of smaller chaebol groups have continued to grow in the last ten years. Lotte Group, Shinsegae Group, and CJ Group, for instance, whose key businesses are not export-oriented manufacturing but domestic market-oriented service industries such as department stores, large retail stores, or cable television, all show increasing sales (Jeong, 2007).

Export and domestic sales of POSCO and Hyundai Heavy Industries Group, whose key businesses are steel, machinery, and shipbuilding, have also continued to rise in the last ten years. But their investment in technological innovation, measured by the ratio of R&D investment to sales, has not grown as much. Why is this so? Apparently, it is mainly because of the sectoral features of these businesses – they do not require increases in R&D investment as much as the electronics or automobile sectors. Lotte (department store and food), KT (telecommunications), GS (retail and construction), Kumho-Asiana (construction, transportation, petrochemicals), and Hanjin (transportation, shipbuilding) have been able to increase sales without increasing R&D investment in proportion to sales growth.

In other words, many of the businesses run by smaller chaebol groups are those that do not need R&D-driven growth, such as retail (Shinsegae, CJ, Lotte, GS), insurance (Hanwha, Dongbu), food and beverage (Doosan, CJ, Shinsegae, Nongshim), chemicals and petrochemicals (Hanhwa, Dongbu, Daelim, LS), gas (LS), and steel (Dongbu). Furthermore, industries such as machinery (Doosan, Hyundai Heavy Industry, Daelim, STX), construction (Hanhwa, Doosan, Dongbu, Daelim, Shinsegae), and shipbuilding (DSME, STX, Hyundai Heavy Industry) rely as much on the tacit knowledge of skilled laborers and technicians, as they do on research institutes and laboratories.

A serious socioeconomic conflict in South Korea today arises from rent-seeking in domestic service markets. Service sectors such as financial services (insurance, credit cards, leasing, and so forth), retail (department stores and large discount stores), transportation (land transport and logistics), broadcasting, educational and medical services, and so on, are mostly domestic market oriented. Until the 1990s, many of them had been under strict regulation in the public interest. Therefore, in these sectors, unlike in export-oriented manufacturing sectors, it is easy to make a profit by rent-seeking behaviors such as deregulation, building monopolies or oligopolies, or establishing crony links between politicians and business. Rent-seeking can be easily practiced, for example, when existing regulations for protecting ecological or financial stability disappear. Deregulation and privatization in real estate can also create crony businesses in construction and other real estate businesses. In fact, corruption scandals, collusion, and cartels occur frequently in domestic market-oriented service sectors. Also, in some manufacturing sectors such as food and beverage, and petrochemicals, which focus mainly on domestic markets, it is easy to establish cartels or other rent-seeking practices.

As many of the smaller chaebol groups engage in such domestic market-oriented industries, they are able to make easy money from neoliberal deregulations and privatizations, making technological innovation unnecessary. Even the four largest chaebol groups have been trying to expand businesses in service sectors. The typical case is Samsung: it already has leading companies in financial services (Samsung Life Insurance, Samsung Securities, and Samsung Card), and is now trying to enter into medical service sectors, which are closely linked with the business of Samsung Life Insurance. Here again, these sectors have been subject to the effects of deregulation and privatization.

Smaller chaebol groups will not drive innovation-based growth, as they will not actively expand, by establishing new subsidiaries or acquiring existing companies, into sectors in which R&D is crucial. This is partly because, according to the theory and practice of shareholder value, diversification of large companies, especially diversification into unrelated business, is a source of opportunism or moral hazard among controlling shareholders or managers; diversification of a business group in particular is criticized as *tunneling* (Amihud and Lev, 1981; 1999). In the discussion within South Korea also, diversification of a chaebol group is regarded as a source of moral hazard (Choi J-P, 1999; Kim G-W, 1999; Kang et al., 1991).

Since, after 1998, South Korea's laws and other institutions regarding corporations, securities, and business groups were reformed according to shareholder value theory, the influence of short-term oriented portfolio investors on the strategic decision-making of listed large companies increased dramatically. Their influence seems most powerful when chaebol groups, as well as large companies in general, want to diversify their businesses. This weakened the risk sharing between subsidiaries of a chaebol group significantly, and hence, risky diversification of chaebol groups into R&D-intensive industries also diminished significantly.

Since the start of industrialization in the 1960s, diversification has played a key role in the growth of big South Korean business and chaebol groups (Amsden, 1997; 2001; Jeong, 2004). And there have been three waves of diversification. The first wave came in the late 1960s and 1970s, when chaebol groups, supported by the government's industrial policy, diversified into heavy and chemical industries. These were export-oriented manufacturing sectors such as electronics, automobile, steel, shipbuilding, and machinery. The government selected key industries and provided various subsidies. Banks, which were either government owned or under government control, were one of the major instruments of the industrial policy; they enabled diversification. For example, Samsung Group, whose core business was textiles and trade in the 1960s, diversified into electronics by establishing Samsung Electronics; Hyundai Group, whose main focus was on construction (Hyundai Construction) diversified into automobiles by establishing Hyundai Motors.

The second wave of diversification came in the mid-1990s, when the Kim Young-sam government abandoned five-year economic planning and partially eased industrial policies. Under five-year planning, the government intentionally allowed only a small number of companies to enter the strategically key sectors, in order to give them an oligopolistic or monopolistic position in the domestic market. The chosen companies could make profits partly thanks to the licensed rent-seeking in the domestic market, even though they often did not earn profits in export markets at that time. This policy of entry licensing was abolished in 1993, when the Kim Young-sam government made 'globalization' the watchword. Then, almost all chaebol groups, including the four largest ones, diversified into export-oriented manufacturing sectors such as electronics, automobile, steel, shipbuilding, and chemicals and petrochemicals (Jeong, 2004). They also diversified into domestic market-oriented service sectors such as merchant banking, securities trade, insurance, construction, retail, broadcasting, and so forth, as the government partially deregulated the financial sector and other service sectors in order to obtain membership of the World Trade Organization and the OECD.

The third wave of diversification, which occurred in the 2000s, was, however, quite different in nature. The first wave had been driven by state interventionism and the quest for entry into export markets, and the second, in the 1990s, was driven by partial deregulation – diversification occurred in both export-oriented manufacturing sectors and domestic market-oriented services sectors. In contrast, the third wave has been driven by complete deregulation; diversification has occurred mainly in domestic market-oriented service sectors. This is because deregulation has allowed South Korean big business to make easy profits in domestic markets through various rent-seeking businesses; under a regime of neoliberalism and shareholder value capitalism, South Korea's large companies and chaebol groups strongly tend to diversify into sectors where they can earn revenues in safe and easy ways, through rent-seeking, rather than in risky investment in technological innovation.

Entry into the domestic market-oriented sectors by chaebol companies and other large companies has brought about socioeconomic conflict. Chaebol groups such as Shinsegae, CJ, and GS, whose core businesses lie in the retail sector (department stores, large discount stores), collide with small neighborhood stores as they extend their reach throughout the country. Moreover, some young successors of chaebol families (Samsung, CJ, Shinsegae, and Hanhwa) have tried to enter into the bakery industry, with the support of the chaebol groups under their respective control, leading to bitter criticism from small bakery owners. There is currently much discussion in South Korea's national assembly and among government officials about the possibility of limiting the entry of chaebol groups and large companies into such businesses, while neoliberal think tanks and other neoliberal-oriented organizations, including the Federation of Korean Industries (the official representative body of the chaebol), oppose any such regulatory rules.

There have been other notable cases of socioeconomic conflict caused by the entry of chaebol groups into domestic markets. Many chaebol groups own companies in the financial services sector – insurance, securities, and leasing – and they have lobbied for additional deregulation. Their quest for more deregulation was not halted even by the global financial crisis that began on Wall Street at the end of 2008. They still maintain that the financial market in South Korea needs to be transformed into one resembling Wall Street.

A serious social conflict occurs in the case of insurance services, because insurance companies, most of which belong either to chaebol groups or to transnational insurance companies, require deregulation in medical services, so that profit-oriented hospitals can be established. If so deregulated, the public health-care and insurance system will be severely weakened. In a country where the social safety net is still in the growth stage and vulnerable to social shocks, any weakening of welfare services will bring about serious social conflict.

3.5 FTAs, rent-seeking and interest politics

The liberal economic reforms of the Kim Dae-jung and Roh Moo-hyun democratic governments (1998–2007) lowered the country's economic growth rate by half. The gap between the rich and the poor widened, youth unemployment increased, and regular jobs decreased; the living standards of the middle and lower classes declined. This led to general dissatisfaction and greatly contributed to the victory of the conservative candidate, Lee Myung-bak, in the presidential election at the end of 2007. The Lee Myung-back government (2008–2012), however, introduced even more free market reforms. It cut corporate and individual income tax rates and announced plans to privatize railroads, electricity, and state-run banks. It also proposed free market reforms of the health and educational sector.

The government's commitment to further neoliberal reforms is exemplified by its negotiation with the United States regarding the FTA.[5] In summer 2011, the Lee Myung-bak government accepted the modifications proposed by the United States regarding beef imports; the US Congress then ratified the agreement. South Korea's National Assembly also ratified the FTA in November 2011, when a majority of members of the ruling conservative party, as well as those of the oppositional Democratic Party, approved the treaty. This again showed that the majority of members of both parties, in spite of differences on political and security issues, has a similar orientation toward the free market economy.[6]

South Korean society was divided by the FTA issue. Proponents of the treaty argued that it would reduce US tariffs, and thus increase Korean exports to the United States. In fact, a majority of large companies, including chaebol, and a considerable number of export-oriented SMEs and venture businesses welcomed the FTA, because they believed that they had comparative advantages in trade with the United States. This seemed important for export-oriented manufacturing sectors like electronics, automobile, shipbuilding, and machinery.

However, opponents argued that the FTA was only favorable to the multinational companies of the two countries, and that it was even more favorable to the United States, in the same way that the North American Free Trade Agreement (NAFTA) had been. Without the FTA, the average import tariff rate was 7.8 percent in Korea and 2.4 percent in the United States, and this means that the positive effect of export increase from the trade agreement would be on the side of the United States (Song, 2012). For instance, cellular phones and semiconductors, two major export items from South Korea to the United States, were already nontariff goods, and the average import tariff rate was 2.5 percent for automobiles and 5 percent for TVs.[7] Furthermore, from the 1990s many South Korean multinationals, including Samsung Electronics and Hyundai Motors, had expanded overseas production sites in the United States as well as in Latin American countries such as Mexico and Brazil, NAFTA member countries, in order to export without paying tariffs. Therefore, it seemed obvious that the alleged positive effect of increasing exports – thanks to the abolition of tariffs by the FTA – was either a fiction or a significant exaggeration.

There was, of course, some opposition to the FTA from business elites. The treaty extends the period for copyright protection from 50 to 70 years after the author's death, and it protects patent rights more strongly. This appears favorable to the United States and unfavorable to South Korea, which has less intellectual property than advanced nations; therefore, many book publishing and pharmaceutical companies opposed it. Furthermore, stronger protection of patents seemed unfavorable to South Korea's strategic effort to promote IT, BT, and NT areas, in which existing patents held by the United States had been important sources of frustration; therefore, some bureaucrats and industrial policy experts did not support the treaty.

In this case, the question arises: why did a majority of South Korea's elite class, including shareholders, owners, and managers of multinational companies, support the FTA with the United States, even though many of them did not believe that the treaty would have positive effects on exports and economic growth? The answer lies in other aspects of the FTA. First, free trade agreements generally explicitly limit state interventionism and protect the rights of investors and companies. Almost all large South Korean companies, including chaebol companies, welcomed the FTA because they believed that it would greatly contribute to the institutionalization of free enterprise and free market principles in the economy.

Second, some South Korean multinationals are already highly competitive in R&D and in producing patentable technologies. Companies of Samsung Group, Hyundai Motors groups, LG Group, and SK Group are typical cases, and naturally they welcomed the stronger protection of patents and other intellectual properties. Also, some large companies, SMEs, and venture businesses engaging in R&D-intensive industries such as IT, BT, and NT, supported the FTA because they believed that they had already developed the capability of producing their own patentable technologies.

At the same time, however, many large companies and SMEs did *not* want stronger protection of intellectual property rights because they had not developed such technological capabilities. For instance, extension of the period of patent protection is favorable to US pharmaceutical companies with original patents of drugs. This is also true of some South

Korean pharmaceutical companies, mostly chaebol subsidiaries, which have made efforts to develop drugs with original patents.[8] However, it is not favorable for the majority of South Korean pharmaceutical companies, which have not developed these capabilities. This type of company produces generic medicines with licensed patents from global pharmaceutical firms. In this way, the FTA will have a strong polarizing effect on companies in the pharmaceutical industry and other R&D-intensive industries.

Third, as mentioned earlier, many large companies, including chaebol subsidiaries, prefer entry into domestic market-oriented service sectors, where they can make money easily through rent-seeking. The FTA with the United States will be very helpful to them because it will expand free market principles in service sectors through privatization and deregulation. For example, large discount stores belonging to chaebol groups (Shinsegae, Lotte, GS) enthusiastically welcomed the FTA because they believed it would place them out of the reach of proposed new regulatory rules intended to protect small neighborhood stores. In the same way, financial service companies, many of which belong to chaebol groups, also welcomed the treaty because they expected additional deregulation of their business.

In this context, proponents of FTAs usually argue that economic growth driven by the manufacturing sectors has reached its limit, and that the service sectors must take the lead in the near future. To achieve this goal, they require an extensive deregulation and privatization of social, public, financial, and other services.[9] Even reports from the OECD have recommended such an extensive liberalization of service sectors (Randall, 2009; Randall and Urasawa, 2012).

Furthermore, South Korean business elites widely expected the FTA to clear the way for additional privatizations and deregulation in public services such as gas, railroad, electricity, water supply, postal service, medical service, educational service, and other welfare services. Therefore, it may be said that 'the FTA with the US is a legal institution which protects only the rights of investors and companies, especially those of multinationals in both the United States and South Korea; it does not serve the public welfare' (Song, 2012). To the critics, the Lee Myung-bak government responded with the argument that 'for the public services such as education, public health, and other social services, there is a wide room in the FTA for policy intervention by the government' (Motie and Mosf, 2011). This is true. But it is also true that over the last 20 years, South Korean governments have made constant efforts to privatize and deregulate public service sectors. Thus, there is no reason to think that the government and politicians will actually exercise their power of policy intervention.

The last reason for the welcome given to the FTA by South Korean business and political elites can be found in individual interests – that is, the elites welcomed the FTA because they believed it would be good for their personal wealth and income growth. This belief is so strong in some supporters that they will not hear about negative effects of the FTA on many industries and on the overall economy. Consequently, the debate in South Korean politics and society about the FTA was driven more by ideology than by concern for industry and the economy in general.

3.6 Summary and conclusion

Neoclassical critics argued that the 1997 Asian crisis revealed structural weaknesses in South Korea's economy. They argued that strengthening free market principles and shareholder values was essential in order to enhance the efficiency of the South Korean economic structure. The liberal reform, however, dismantled the growth engine behind South Korea's economic miracle. Large companies, including chaebol firms, shifted their focus from long-term to short-term profitability. Now they have an explicit commitment to shareholder value.

Long-term investments made by South Korea's large companies today tend to be polarized. A small number of large companies, with abundant profits and internal reserves, are leading long-term investment in facility and R&D; however, most remain virtually uninvolved. The passivity of a majority of large companies in long-term investment is the key reason for sluggish growth in the South Korean economy. It is apparent that the industrial features of the businesses of this majority, which includes companies belonging to smaller chaebol groups, do not require increases in R&D and facility investment, as they engage in domestic market-oriented industries, in which they can make easy money from deregulations and privatizations, making technological innovation unnecessary. In addition, the FTAs with the United States and the EU are expected to create further polarization between a small number of multinationals with capabilities of producing patentable technologies and others without such capabilities.

Nonetheless, a majority of South Korean business elites and politicians welcomed the FTA because they believed that it would greatly contribute to the institutionalization of free enterprise and free market principles in the economy. In fact, many large companies, including chaebol ones, believed that the FTA would extend free market principles into service sectors, in which they can make money easily through rent-seeking. In conclusion, it is fair to say that they supported free market principles, shareholder value capitalism, and the FTA for ideological and personal interests rather than from concern for industrial catch-up and economic growth.

Notes

1. South Korea's policy financing institutes are all products of the developmental state era.
2. Press release of the Financial Services Commission, November 23, 2011.
3. Among the 15 largest R&D intensive companies, Samsung Electronics, Samsung SDI, and Samsung Electro-mechanics belong to Samsung Group; LG Electronics, LG Chemistry, and LG-Phillips belong to LG Group; Hyundai Motors and Kia Motors belong to Hyundai Motors Group; Hynix Semiconductors previously belonged to Hyundai Group and now belongs to SK Group; SK-Telecom, previously under public ownership, now belongs to SK Group; Ssangyong Motors previously belonged to Ssangyong Group; KT and POSCO were previously under public ownership; KEPCO is still under public ownership. The only exception is Pantec & Curitel, a cellular phone manufacturer that was established in the early 2000s.
4. For example, a US-based private equity fund drove Daewoo Electronics, once a subsidiary of Daewoo Group, to a separation into several business units in order to facilitate a buyout.
5. The FTA negotiations in summer 2008 triggered nationwide resistance from angry citizens, when it was reported that beef imported from the US had a serious risk of BSE (mad cow disease). Opposition to the reform program grew even stronger with the advent of the global financial crisis in fall 2008.
6. It was in fact the Roh Moo-hyun government that, from 2006, had initiated the Korea-US FTA negotiation, and the government was ready to sign the official agreement negotiated with the Bush administration in June 2007. However, the US Congress opposed ratification and required more import of beef from the US.
7. From the official home page of the South Korean government regarding the FTA: http//www.fta.go.kr/korus/.
8. LG and SK established pharmaceutical companies long ago; Samsung is trying to enter this industry.
9. This kind of view is seen in numerous official speeches and announcements by ministers and other high-ranking government officials. Also, numerous research reports from state-run think tanks such as Korea Development Institute share the same views.

4
Private Chinese Multinationals and the Long Shadow of the State
Andreas Nölke

4.1 The rise of Chinese multinationals – public and private

The recent rise of Chinese multinationals is rather remarkable. While Chinese multinationals were completely insignificant in 2003 (Yang and Stoltenberg, 2013, p. 72), they range among the most prominent global companies in 2013. As of the latter year, 89 of the 500 largest global companies measured by total revenues are based in China or Hong Kong, with a further six based in Taiwan (Fortune Global 500, 2013). Although the market value-based listing conducted by the *Financial Times* tends to underestimate Chinese companies due to its requirement of at least 15 percent of shares being held by dispersed shareholders (thereby, for instance, excluding fully state-owned companies), it still lists 45 of the top 500 global companies by March 28, 2013 as being based in China, Hong Kong, or Taiwan (FT Global 500). Chinese companies did not only acquire prominent Western brands such as Volvo and the IBM personal computer division, but they also have become Western household names on their own, as indicated by cases such as Haier or Huawei.

The prominent role of the Chinese state in regulating and supporting business is very well known regarding its state-owned enterprises (SOEs; Yi-Chong, 2012). Over the last few years, several econometric studies classifying Chinese companies according to their corporate ownership have demonstrated that Chinese state-owned and state-controlled companies follow the strategic needs of their home country government, for instance, by investing in natural resources, including host countries with difficult institutional contexts (Kolstad and Wiig, 2012; Duanmu, 2012). Similarly, the subsidization of Chinese state companies by Chinese state banks is a much-lamented feature of Chinese capitalism, at least from the perspective of US competitors (Martin, 2012). Correspondingly, it is hardly surprising that observers 'argue that the case of China demonstrates the profound influence of institutions on business' (Yang and Stoltenberg, 2013, p. 73). Much less well known, however, are the varied ways in which the Chinese state allies itself with private Chinese multinationals.

As of 2003, private Chinese companies are no longer prohibited from investing abroad (Liang et al., 2012, p. 134). Private corporations have larger shares in Chinese manufacturing than SOEs or foreign companies (ten Brink, 2013, pp. 194–195). And by now, they also comprise about a third of Chinese outward foreign direct investment (OFDI) stock, mainly in manufacturing. But these do not include most of the largest Chinese multinationals, which partially explains why those private multinationals are less known among the Western public (Lin, 2010, p. 367). Western observers are often upset by the existence of very large Chinese state-owned companies, which are potentially seen as a threat to Western interests. Still, for neither state-owned nor state-controlled companies such as Huawei does the state matter a lot (Breslin, 2012, p. 38; see also Ozawa, this volume). This includes various promotional measures in the context of the 'going global' policy, the close cooperation between provinces and local multinationals, for instance with regard to access to credit and – in the broader picture – the guarantee for continuing access to the most important country-specific advantage, which is abundant and inexpensive labor. Based on *guanxi* (for instance, close and regular informal contacts between companies and government), private Chinese multinationals share many features of state-owned / controlled companies. Given these features, private Chinese multinationals are an important feature of Chinese state-permeated capitalism.

This chapter first provides a survey of the various forms that the close linkages between 'private' Chinese multinationals and the Chinese state take. Based on a theoretical framework that combines concepts from comparative capitalism with those of global political economy, the second part of the chapter focuses on domestic support measures, whereas the third part addresses the cooperation between Chinese multinationals and the Chinese state with regard to international relations. Given the early stage of research on the topic, the chapter has an explorative character, and is not meant to provide a systematic empirical overview. The purpose rather is to stimulate further research on this much less known feature of Chinese state capitalism.

4.2 State-business relationships in large emerging economies: State-permeated capitalism in the global political economy

The point of departure of my more general argument is an ongoing lack of convergence between Chinese capitalism and other (Western) modes of capitalism. In order to clarify this argument, the debate on comparative capitalism (Jackson and Deeg, 2006) is highly useful. Within this debate, the focus is on the study of institutions that are important for the operation of business, such as corporate governance, corporate finance, labor relations, education and training systems, and systems for the transfer of innovations. More specifically, it is argued that we can identify not only differences between the institutions of national business systems (Whitley, 1999) but also certain types of capitalism in which these institutions show remarkable complementarities, thereby contributing to the dynamic development of these economic systems.

From the comparative capitalism perspective, the dominant role of state agencies and national capitalists is not unique to China, but rather typical of the general type of capitalism that has been evolving in the big emerging economies. Elsewhere (Nölke, 2010; 2012), I have named this type of capitalism 'state-permeated market economy' (SME), as a way of extending the existing typologies within comparative capitalism beyond the established types of 'coordinated market economies' (CME) and 'liberal market economies' (LME) (Hall and Soskice, 2001a). The SME variety of capitalism is dominated by dense informal relationships between public authorities and major domestic corporations, which function as the central coordination mechanism of the economic system. In marked contrast to the 'dependent market economies' (DME) of East Central Europe (Nölke and Vliegenthart, 2009), these political economies are rather dominated by national capitalists, not those of global financial markets, and thus are able to pursue long-term national development strategies. Dominance by national capital inter alia can be illustrated by looking at the relationship between foreign direct investment (FDI) inward stock and gross domestic product (GDP). Data indicates that large emerging markets such as China and India show a much lower degree of foreign ownership than established LMEs (US, UK), CMEs (Germany), and DMEs (Czech Republic and Slovakia); only the Japanese CME has similar features.

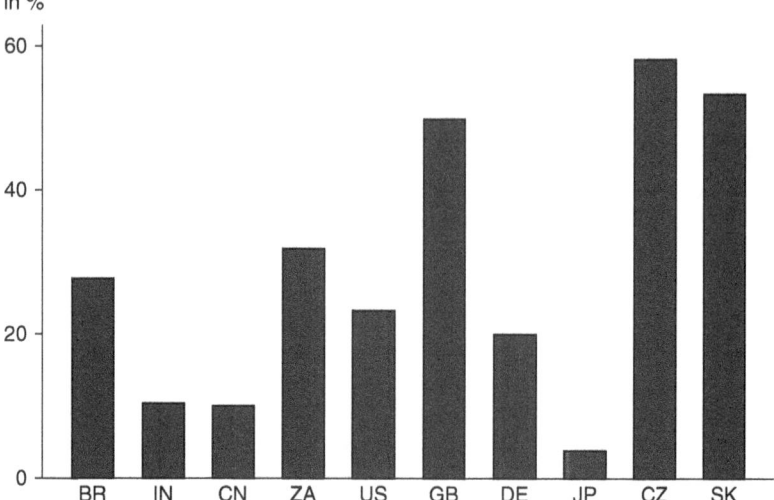

Figure 4.1 FDI inward stock of GDP, 2011 (%)
Source: Elaborated by author, based on UNCTAD World Investment Report 2012 (UNCTAD, 2012).

I consider the model of state-permeated market economies as typical for *large* emerging markets, such as witnessed in the BRIC (Brazil, Russia, India, and China) countries (van Tulder, 2010). Due to the large size of domestic markets, emerging market governments have a good negotiation position toward foreign investors and governments. Therefore, no 'sellout' is necessary: state actors do not have to give in to the demands of foreign multinationals, but may impose conditions upon the latter, for instance, with regard to the transfer of innovations toward domestic manufacturing. Moreover, the size of consumer demand on large domestic markets allows for a certain isolation of companies from fluctuations on global markets and also enables growth strategies first based on production for domestic markets, and later for international expansion (Lu et al., 2010, p. 241).

From the perspective of this model, the emergence of multinational corporations (MNCs) from large emerging markets is based on a number of very specific institutional factors and complementarities (Taylor and Nölke, 2010; Nölke and Taylor, 2011). These factors include long-term stability with regard to corporate governance and corporate finance, necessary in order to pursue catch up-strategies; low labor costs and an abundant supply of workers with at least basic qualifications in order to compete on markets for goods with an intermediate level of technological complexity; and a system of innovation transfer that is based on reverse engineering.

Linkages between the domestic institutions of state-permeated capitalism and the global political economy, however, are not limited to FDI. At least equally important is the relationship between domestic and international institutions. The comparative capitalism framework, however, does not cater to these issues, given that it tends to treat national economies as closed containers. Correspondingly, we need to combine comparative capitalism with inputs from global political economy (Nölke and Taylor, 2010; Nölke, 2011a; 2011b). From this perspective, the core assumption is that emerging market multinational corporations operate in closer collaboration with their national governments regarding international institutions than do Western MNCs. Thus they are more inclined to further their interests through governmental channels, rather than by direct (transnational) participation in global economic institutions. Arguably, many smaller Western companies rely on their governments in order to further their interests in global negotiations too, and the same argument might be made for MNCs from Western countries with very close government-business relationships such as France. Still, it is clear that most Western MNCs, in particular those of Anglo-Saxon origins (but also German and Japanese ones), have made it their habit to participate in global economic governance arrangements themselves, either as lobbyists during the negotiation of global agreements or as participants in private self-regulation. In all of these cases, the substance of business preferences and the mode of their participation in global economic institutions appear to be interrelated – preferences for liberal regulations go hand in hand with a rather independent role of business as transnational lobbying power and self-regulator, whereas a strong background in state support seems to be linked to a preference for global business regulation in intergovernmental settings.

4.3 Private Chinese multinationals and domestic state support measures

China appears to be the vanguard case for the evolution of state-permeated capitalism in large emerging economies. While the prominent role of SOEs in Chinese capitalism is well known, much less familiar are the various ways and means of cooperation between private Chinese companies and the state. The latter provides crucial support for the growth and outward expansion of Chinese multinationals in a number of fields. As far as studies from international business look at these institutional issues at all, they usually focus on FDI promotion policies (Ren et al., 2010; Xue and Han, 2010). The comparative capitalism debate, in contrast, allows us to map these support measures in a somewhat more systematic way, since it highlights distinct broad domestic institutional spheres that are important factors in supporting the growth of companies, that is, issues of corporate governance and control, corporate finance, industrial relations, and the regulation of interfirm relations, for instance, by competition policies and other sector-specific regulations. Overall coordination between private companies and state authorities takes place through various formal and informal consultation mechanisms.

Overall coordination between private Chinese multinationals and state authorities: It is by now well known that the managers and owners of private Chinese businesses cultivate close relationships with representatives of the state and the party (ten Brink, 2013, pp. 204–213). Partially, this takes the conventional form of consultation and lobbying, but more important are informal means of influence. Whereas the latter was always the most important form of coordination in the case of SOE, they become increasingly important on the side of private companies as well. Not only managers of SOE are party members, but increasingly the owners and managers of private companies as well (or their family members). Frequently based on the reciprocal principles of guanxi, these informal and personal means of coordination are crucial for the coherence of state support for the expansion of private Chinese multinationals, by allowing for a fast reaction to economic changes, based on a high degree of mutual trust: 'These networks...appear to facilitate information flow from the bottom up as well as from the top down. They foster relational exchange and collaboration on many levels of the production and policy-implementation process' (Lin and Milhaupt, 2013, p. 707). Although guanxi goes back to Confucian roots, it has taken on a new meaning as a mediating institution between private capitalist accumulation and Leninist state control (McNally, 2011, p. 3). However, when we speak of 'the state', we should always bear in mind that this type of 'institutional clientism' (Xing and Shaw, 2013, p. 105) is not necessarily the central state. For many private Chinese companies, even more important are close relationships with local governments, in particular since these governments control access over core input factors such as land – and, in turn, depend on the viability of the private local economy with regard to tax revenues (Breslin, 2012, pp. 41–42).

(Indirect) state control of private Chinese multinationals: More than 50 percent of the Chinese multinationals listed on Fortune 500 are

SOEs controlled by the central government (Lin and Milhaupt, 2013, pp. 699–700). Except for financial companies (banks and insurances), these companies typically are responsible to the State-Owned Assets Supervision and Administration Commission of the State Council (SASAC). Other Chinese companies on the Fortune 500 are SOEs that are under the control of local or provincial governments. Still, even those remaining companies that seem private are often indirectly controlled by the state. Determining the exact ownership structure of Chinese business corporations is a difficult, if not impossible, task (Breslin, 2012, pp. 35–36). While many Chinese multinationals formally are private, many still are controlled by the state, via complex control chains: 'The state-dominant structure...lies in the fact that the state is in the ultimate and absolute control of 81.6 per cent of all publicly quoted companies via two control patterns: (1) government direct control of 9.0 per cent of the quoted companies, and (2) government indirect control of 72.6 per cent of the listed companies via stock pyramids' (Liu and Sun, 2005, p. 48). Correspondingly, one needs to trace the complex control chain of listed Chinese companies in order to identify the ultimate owner. Doing so reveals the strong control of the state over most of the 'private' Chinese multinationals. Most of this control is indirect, exercised via – formally private, but de facto state-owned – investment holding companies, or via state-controlled (parent) industrial companies (Liu and Sun, 2005, p. 53). However, this does not mean that there are few private Chinese multinationals in general. Official Chinese OFDI statistics also underestimate the number of these companies, given the widespread practice of ownership and control via offshore holding companies in tax havens or Hong Kong. Many private Chinese multinationals officially are located in Bermuda or the Cayman Islands (Ning and Sutherland, 2012).

Direct financial support by (para-)state bodies, such as development banks or pension funds: Private Chinese multinationals also receive financial support from the Chinese state, arguably to a higher degree than most Western multinationals. Correspondingly, 'Western governments are also suspicious of the subsidies, low-interest loans and generous export credits lavished on favored champions, including Huawei' (The Economist, 2012b, p. 2). Financial support does not only include centralized support by the big national banks but also the close cooperation between provinces and local multinationals with regard to access to credit. Recent studies estimate that state subsidies in some sectors of manufacturing may even exceed 30 percent of industrial output (Haley and Haley, 2013). These advantages in terms of resource endowments are not only available to SOEs but also to the private ones (on a more limited scale), since the latter also spend a lot of time 'cultivating relationships with the government' (Liang et al., 2012, p. 142). Access to finance is one of the institutional spheres in which a close relationship with state actors matters most for private Chinese companies (Breslin, 2012, p. 41). The acquisition of IBM's PC division by Lenovo, for instance, was only possible because of a loan by a state bank (Lin, 2012, p. 371). However, going abroad (at least to Hong Kong) can also be a strategy in order to compensate for the preferred treatment of competing SOEs: 'A large number of Chinese firms invest in Hong Kong to establish financing channels because the financing opportunities at home are limited and mostly occupied by SOEs' (Liang et al., 2012, p. 136).

State control of the costs of labor: As is well established by now, low labor costs in China have been a major source of comparative advantages for Chinese multinationals as well as Western multinationals investing in China. As far as the state assists in keeping labor costs low, this can also be seen as a state support measure for private Chinese multinationals. Important factors in this context are the avoidance of comprehensive sector- or nationwide self-organization on the side of labor, as well as the segregation of the labor force, inter alia based on the *hukou* system of registration (ten Brink, 2013, pp. 281–309). More recently, however, unorganized social unrest has risen considerably, and the central government has increased its activities for some time via comprehensive consultation mechanisms. Based on these developments, labor costs inter alia have recently have risen somewhat, thereby inducing private Chinese multinationals to invest in Southeast Asia, in order to exploit the still lower labor costs in these countries (Liang et al., 2012, p. 136).

Competition policy and sector-specific regulation: China's policy toward regulation differs considerably between sectors. Whereas some sectors are deeply liberalized, other sectors remain strictly under state control (Breslin, 2012, p. 39; Hsueh, 2012). The latter not only pertains to SOEs but also to private ones. Generally, state firms control the following sectors: 'oil, gas, and mining; the production of basic producer goods such as nonferrous metals, steel, and petrochemicals; essential network industries in telecommunications, transportation, and utilities; and all major banking and financial institutions in China' (McNally, 2012, p. 753). However, this focus of public control on critical industries also means that private Chinese multinationals are encouraged to freely expand in other sectors that are deemed to be noncritical – but also need to be able to compete with foreign companies that equally profit from the liberalization of these sectors. Moreover, some private Chinese companies go abroad since they are not eligible for the preferential treatment given to those critical industries and / or suffer from political interference on the national level (Ren et al., 2010, p. 15). Although China formally enacted an antitrust law in 2008, this law in practice is not implemented in stringent ways, but rather follows political, sector-specific prerogatives (Lin and Milhaupt, 2013, p. 723). Finally, sector-specific state measures for protection and liberalization also vary over time, thereby adding to the confusion of Western observers. Correspondingly, the Chinese government reinstated tax deals for private exporters in the Coastal provinces in 2008, even before the global economic crisis affected these exporters (Breslin, 2012, pp. 39–40).

OFDI promotion and supervision policies: Last, but not least, China uses particular policies in order to stimulate OFDI, similar to many other countries. Since 1979, China has developed these policies – the permission of OFDI was one of the then Fifteen Measures of Economic Reform articulated by the State Council – culminating in the 'going out' or 'going global' strategy (Ren et al., 2010, pp. 7–13; Shambaugh, 2013, pp. 174–183; Yang and Stoltenberg, 2013, pp. 73–75). These policies (admittedly far more important for SOEs than for private corporations) today include direct financial support (including the 'International Market Developing Funds of Small- and Medium-Sized Enterprises'), some risk-safeguard policies (for instance, accident insurance policies), and an information service network (Xue and Han, 2010, pp. 319–321). Further reforms are ongoing, including more liberal approval procedures and additional means for funding private OFDI (Hanemann and Rosen, 2012, p. 46). However, some private Chinese companies still try to evade some of the domestic approval requirements and potential interference by state authorities by going abroad, in particular by using offshore holding companies (Ning and Sutherland, 2012). Nevertheless, in comparison with other emerging markets such as Brazil, China's state OFDI support for private multinationals today is very comprehensive and proactive (Goldstein and Pusterla, 2008, pp. 19–20).

Generally, China has pursued a more sophisticated policy with regard to both inward and outward FDI than both the protectionist states of the first wave of state capitalism and the developmental states of the second wave. Instead of severely limiting FDI in order to promote export-oriented industrialization, it has taken a more liberal approach, while still retaining control over strategic issues:

> In strategic sectors – those important to national security and the promotion of economic and technological development – the government centralized control of industry and strictly manages the level

and direction of FDI. In less strategic sectors, the Chinese government relinquishes control over industry, decentralizes decision making to local authorities, and encourages private investment and FDI. In other words, taking a purposive orientation toward industrial and FDI policies, China permits large-scale FDI to structure foreign competition in ways that allow it to transfer foreign technology, increase the national technology base, encourage indigenous technology and production capacity, and promote domestic business. By exercising this bifurcated strategy, China manages to retain political control and regulatory capacity and to modernize, industrialize, and transform its economic system in the context of international integration. (Hsueh, 2011, pp. 3–4).

4.4 (Private) Chinese multinationals, the state and international institutions

The role of Chinese multinationals with regard to global governance is a hitherto unexplored territory, irrespective of whether they are private or public. Arguably, the rapid expansion during the last 10–15 years has kept these companies (and their academic observers) quite busy, thereby not allowing for the allocation of substantial attention and resources for engaging international rules or institutions. Except for the specific issue of the political repercussions of Chinese investments in Africa, Chinese multinationals still seem to be rather invisible as actors of global governance. Unless specifically mentioned, the following observations apply both to public and private Chinese multinationals.

Low visibility in global economic negotiations: In their comprehensive survey of the implication of the rise of India and China for global economic governance, Kaplinsky and Messner (2008, p. 19) do not identify any meaningful role for Chinese or Indian MNCs as actors within these arrangements. Still, they give us a clue why this is the case, in highlighting the 'different combinations of state and capitalist development compared with the industrialized world'. Chinese MNCs have very strong linkages with public authorities, and therefore do not need to participate in global economic governance arrangements on their own. This observation confirms the results of earlier research on Western actors: studies on the participation of various social actors in transnational policy networks have demonstrated that those actors that are used to cooperating very closely with the state on the domestic level, such as labor unions, tend to follow the same pattern regarding their involvement in international institutions, that is, they mainly express their preferences via their national governments and do not invest heavily in transnational associations. Those social interests that are used to operate at somewhat more of a distance from the state, such as nongovernmental organizations (NGOs) and (Western) MNCs, in contrast, are better organized at the transnational plane and participate actively in transnational policy networks and transnational private self-regulation (Nölke, 2004; Graz and Nölke, 2008). Chinese MNCs, however, tend toward the former, given their particularly close relationship with the state.

State-directed private governance: In many fields of standard setting, business itself has a decisive role regarding technical requirements. Multinational companies are very important actors in this field. However, usually these standard-setting activities are dominated by major Western companies. In order to prevent the evolution of standards that 'create intellectual hegemony by foreign professional / technical civil societies, which would in turn control the direction of China's product / industrial development without considering the technical levels of (and / or without considering a need to cooperate with) local producers' (Wong, 2013, p. 179), the Chinese state intervenes into private governance. Correspondingly, the Chinese authorities orchestrate homegrown Chinese standards, with the target of establishing alternative global standards (Wong, 2013, pp. 179–181). Similarly, corporate social responsibility standards for the textile industry only became acceptable to Chinese business after the China National Textile and Apparel Council developed a specific Chinese standard; previous Organization for Economic Cooperation and Development-based standards were clearly opposed (Weikert, 2011, pp. 193–194). Even in the context of ecological and food safety standards, an issue area that is dominated by self-regulation schemes organized by MNCs and NGOs, the participation of China is top-down and government controlled: while China is one of the largest producers of organic agricultural products in the world, it stubbornly refuses to participate in the established private schemes and prefers to set up its own state-directed certification system, Green Food (Basu and Grote, 2006), in marked contrast to the strong participation by western MNCs in various forms of transnational private self-regulation.

State support for access to foreign markets, in particular in Africa: The crucial support of the Chinese government for enabling Chinese public companies to get access to natural resources in Africa, for instance, in the context of resources-for-infrastructure swaps, is already well established, inter alia in the form of resource-for-infrastructure swaps (Konijn and van Tulder, forthcoming). What is much less known is the state support for private Chinese multinationals in their African operations. State-supported projects work as 'door openers' for (smaller) private Chinese companies, based on the utilization of established contacts with African politicians and administrators (Scholvin and Strüver, 2013, p. 4). By 2012, private investment projects made up some 55 percent of Chinese OFDI projects in Africa, mainly in manufacturing and services (Shen, 2013, p. 2).

State-supervised integration into transnational class networks: Finally, although we do not yet have systematic empirical evidence about the integration of Chinese business leaders into (so far Western-dominated) institutions of global capitalist class networks, such as the Trilateral Commission or the World Economic Forum (WEF), it is obvious that the state and the party supervise this form of participation in transnational governance. For many decades, managers and owners of Western multinationals have been among the most important participants within these networks (Gill, 1991; van der Pijl, 1998; Graz, 2003). More recently, these networks have extended their reach to emerging market capitalists, as witnessed by the renaming of the former Japanese subgroup of the Trilateral Commission first as the Pacific Asian Group (2000) and then as the Asia Pacific Group (2012), as well as by the specific emerging markets meetings organized by the WEF. However, the fact that the ongoing series of 'Annual Meetings of the New Champions' of the WEF has taken place in China since its inception in 2007 (alternating between Dalian and Tianjin) not only indicates that global networks seek to integrate managers and owners of private Chinese multinationals but also that the Chinese state seeks to exercise a certain degree of control over this integration, by organizing these meetings in mainland China.

4.5 Conclusion

The chapter has demonstrated that not only state-owned Chinese multinationals but also private Chinese cultivate a very close relationship with the state. This close relationship can be seen both with regard to domestic economic regulation and in activities regarding transnational regulation. Thus, the careful conclusion by students of international business that 'even FDI by privately owned Chinese firms reflect political objectives, due to the incentives they face when investing abroad' (Kolstad and Wiig, 2012, p. 29) appears to underestimate the degree of state control over private Chinese multinationals. Clearly, 'government support in China is more than background conditions, but an active agent' (Lu et al., 2010, p. 242). Given that private companies are a least likely case (Klotz, 2008) for the argument of a strong relationship between Chinese multinationals and the state, this observation gives considerable support for the thesis of comprehensive state permeation of Chinese capitalism: 'China has not become a liberal market economy' (Hsueh, 2011, p. 263).

These findings are embedded within the broader picture of the current evolution of capitalism in large emerging markets. The close relationship between private Chinese multinationals and the Chinese state is a typical example of the emergence of state-permeated capitalism in large emerging economies such as Brazil, China, or India. Close relations between major companies and the state can be counted among the distinguishing facets of these economies. However, the specific type of state capitalism 3.0 currently established in China and other large emerging economies is somewhat different from earlier forms of state capitalism. In contrast to the previous type of state capitalism 2.0, it is not coherently directed by a central planning body such as the Japanese Ministry of International Trade and Industry, but rather by competing coalitions between (local / regional) state agencies and national capitalists: 'China scholars find the Chinese state lacks both the internal coherence and strong ties to a docile society characteristic of the "embedded" developmental state' (Hsueh, 2011, p. 14; cf. McNally, 2012, p. 754). And in contrast to the first wave of state capitalism in the late nineteenth century, it is much more sophisticated, not only relying on tariffs as protectionist measures. The fragmentation and sophistication of Chinese state capitalism not only makes it difficult for Western policy-makers to pinpoint Chinese strategies and develop appropriate measures for dealing with these strategies (Jiang, 2010, pp. 9–10). It also creates the need for further studies that support a more thorough understanding of the Chinese version of state capitalism 3.0.

5
Russia's Multinationals: Network State Capitalism Goes Global
Jonas Grätz

5.1 Introduction

In the last few years, Russian multinationals have been subject to increasing attention, due to the spectacular growth of Russian foreign direct investment (FDI) during the 2000s, which set a new world record (Andreff, 2013). Efforts at explaining this extraordinary growth focused on separating real FDI (productive activities abroad) from its 'fake' cousins and on trying to adapt theories of multinationalization by introducing home-country variables. This chapter will build on this literature and ask what drives Russian multinational corporations (MNCs) abroad and what role state actors have in their investment behavior. In analogy to Mikler's (Chapter 1) concern about the impact of the home-country context on MNCs, this chapter provides a thorough analysis of the domestic politicoeconomic context, of government capacities and policies, and investment behavior of the MNCs. Due to space constraints, the chapter will focus on the oil and gas industries, but will also include some evidence from the ferrous and nonferrous metals industries.

The chapter will proceed as follows: first, it will give some theoretical background on Russian MNCs, highlighting the domestic context as an important driver that may override other drivers, such as industry-specific variables. A description of government policies and capabilities will come second. The third and largest section will give a short overview of Russian FDI and then give detailed descriptions of the investment behavior of Russian MNCs from the oil and gas industries.

5.2 Explaining the emergence of Russian MNCs

The literature on Russian MNCs has converged on a number of issues: geographic and cultural proximity are strong factors in explaining the direction of outward FDI to the Commonwealth of Independent States (CIS) (Andreff, 2013; Annushkina and Colonel, 2013; Kalotay, 2008; Kalotay and Sulstarova, 2010; Kuznetsov, 2010), whereas the advantages garnered from their natural resource base and oligopolistic or monopolistic advantages in the home market have been used as an explanatory factor for the ability of Russian MNCs to compete globally. Hence, a strong industry bias skewed toward extractive industries has been noted in Russian outward FDI (Annushkina and Colonel, 2013; Kalotay, 2008, p. 102; Mccarthy et al., 2009). Furthermore, the managerial experience of Russian managers gained during the transition and their corresponding flexibility have been purported as giving them an edge over developed country MNCs when internationalizing into developing countries (Kalotay and Sulstarova, 2010; Kuznetsov, 2010). While all these factors are important, a consensus has emerged that a focus on the domestic context is needed to understand both the relationship between inward and outward FDI, showing the profile of a developed country rather than an emerging market, and the active investment behavior of Russian MNCs abroad (Andreff, 2003, p. 91; Crossland, 2013; Kalotay, 2002; Sauvant, 2005).

Looking at the domestic context, there is growing consensus in the literature that Russia's economy today resembles some form of state capitalism (Andreff, 2013; Mccarthy et al., 2009). Assertions that 'market reform succeeded' (Åslund, 2007) in Russia are more political advocacy than a description of reality. It is true that most assets were privatized during the 1990s, but this did not lead to a dispersion of ownership. The most important industrial assets are in the hands of a few families or the state, with a growing tendency toward state ownership. Thus, more appropriate analyzes highlight the economic dualism of markets operating in some 'nonstrategic' sectors of the economy, such as consumer goods or telecoms, whereas in most other sectors political patronage and network relationships, as well as the interests of state elites, are undermining market competition (Easter, 2008; Mccarthy et al. 2009, p. 173).

The roots of the hybrid Russian system lie in Russian society's weak solidarity, which is characterized by an atomization of social relations (Tatur, 1998). Slowly, this is changing, but only in the more developed regions. Thus, elites have great leeway to assert their interests. The Russian order can be characterized as driven by three differing interests: actors interested in market competition (mainly individuals in the role of consumers), 'oligarchs' possessing huge assets interested in self-preservation and perpetuation of rents, and state actors interested in the preservation and strengthening of their power and personal profits (Annushkina and Colonel, 2013; Puffer and McCarthy, 2007). There is a further dimension of some importance – political elites at the regional level – but today they are either a proxy for the interests of the 'oligarchs' or for realizing the interests of political elites at the federal level. Whereas in the 1990s oligarchs largely called the tune, market reforms seemed to make progress for brief periods in the early 1990s and 2000s. Starting in 2003, this has been eclipsed by the advance of '*siloviki* capitalism' (Puffer and McCarthy, 2007), in which people with a background in the security services are using state tools to advance state and personal interests as defined by them. Businesses have to follow state interests to a greater extent than before. As long as the elites deliver some economic performance – which is premised on high commodities prices – they do not have to fear popular discontent. Furthermore, the *siloviki* pillar is strengthened by the popular perception that a strong state and state control of the economy are in any case better than private control (Sutela, 2012, p. 194). This view has been underscored by the fact that strengthened control by state actors has resulted in greater domestic investment as compared to previously. But still, investment in the Russian economy compared to gross domestic product (GDP) is less than in most transition economies.

Thus, in comparison to the 1990s, the material capabilities of the state have improved, but institutions have not been strengthened. The state operates according to the equation 'strong actors – weak institutions'. The result is that the state is weak in infrastructural terms, but relatively strong in some aspects of coercive power. Weak institutions, high centralization, and competition between participants result in incoherent policies and highly uneven attention of state actors to the different players. As political power is less institutionalized than in stable orders such as the liberal or coordinated market capitalisms (see Mikler in this volume), the economy is subject to political interests. To stay within the terminology of this volume, the Russian order shall be labeled 'network state capitalism'. It is a form of illiberal capitalism, as it defies rules in pursuit of network power and cohesion. This sets the Russian case apart from other forms of state capitalism – not only from democratic state capitalisms but also from more institutionalized orders such as the Chinese version of party state capitalism that has a larger capacity to strategically transform the economy (see Ozawa in this volume).

The literature identified four pathways in which the domestic context leads to larger outflows of 'real' FDI. Two of them are on a structural level, influencing the size of the firm and its capabilities, and two of them on the level of motivations. First, on a structural level, weak institutions and formal restrictions on inward FDI act as entry barriers to foreign and domestic competitors (Durnev, 2010; Khanna and Palepu, 2006; Stal and Cuervo-Cazurra, 2011). Weak institutions and the network relationships that supplant them, as well as the high direct participation of the state are privileging incumbents over new entrants. This allows for privileged firms to increase their size far beyond what would be feasible in a competitive market, and thus to leverage their home-country monopolistic advantages in the internationalization process (Hymer, 1976; Tulder, 2010). Thus, political order and political preferences (Liuhto, 2007; Putin, 1999) make for a bias in favor of large domestic capital. This comes at a cost to economic efficiency, but, as both Mikler and Ozawa (in this volume) point out, MNCs often operate in an oligopolistic environment, providing some rationale for promoting size. Second, state promotion might help companies establish a global presence. State actors may be willing to support companies in establishing contacts with foreign states, in gathering intelligence, by giving financial support, or by other means (Andreff, 2013). Third, on the level of motivations, weak institutions and political control also open up new avenues for state actors to use the companies in their own interest, as a quid pro quo for securing property in Russia or in exchange for other favors. Thus, it may also happen that companies venture abroad for purely political reasons, or may combine political and economic goals (Grätz, 2013b; Liuhto and Vahtra, 2007). And last but not least, weak institutions may push companies to go abroad, as property rights are insecure in principle. International investments in safe jurisdictions may act as an insurance policy against infringements by domestic authorities. Or they may act as a 'golden parachute' for the possibility that one gets kicked out of the plane (Vahtra and Liuhto, 2004).

These domestic influences are shaping the magnitude and persistence of Russian outward FDI. While industry variables and cultural proximity as highlighted by the literature may be important in some cases, they might also be overridden by the push factors of the domestic context, especially if political interest is involved.

5.3 National champions: government policies toward MNCs

The Russian government neither formulated formal policies to support MNCs nor developed appropriate government agencies tasked with assisting foreign investment abroad. This corresponds with the general institutional weakness of the Russian state. Russia thus possesses large MNCs, but it cannot effectively formulate and implement a national development strategy as described by Ozawa (in this volume). Instead, it relies on informal policies, both for passive support i.e., protection from foreign competition, and for active support i.e., helping MNCs achieve a global presence. Via their networking capabilities large companies can get the most out of government. At the same time, networks imply that state actors may use corporations to implement their goals as well.

Current government policy was broadly formulated by Vladimir Putin in 1999. In an academic article he highlighted the central role of natural resource industries as an engine of growth and development in Russia. Huge companies formed on the basis of resource endowments should fulfill a number of tasks: acting as stable providers of revenues for the state budget, stabilizing labor conditions, developing new technologies – especially by transferring military know-how to the civilian sector – modernizing the economy, and integrating Russia with the CIS and the world. Where necessary, the state should interfere in order to reach these goals (Balzer, 2005; Putin, 1999). Hence, global integration of Russia should take place from the inside out, with indigenous multinationals that challenge the established players. What is lacking in this concept is an understanding of how to reap the opportunities presented by globalization.

Successive policy documents followed in these steps. The foreign policy and national security concepts state that Russian companies have to be protected against foreign competition, while the state should support Russian companies in venturing abroad and should punish foreign attempts at hampering their expansion. Echoing Vernon's ideas (Vernon, 1972), Russian MNCs are seen as one of the tools that the Russian state has at hand to realize its interests (Russian Federation, 1997; 2000a; 2000b; 2008a; 2008b). Thus, there is a general idea that the multinationalization of domestic capital deserves state support, as it is the key to Russian economic integration with the world and will enhance Russian influence abroad.

Conversely, economic integration by way of foreign investment in Russia should be controlled to safeguard Russian autonomy from foreign influence. This was formalized in the 2008 law limiting foreign investment in companies of strategic significance. It designates 42 types of activities, investment in which requires approval by a government commission. This includes activities pertaining to natural resources, the defense sector, and media and telecommunications, as well as natural monopolies, actually rendering approval necessary in a great number of cases (Syrbe et al., 2012).

The 'Strategy 2020' contains recommendations for future policies. The document, containing analysis and policy recommendations numbering almost 900 pages, urges support mainly for export diversification. The state should strengthen capabilities to support exports with market information an organizational and financial support. In addition, a state-owned bank dedicated to supporting exporters should be founded (Strategy, 2012). Not much is being said about outward FDI, however. The document just mentions diplomatic backing for Russian MNCs and support for alliances between Russian and non-Russian MNCs (Strategy, 2012). The document thus formulates some elements of better institutions that support Russian outward FDI, but falls short of formulating a coherent strategy on how to interact with the global economy.

5.4 Protecting and promoting Russian capital: government actions

As the formal government policies for supporting Russian MNCs remain weak on paper, a look at government capabilities and actions may help shed greater light on actual policies. When it comes to supporting foreign expansion, the state's most important measures to support Russian MNCs are financial support, information provision, and diplomatic support. Secret services may also be employed to support corporate strategies abroad.

Financial support for companies venturing abroad has been selective and accessible only to well-connected firms. It came mostly in the form of anticyclical support for existing multinationals during the financial crisis, in order to prevent them from falling into foreign hands. In addition, fully state-owned multinationals received support to achieve policy goals abroad. Mostly, money from the oil stabilization fund was used. These reserves proved effective as an anticyclical tool, both to support domestic business and to snap up cheap assets abroad from cash-strapped corporations. The support was rendered via state or state-affiliated banks, such as Vneshekonombank (VEB), Vneshtorgbank, Sberbank, or Gazprombank. Similarly to China, the Russian banking sector is dominated by state-owned banks, the market share of which grew from 35 percent in 2000 to over 55 percent in 2011 (Vernikov, 2012, p. 253), but it is much weaker than Chinese banking. During the financial crisis, VEB lent more than US$ 50 billion (about 4 percent of annual GDP) to big, mostly 'oligarch'-owned companies in the ferrous and nonferrous metals industries, but also to state-owned oil producer Gazprom Neft (Åslund, 2012, p. 247; Čečel' and Pis'mennaja, 2010;

Vnešėkonombank, 2010). Thus, the state is definitely giving the necessary support to Russian businesses when they are in crisis, not only to keep them from going bankrupt but also to avoid foreign participation. But support comes as an ad hoc response to opportunities and threats and is not institutionalized.

In comparison to the relatively weak financial sector, Russia's bureaucratic capacities in information gathering, covert action, and diplomacy are rather high. From the Soviet Union, Russia inherited sizable bureaucracies. For information collection and covert action, the several security services, such as the foreign intelligence service SVR and the military foreign intelligence service GRU, have been revitalized after a certain downscaling during the 1990s and still assume a political role (Anderson, 2007, p. 269). According to the German national intelligence service, the SVR has 13,000 staff, whereas the GRU comes in second with 12,000 staff. Russian security services are perceived as being the most active in human intelligence by a number of European Union (EU) security services. They are also perceived to be particularly seeking intelligence in economic matters, such as energy policy and decisions and energy markets (BIS, 2012; BMI, 2013; TSO, 2012, p. 27).

The Russian foreign ministry can bring to bear considerable skills and prowess in diplomacy. However, in contrast to the security services, the foreign ministry does not seem to enjoy great support in the current Russian elite, as can be inferred from recent remarks by Putin that there are certain 'clans' present in the ministry (Kremlin.ru, 2012).

The measures of support for Russian business vary hugely according to the importance of a given industry or company to the political leadership. Besides the standard instruments of economic diplomacy, asset swaps are particularly prominent. Here, the Russian political elite uses its discretionary power to open investment opportunities in Russia to further the international expansion of Russian MNCs. Asset swaps are often negotiated with the participation of President Putin. Again, particular emphasis is put on the energy sector (Žiznin, 2005).

In addition to the relatively limited tools of economic diplomacy, Russian state actors can use a wide array of tools of 'economic statecraft' (Baldwin, 1985; Grätz, 2013b; Stulberg, 2007). Such actions seek to enlarge and exploit the economic dependence of third states on Russian supplies in order to weaken their bargaining power (Hirschman, 1945). This may take the form of carrots such as lower-than-average energy prices or the postponement of debt recovery. Also, it may include sanctions such as blockades of energy deliveries, the sudden hiking of prices, or the blocking of access to the Russian market. These tools might be used for the sake of corporate profit or for political goals, or both.

Naturally, these instruments will only work if there is significant economic vulnerability of the target state toward Russia. To use these tools, Russia needs background conditions of scarcity and the lack of options for diversification (Newnham, 2011). These tactics might be integrated into a broader framework of strategic manipulation, in which Russia precludes certain options in order for its own proposal to be selected voluntarily by the target (Stulberg, 2007, p. 47). Table 5.1 summarizes the above discussions with a list of instruments that have been used.

If compared to more institutionalized states, the agency costs of using companies for economic statecraft are lower (Newnham, 2011; Stulberg, 2007, p. 48). Weak institutions and the corresponding risk of losing control over the rents generated in the natural resources industries, in turn, generate a further rationale to keep weak institutions and networks in place (Kalyuzhnova and Nygaard, 2008).

The next sections will give an overview of Russia's multinationals and then analyze the largest multinationals from the oil and gas industries.

5.5 Russian FDI and Russian MNCs

Before the discussion of Russian MNCs, some clarifications about FDI figures are in order. The magnitude of FDI from Russia is likely to be grossly overstated by the figures commonly reported, as the Russian pursuit of tax havens as investment destinations is extraordinary in global comparison (Hanson, 2010, p. 640; Kuznetsov, 2007b, p. 3; Pelto et al., 2003). About half of the outward FDI stock reported by the Bank of Russia is located in tax havens like Cyprus, the Virgin Islands, Luxembourg, and the Bermuda Islands (CBR, 2010). In 2011, the outward FDI stock was reported at US$ 362 billion, while inward FDI stood at US$ 456 billion. A part of outward FDI is likely to be real investments, but much of it is likely to be capital roundtripping or nonproductive investment. An indicator for the significance of roundtripping investment is the fact that 40.8 percent of inward investment originated in Cyprus, Luxembourg, and the Netherlands from 2006–2009 (Rosstat, 2010a; 2010b). In addition, 20–25 percent of Russian outward FDI is likely to go into real estate rather than constituting productive investment (Kuznetsov, 2011). Similarly, inward FDI figures overstate the amount of real inward FDI, as a significant amount is of Russian origin and is 'roundtripping' for reasons of tax minimization and asset protection. Thus, the Russian FDI profile is of less impressive magnitude than suggested by the internationally available figures. At the same time, the relationship of real outward

Table 5.1 State instruments to support Russian MNCs

external target: coercion
blockade of valuable good or threat of
subversion of policy goals by covert action
worsening of given economic condition or threat of
external target: inducements
loan toward third state
debt restructuring
provision of risk capital by company
selective opening of investment opportunity (asset swap)
targeted awarding of orders to foreign industry
provision of enhanced market access
rent provision (e.g., by gas transit)
security policy concession (*issue linkage*)
domestic policy concession (*issue linkage*)
external target: strategic manipulation and influencing framework conditions
adding / subtracting options for the target (e.g., market foreclosure)
attribution (changing the perception of values of policy options, e.g., by generating competition between states and/or companies)
networking and co-optation with elites in target country
building of local support networks
influencing public opinion
uploading bilateral problems to a multilateral level
internal resources and instruments
using state to support business
coordination by state actors
informational support
credit provision
border taxes and other export/import restrictions
selective tax cuts

Source: adapted from (Grätz, 2013b).

FDI to real (non-Russian) inward FDI is likely to be less skewed toward the former than suggested by the figures. The bottom line is that Russia might have a more normal 'real' FDI profile than had been thought. At the same time, the ratio of all sorts of outward to inward FDI is still much higher than for other emerging or transition economies.

Inward FDI figures from the state statistics service Rosstat are not compiled on a balance-of-payments basis but on surveys from companies, and are thus regarded as much closer to the truth (Kuznetsov, 2011). Rosstat reports a stock of US\$ 132 billion for the first quarter of 2013 (CBR, 2012; Rosstat, 2013). This figure is only slightly higher than the amount of US\$ 111 billion reported in the latest report on the 20 largest Russian multinationals compiled on behalf of the Vale Columbia Center on sustainable international investment (IMEMO and Vale, 2013). These multinationals are thus likely to make up the bulk of real Russian outward foreign investment.

The list of Russia's 20 largest multinationals (see Table 5.2) shows that Russian outward FDI is clearly skewed toward the oil and gas and ferrous and nonferrous metals industries: 14 of the 20 largest Russian MNCs are from these industries, while only 10 of them are among the top-20 Russian companies by revenue. They hold more than 87 percent of foreign assets among the top-20 foreign investors (IMEMO and Vale, 2013). These figures get even more skewed when considering that the two shipping companies on the list, FESCO and Sovcomflot, have to be labeled 'pseudo-TNC', as they are only registering their ships abroad for tax and insurance reasons, but do not actually maintain a presence there (Kuznetsov, 2007a; 2007b). On the other hand, oil company TNK-BP has merged with Rosneft, freeing one slot on the list. Its place has been filled by Renova, which is missing in Vale's list for curious reasons, as it has not divested its substantial international holdings.

Most of the companies are listed at the stock exchange, although even for the listed companies the free float is less than 50 percent. Many of them have one large blockholder, either a family or the state. Crossholdings by different families are also common. Listing has been motivated primarily by the need for capital from international markets to support expansion, given the low level of development of domestic capital markets. Listing comes with improvements in information disclosure to the public, rendering the gathering of information far easier than is the case for many Chinese multinationals, for example. The next section will give an overview of the international investments of the multinationals from the gas and oil industries. It will then briefly touch on the ferrous and nonferrous metals industries, which could not be included here due to space constraints.

5.6 The oil and gas industries

As Russia is the world's largest hydrocarbons producer, oil and gas are the backbone of the Russian economy and the state budget. When compared to the metals industries, oil and gas have proven to be relatively robust, as prices quickly rebounded after the initial wave of the economic crisis. Oil and gas revenues flow to the state's reserve fund and have been funneled to state banks that used the money to support the multinationalization of state-owned companies or private multinationals

Table 5.2 Largest Russian multinationals US$ million, 2011

Name	Main industries	Status	Foreign assets	Rank Ekspert-400
LUKoil	Oil / gas	Private / listed	29159	2
Gazprom	Gas / oil	State / listed	21767	1
Evraz	Iron / steel / coal	Private / listed	8210	13
Mechel	Iron / steel / coal	Private / listed	6365	18
Sovcomflot	Shipping	State / unlisted	5838	162
Sistema	Telecoms / oil / retail / media / electronics	Private / listed	5207	7
Severstal	Iron / steel / coal	Private / listed	5194	14
Rusal	Aluminum	Private / listed	4611	20
NLMK	Iron / steel	Private / listed	4226	21
Rosneft	Oil / gas	State / listed	4000[a]	3
ARMZ	Uranium ore	State / unlisted	3731	–
Renova	Technologies, engineering	private / unlisted	~3000[b]	–
TMK	Steel pipe	Private / listed	2494[c]	36
MMK	Iron / steel / coal	Private / listed	2101	28
Norilsk Nikel	Nonferrous metals mining	Private / listed	1968	17
Zarubezhneft	Oil / gas	State / unlisted	1834	–
NordGold	Gold mining	Private / listed	1695	–
Inter RAO	Electricity	State / listed	1433	12
FESCO	Shipping	Listed	747	215
Acron	Agrochemicals	Private / listed	721	104

Source: IMEMO/Vale (2013), Ėkspert (2012).
[a] Combines reported assets of Rosneft and the former TNK-BP.
[b] Estimate based on June 2013 market value of stakes in Swiss companies OC Oerlikon and Sulzer.
[c] Includes estimated cost of stake in IPSCO/Oman purchased in 2012, see Džumajlo (2012).

in other industries. Also, the oil and gas industry is a key demand driver for the Russian steel industry, at least as long as Russia relies on pipelines to bring its products to market. Accordingly, the political actors show a keen interest in those companies.

Oil and gas multinationals are also the largest Russian companies and international investors, and state involvement is high. The relationship to political actors also explains their access to oil and gas resources in Russia. The reserve base in Russia of those oil and gas multinationals that are strongly networked with state actors grew more rapidly as compared to those multinationals that are less densely networked (Grätz, 2013a). The following section is mostly based on Grätz (2013b), so further references will be given only when necessary.

Gazprom is certainly the most well-known Russian multinational. The state holds the majority share, and its management was mainly brought in by Putin in 2002. The dense network between Putin and the Gazprom management, in which key posts consist of his acquaintances, make for a high degree of cross-fertilization of worldviews and corresponding priorities. Gazprom is essentially the incorporated Soviet gas ministry, without its corresponding arms in the newly independent states, although it has regained control over some of those assets, notably in Belarus and Kazakhstan. It is the world's largest natural gas producer, and a major oil producer, since it snapped up the oil assets of Roman Abramovich in 2005. In a nutshell, Gazprom's global strategy can be characterized as being based on the assumption that it operates in an oligopolistic market where its corporate decisions can have substantial influence on market structure and pricing. This has been true for much of the 20th century, but as technology evolved and made gas a less scarce and not only a regionally but also a globally traded good, the gas landscape has been thoroughly transformed. Gazprom's political value is also derived from the fact that it supplies goods to oligopolistic or even monopolistic markets where consumers cannot find a substitute. The rigid structure of pipeline transport has been the key conduit of economic and political power in this regard. Hence, pipeline assets make up the bulk of Gazprom's investment. Assets are mostly located in Europe and the CIS. Gazprom's international holdings are too diverse and far-ranging to be fully accounted for in this article.[1] Instead, the section will highlight some of the investments in which political actors have played a role in facilitating success or in pushing Gazprom toward politically desired investments. Gazprom's investments and actions are often directly coordinated by political actors, most prominently by Putin, and motivated by a mix of commercial and political goals. This became apparent, for example, in the South Stream project, a hugely expensive pipeline project designed to bypass Ukraine when delivering gas to South Eastern and Central Europe. The economic driver of the project is the desire to cement Gazprom's position as a monopolistic supplier in the target markets, whereas the political driver is the desire to reduce Ukrainian bargaining power in order to bring the country closer to Russia, and to strengthen Russian influence in the Balkans. The pipeline consists of an offshore section that runs through the Black Sea and an onshore section through several EU member states. The strategic context was marked by the EU-backed Nabucco-project, aimed at reducing the market power of Gazprom. As Gazprom's goals were antagonistic to the goal of diversification, and as the multinational demanded local participation in financing and special conditions for its projects, cooperation with governments had to be established. This has been done both by manipulation of the context for decision-making (subtracting or adding options, or altering the representation of risks for the target actor) and a mix of inducements and coercion. Manipulation of the context was done mainly by generating competition between countries for the project by negotiating simultaneously with several countries, thereby suggesting the pipeline would be built anyway. This emphasized the foregone transit revenues and benefits for the economy of a noncooperative solution, rather than the drawbacks of the project. Economic coercion was applied to Hungary, for example. Gazprom's January 2006 reduction in delivery to Ukraine resulted in supply shortfalls that necessitated emergency measures in Hungary, making the dependence on Russian supplies clear to everyone. This resonated in Hungarian politics. What followed was a cooperation proposal by Putin in the form of the new pipeline, bypassing Ukraine. Hungary agreed to host part of the pipeline and was immediately rewarded with greater market access for Hungarian products in Russia, which reduced Hungary's trade deficit with the country. Later, when Russian political actors tabled the proposal for an intergovernmental agreement that would exempt Gazprom's investments from EU rules on third-party access, Hungarian politicians tried to renege. But they were quickly brought in line when Russia negotiated with neighboring states about bypassing Hungary. In the end, the agreement was signed, contradicting EU law, and the investment decision for the pipeline was taken. Meanwhile, examples of purely political motivations can be found in Venezuela. Here, it was about supporting an ally in the quest for a 'multipolar world order'. At the behest of political actors, Gazprom invested in risky exploration projects in the country, although these projects were earmarked for the domestic market only. In summary, Gazprom can hardly be distinguished from Russian political actors, and corporate and state goals often merge. The strong integration begets the formation of 'Russia, Inc.' (Gaddy and Kuchins, 2008; Illarionov, 2006), where state interests may be captured by profit-making interests of the corporation, while the corporation may often be instrumentalized for political goals.

Rosneft is the second-largest Russian company. It is state owned and mainly engaged in the oil business. Gradually, it came under control of a group led by Igor Sechin, a very influential former security service officer and confidant of Putin, who eventually took over the post of chief executive officer (CEO) in 2012. With Sechin's help, Rosneft grew from a small state-owned entity to the dominant Russian oil producer, extracting over 40 percent of Russian oil. This was accomplished by taking over the assets of private competitor Yukos in 2004 after its former owner, Mikhail Khodorkovsky, ended up in a Siberian prison colony. The owners of TNK-BP were treated differently and remunerated decently when Rosneft took over the company in 2013. The growth of Rosneft by takeovers exemplifies the extraordinary instruments of state actors in the Russian context. Meanwhile, the internationalization of Rosneft is only beginning, and has been shallow compared with most of its competitors. But due to its positioning as the leading oil company in Russia with the best political connections, Rosneft emerged as the key partner for international oil companies looking to Russia for investments. This position is ideal for asset swaps as the key mechanism for internationalization. The first such deal was concluded in 2011, when Rosneft took over the shares of Venezuela's PDVSA in a joint venture with British Petroleum BP, which owns stakes in four German refineries and a strategically important oil pipeline. BP did not exert its right of first refusal, since Rosneft offered investment opportunities in the Russian Arctic offshore and the formation of a broader business alliance that would entail mutual ownership ties between Rosneft and BP (Neff, 2011). The blocking of the latter deal by the Russian shareholders of TNK-BP did not frustrate the refinery investment. And, as we now know, the Russian owners of TNK-BP did not prevail over Rosneft, but were slowly but surely maneuvered out of business. An asset swap has also been carried out with ExxonMobil, swapping access to Russian tight oil resources, acreage in the Russian Arctic, against access of Rosneft to the Mexican Gulf and technology transfer. Other such deals with major international oil companies are in preparation. There is a large, politically motivated upstream investment into Venezuelan heavy oil The Russian strategy toward Venezuela has been largely defined by Sechin in his former role as a government member; hence, Rosneft emerged as a key investor in the Latin American country. Rosneft is leading a consortium of Russian oil companies investing in heavy oil projects, and has taken over separate obligations under another heavy oil project in the Orinoco basin. In sum, Rosneft is the emerging Russian national oil champion, succeeding based on the superiority of its connections and because of its performance in realizing both the political and economic goals of the state.

LUKoil is privately owned and has been an early bird in internationalization. Around 30 percent of shares are owned by the management, the CEO Vagit Alekperov being the main blockholder. Other shareholders are unknown. Alekperov rose from the oil fields of Baku to become the deputy minister of the Soviet ministry of the oil and gas industry and helped shape Soviet policy to form several large vertically integrated 'concerns'. LUKoil was one of them, and was subsequently privatized. Alekperov has been in charge since the beginning, and has shown great appetite for reintegrating business chains in the CIS with the help of his company. He also envisaged LUKoil as a global multinational and a competitor for international oil companies. LUKoil's drive for investing abroad has been encouraged by the growing role of state-owned companies in the Russian oil and gas industries, which have been snapping up the best fields. In terms of upstream integration, Kazakhstan has been the mainstay of LUKoil. Here, the multinational is a minor investor in the huge but expensive Karachaganak oil and gas consortium, and it controls several other oil fields. In Uzbekistan, LUKoil has invested heavily in gas production, a profitable investment supported by political actors in order to strengthen ties between Russia and Uzbekistan. But as soon as 2014, LUKoil's focus on foreign upstream will move from the CIS to Iraq, where it has a 75 percent stake in the large West Qurna-2 oil field. LUKoil was already a partner in the field in the 1990s, when it was the only Russian oil company capable of international expansion. After the regime change in Iraq, Russian political actors supported LUKoil's bid to reenter the field, as LUKoil had the best relations in the Iraqi oil industry. In terms of downstream integration, the multinational started to invest in Bulgarian and Romanian refineries in the 1990s. It now dominates the Bulgarian market for refined products and has a growing position in the West Balkans. This is also due to the fact that LUKoil invested in further refineries in Italy and the Netherlands in the late 2000s. The latter deal was facilitated by Putin, who coordinated an asset swap by opening up investment opportunities for French oil company Total in Russian gas producer Novatek. In exchange, LUKoil received access to the refinery owned by Total. LUKoil also owns petrol stations in different countries, including the United States. In sum, LUKoil can score points with the Russian political elite by investing internationally and posturing as an oil multinational, but it has come under increasing pressure in Russia through the competition of state-owned oil and gas companies with better connections. It is of value to political actors as it is privately owned, and hence may arouse less suspicions abroad than state-owned companies, yet still bring the benefit of weakening the corporate control of Western companies. But as competition mounts in Russia, some of its investments look rather like 'system escape' than like sensible investments from an economic standpoint. This is especially true for investments in filling stations as well as in some refineries.

Zarubezhneft is the most internationalized among the Russian oil companies. It is small and fully state-owned. Its internationalization is due to the fact that it was founded in 1967 as a Soviet vehicle to help allied countries with oil developments, using Soviet technology and expertise. Currently, it is run by figures close to Sechin and associated with Rosneft (Makarkin, 2013; Mel'nikov and Solodovnikova, 2013). The company has a long relationship history with Iraq and Vietnam. Today, it has a growing role in strengthening the economic relationship with key Russian allies outside the CIS, such as Vietnam, Cuba, and the Serb Republic in Bosnia and Herzegovina. The joint venture Vietsovpetro with the Vietnamese state oil company has existed since 1981, and is expected to be active at least until 2030. It is producing oil and gas in the Vietnamese shelf and has several new blocks to develop. The good position of Zarubezhneft in Vietnam is also due to the fact that it could propose asset swaps: Since 2008, the joint venture Rusvietpetro has been working on 13 oil fields in Russia. In exchange, Zarubezhneft got access to further blocks on the Vietnamese shelf (Nestro, 2013; Solodovnikova, 2013). Less profitable investments are being made in Cuba, but they are part of Russia's strategy of raising its profile in Latin America. Cuba is a key ally of Venezuela. Here, the multinational is providing substantial risk capital. Since 2009, it has been exploring the Cuban shelf, but has not found hydrocarbons so far. It temporarily suspended its drilling program in 2013, but says it will resume in 2014 (Moscow Times, 2013). Zarubezhneft's investments in Bosnia and Herzegovina are also politically driven, as the company targets the Serb Republic in Russia's effort to bolster Serbs in the region. Since the end of the war, it has reconstructed a small refinery and invested in petrol stations. Financial support for these investments came from state-owned VEB, underlining the political rather than economic drivers (Nestro, 2012). Zarubezhneft is thus complementing the Russian oil sector with an internationally experienced player that is politically driven and realizes projects in the foreign policy interests of Russia.

Summing up, Russian oil and gas multinationals come in great variety and thus have a relatively good division of labor from the viewpoint of state actors favoring global expansion. There are private players eager to build a global presence on their own, as prospects in Russia are not so good. There are majority state-owned players subject to the discipline of the stock exchanges and bond markets that can still be used for facilitating politically driven investments. And then there is a nonlisted, state-owned player like Zarubezhneft to pick up the pieces that the others left behind – relatively small-scale projects abroad that need a high degree of political backing or politicized capital. Competition between those players in Russia is still helping keep the power of the individual actors in check. The involvement of state actors and state interests is far more apparent than in the other industries.

The case studies of companies from the ferrous and nonferrous metals industries had to be excluded from this chapter due to space constraints.[2] Nevertheless, it is worthwhile to integrate some of the insights into this chapter. Whereas the ferrous metals industry does not feature any state-owned MNCs, the nonferrous metals industry does. In the ferrous metals industry, the expansion was largely toward downstream markets in the United States and the EU. Thus, rather than cultural or geographical proximity, market access, system escape, and the impact on global markets have played a role for downstream expansion. Political actors supported only some of the companies, mostly by credit provision during the financial crisis of 2008. State support could override industry drivers after the financial crisis, as Russian MNCs would have had to retreat.

State support was more apparent in nonferrous metals, which was also used to override industry drivers. As Russia partly lacks resources, upstream integration was an important industry driver in the run-up to the financial crisis. It was amplified by the political desire to control a greater market share in order to influence world markets. In uranium mining, this goal was also supported with the help of various tools, including covert action by secret services and a family clan.

5.7 Conclusion: Russia Inc. and Co.

This chapter has argued that the domestic context in political economy terms has decisive influence on the international investments of Russian MNCs. Industry variables can explain variations between industries, but the domestic context is decisive both for determining the domestic size of the multinational and the degree of its multinationalization. The Russian domestic context has been termed network state capitalism, as it is based on networks and thus defies institutionalization, which is important for ideal-typical versions of state capitalism.

The cases of the largest Russian MNCs from the oil and gas industries have revealed both the general outward orientation of Russian capital and the remarkable variety of actors. On the former note, network state capitalism explains the more rapid, premature expansion of Russian MNCs when compared to a more optimal path, where inward FDI and investments in the domestic economy are much higher than outward FDI. Russian multinationals expand more rapidly mainly out of two motives: first, the politically unintended reason of system-escape investments aimed at reducing the risks associated with a home base in Russia. Second, the politically intended reason of international expansion either out of economic motivation to ensure oligopolistic or monopolistic influence on global markets, or out of political motivation to support host country governments or enhance foreign countries' dependence on Russia. Regarding the variety of actors, network state capitalism also offers a variety of types of multinationals that complement each other. Hence, Russian political actors can to some extent choose between different actors dependending on a given context in the host state. In statist economies, state-owned actors will be preferred, whereas listed and privately owned multinationals will be preferred in market-based economies. In general, the networked nature of relations means that Russian political actors can use also strongly networked private MNCs for their goals, just as the latter can expect help in times of economic trouble.

For those multinationals that are neither state owned nor well networked, going abroad is a way of insuring against the vagaries of the Russian politico-economic order. In addition, they try to shore up domestic political support by multinationalizing, as political actors tend to see large Russian multinationals as a symbol of national power. Industry variables are not so important to explain their behavior, as they are prone to internationalize even in areas where Russia has strong competitive advantages, such as oil resources. They did not get a huge degree of support from state actors.

Privately owned multinationals with good networks with the state have acted as 'national champions'. They have shown a tendency to overexpand internationally in pursuit of market power, while generally following internationalization patterns based on industry variables. Overextension was rewarded by the state, which bailed them out in times of crisis.

Last, there is a growing number of state-owned multinationals. Here, industry variables are sometimes being amplified with the help of state actors, especially if greater control over markets and target states can be reached, and sometimes play no major role, implying that political goals are in the driver's seat. Gazprom is an example where there is an industry drive for downstream expansion, which has been supported with state tools. Gazprom's upstream expansion, to the contrary, has mostly been driven by political interests alone. The same is true for Rosneft and Zarubezhneft.

For host economies, the presence of 'system-escape' multinationals is beneficial at least in the short run, as they are desperate for investment opportunities and thus may keep companies running that would have gone bankrupt otherwise. But investments in nonferrous metals industries as well as the oil and gas industries may be politically sensitive, as Russian companies often aim to influence markets. There is also the problem that Russian multinationals may be so closely integrated with various state organizations that unexpected, nonmarket tools may be used.

In sum, Russia's network state capitalism is clearly favoring state-owned MNCs, but there is no clear formal mechanism linking MNCs and the state. Hence, networks are central for the degree of integration between state and MNC. Networks may thus override state ownership and lend strong support to even private MNEs. Today's network state capitalism has resulted in a higher share of investments in the domestic economy as compared to the earlier version of oligarchic capitalism. But greater influence by state actors came at the cost of institution building. Prevailing competition between different economic and political factions and the deficiencies in the institutionalization of the state mean that Russia can neither follow the path of East Asian developmental states, nor implement a more rational fusion of state power and capitalism like in China (see Ozawa, Nölke in this volume). Ultimately, this will only change if Russian society grows stronger to the point where it can challenge entrenched networks and build a more institutionalized state.

Notes

1. But see Grätz (2013b) and Poussenkova (2010) for details.
2. See Grätz (2013c) for more details on these case studies.

6
Sector Creation and Evolution: The Role of the State in Shaping the Rise of the Indian Pharmaceutical Sectoral Business System

Heather L. Taylor

6.1 Introduction

The emergence of emerging market multinational companies (EMNCs) as a driving force of change in the political, social, and economic landscape of the world economy has grabbed the attention of policymakers, academics, and the media alike in recent years. While the appearance of multinationals from developing and emerging markets is not a new phenomenon, their bold international expansion into the global economy and the rapid growth of Outward Foreign Direct Investment (OFDI) from their home economies into advanced economies has garnered the attention of many. Consequently, the fact that EMNCs have been making their marks in international commerce by competing successfully in global markets and acquiring assets in both advanced and emerging economies challenges the trend, and in many cases the assumption, that only advanced economies produce such companies. EMNCs are becoming a significant means for the transfer of capital, technology, management, and other assets within and between developing, emerging, and advanced economies, and they are creating new engines of growth in respective emerging markets and being publicly challenged.

Illustrating some of the aforementioned trends and changes, this study considers the rapid international expansion of Indian Multinational Companies (IMNCs), specifically in the pharmaceutical sector between 1990 and 2010, in order to explore the drivers of outward expansion through FDI in the sector; the institutional foundations of industrial comparative advantages; and the influential features of the pharmaceutical-sector business system. By detailing the features of the economic organization and institutional system of the pharmaceutical sector, this chapter is intended to be the basis for future research that will detail the types of institutional business systems within emerging markets and their influence on the sector-specific, competitive relationships between firms and determinants of the internationalization process. To understand how these features influence and are influenced by firms in both advanced and emerging economies, this study applies an historical meso, sector-centered approach, to the analysis of the evolution of the pharmaceutical industry in India in order to develop an initial sketch of the Indian pharmaceutical sector system today.

The domestic and sectoral institutional contexts and trajectories of economic development and organization in emerging market economies have differed substantially from those in advanced economies. An approach recognizing that interests of multinationals are not only embedded in but also have developed out of these contexts allows one the possibility to discuss whether EMNCs in general, and IMNCs more specifically, have fundamentally different business models, internationalization strategies, and interests. Additionally, such an approach allows one to consider the important roles sociopolitical, geopolitical, politicoeconomic, and other historical and contemporary contextual factors play in EMNC development and their evolution into global competitors in specific sectors.

In line with the theme of this volume, the role of the state and public policy plays a central part in the analysis of the Indian pharmaceutical sector. Particularly, a historical contextualist account with specific emphasis on the public policies that created and influenced the development of the sector and its evolution postliberalization (1990) is provided and then later used to develop an initial overview of the current Indian pharmaceutical sectoral system. A great deal of emphasis is placed on the role of state support in the Indian pharmaceutical sectoral system because, despite the fact that many advanced economy states have also supported MNC growth in specific sectors, the path that the Indian state in particular has taken to foster sector and firm growth has substantially differed from those of their advanced economy counterparts in this sector. In most cases, emerging market states have not allowed industry specialization to evolve 'out of' and 'along with' an institutional environment consolidated over periods of prolonged economic development. Rather they often (overtly) chose key industries in which their economies would specialize at specific moments. These choices were often made prior to the existence of an institutional environment or even an industry base that could support further growth and development of these industries. Thus, and as is the case with the Indian pharmaceutical sector, public policy and state support have been crucial in enabling the start of rapidly developing domestic institutional environments. This indeed confirms the type of state-industry relation (see Ozawa in this volume) that has evolved in the Indian pharmaceutical sector, whereby the state has 'fostered, governed and even controlled' the development and growth of the sector and the firms within it (see Ozawa in this volume). Furthermore, this point also serves to highlight the extent to which the indigenous firms in the Indian pharmaceutical sector that have evolved into MNCs have remained deeply embedded within their socioeconomic institutional environment as a result of the manner in which the state created, governed, and controlled the development and growth of the sector and its firms (see Mikler in this volume).

In terms of the literature base that has developed on IMNCs, there has been a sizeable amount of work on the competitive advantages of Indian firms and the industries in which the Indian economy has specialized (CRISIL, 2006; Das, 2007; Gupta A., 2006; Gupta V.-K., 2006; Pradhan, 2003; 2007; 2008). These studies indicate that the competitive advantages of Indian firms largely revolve around low production costs, flexible production systems, a relatively lax regulatory environment, ease of communication given strong English language capabilities, and a weakly enforced intellectual property rights (IPRs) regime. While a variety of industries operate in the Indian economy, outward expansion into advanced economies and most research has typically focused on the information technology (IT), pharmaceuticals, auto and auto parts industries. Outward growth of IMNCs has often been summarized in terms of their specialization in 'skill-intensive intermediate products and services' (Das, 2007, p. 140). A limited literature on specific institutions supporting these specialization patterns has also begun to evolve (Bergman, 2006; Chadha, 2005; Chadurvedi, 2007; Holmström, 2001; Nölke and Taylor, 2010; 2011; Sampath, 2006; Sarathy, 2006; Taylor and Nölke, 2009; 2010).

To date, not much literature has been dedicated to assessing the Indian production system and the institutional complementarities within the system (Mayer-Ahuja, 2006). To be sure, there is not just one Indian variety of capitalism or one Indian national business system. India's economy is indeed highly fragmented, with important differences between industries and regions. Unfortunately, relatively little literature analyzes the social embeddedness of the firm in specific industries in terms of the sources and regulation of the transfer of innovations, actors and networks, competition policy, and the types of interfirm / intrafirm linkages Furthermore, there is a lack of studies linking institutional and political factors with the sectoral position of Indian multinationals. While much research has been devoted to IMNC internationalization and resource building, the particular structural characteristics of industries in which these firms operate have been neglected.

6.2 A middle-way sectoral-system framework

This chapter develops a sectoral business system model for focusing on the interactive nature of relationships between actors (firms and nonfirms), demand, innovative activities, and institutional contexts throughout an institutional system. Here a system can span multiple levels, but for the purposes of this chapter it will be restricted to the Indian national sectoral level. Considering the national sectoral environment only is crucial, because Indian firms remain deeply embedded within their socioeconomic institutional environment at home, even when operating abroad (see Mikler in this volume). These contexts support the development and growth of firms' competitive advantages and sector-specific specialization patterns through the institutional complementarities in the following areas: corporate governance, financial flows and capital markets, industrial relations and work systems, intrafirm linkages, and the transfer of innovation in the economy, as well as the role of the state and public policy.

By looking at IMNCs in specific sectors, a comprehensive and unique approach to particular socioeconomic institutional environments is allowed to develop and contributes to an understanding of the rise and internationalizing strategies of IMNCs. The question of why and how institutions matter has remained mysterious because, to date, analytically and theoretically, ideas surrounding the influential role of domestic institutional environments in EMNCs and their influence on internationalization have been limited in international business studies. While more recent studies on EMNCs have begun to incorporate 'institutions' into their analysis, the majority confines this to analyzing the quality and/or regulatory role of institutions. This implies that the role of institutions in these studies has been taken for granted and incorporated only as a background context to the general phenomena under consideration. In contrast, it is argued here that the rise of EMNCs and their particular competitive advantages can only be fully understood when embedded in the institutional context of economic coordination from which they were born. Furthermore, through precisely analyzing the relationship between the institutional context and the firm, we can generate an understanding of the industrial comparative advantages of these firms when expanding abroad. In the case of India, the majority of research on IMNCs has focused either only on context or only on action in their analyses of internationalization, with action as 'strategic intent' being the primary focus in many of these works.

The approach presented here differs from these previous studies in that it places both context and action at the center of the analysis on the rise and outward expansion of IMNCs. In order to study variances in IMNCs and their internationalization in the domestic sectoral institutional context, two interrelated frameworks grounded in institutional theory serve as the foundation of to create a meso-sector-centered evolutionary institutional framework. This analytical framework will serve in future research as a means to explore the sectoral-level institutional environment in which the internationalizing process occurs at the levels of both the home and the host country, and the institutional embeddedness of firms as they are internationalizing. These two frameworks, varieties of capitalism (VoC) and national business systems (NBS), are briefly presented below.

The VoC approach[1] is a sociological and political economic method of understanding firm behavior within capitalist environments. This firm-centered approach, elaborated by Hall and Soskice (2001a) has become the hallmark of the study of comparative capitalism. Hall and Soskice conclude that there are currently two types of advanced capitalist economies: liberal market economies (LMEs) and coordinated market economies (CMEs). The VoC approach is based on the understanding that the form of economic organization embodied in any given national economy is determined by the organization of business relations within it, and this helps explain differences in the types of firm- and industry-competitive advantages that also contribute to specific specialization patterns within respective countries. The centrality given to the firm within this approach is due to its important role in economic growth or decline within nations, and therefore competitiveness is a core issue analyzed within VoC.

According to VoC, the ability of a firm to innovate is directly tied to the ability of and the way in which firms overcome coordination problems. Since the way in which this is done differs because of the national institutional arrangements, Hall and Soskice construct ideal models around coordination problems and the way that each form of capitalism is able to overcome them. The points of departure used to investigate competitiveness are comprised of five interdependent characteristics of the capitalist environment in which they find themselves (Hall and Soskice, 2001a, pp. 17–33; see also Jackson and Deeg, 2006, pp. 11–20), namely

1. the financial system, i.e., the primary means to raise investments;
2. corporate governance, i.e., the internal structure of the firm;
3. the pattern of industrial relations, i.e., working conditions, wage systems, labor relations;
4. the education and vocational training system; and
5. the preferred mode for transfer of innovations, the relationships between firms (intrafirm).

The two models differ regarding their basic mechanisms for solving coordination problems within national economies. In LMEs, the most important form of coordination is competitive market arrangements and formal contracts. In CMEs, nonmarket forms of coordination such as interfirm networks and national or sector associations play a crucial role (Hall and Soskice, 2001a, p. 8, pp. 33–36). Both models, however, tend to leave the state completely out of the picture. Another major problem of the firm-centered approach is that it tends to perceive reality as static, and does not take into consideration the possibility of the evolution of systems of capitalisms, resulting in snapshot analyses of unrealistically stable environments.

Finally, despite the VoC framework's being a firm centered approach, relatively few efforts have been made to bridge the framework's explanations of the comparative advantages of whole national production systems with the institutional competitive advantages of firms in those respective production systems. This point is particularly relevant because it also sheds light on the relative absence of more in-depth firm case studies in the empirical application of the VoC framework to microlevel processes of firm strategy. Thus, supplementing the VoC framework with international business literature on firm strategies will provide a more comprehensive approach to understanding how the institutional comparative advantages of national production systems at a macrolevel are related to the industrial competitive advantages of firms in specific industries at a mesolevel and in turn how both are interlinked with firm strategy, preferences, and interest formation at a microlevel. Furthermore, while VoC helps explain the sector-specific patterns that are created as a result of these institutional complementarities, there has been little work that details the sectoral-institutional domains that operate in many unique industries.

The comparative NBS framework pioneered by Richard Whitley (1992; 1999; 2001; 2007) sets out to describe the characteristics of business systems as a means to understand modes of coordination and how they came to be established. In the NBS framework, 'emphasis is on the interdependence of economic organization and institutional contexts, coupled with significant similarities in some major institutional features across market economies' (Whitley, 2001, p. 27). Unlike the VoC framework, the NBS approach explicitly incorporates an evolutionary aspect of business system development in order to explore the underlying institutions of economic coordination in market economies. These institutional features and characteristics frame patterns of economic coordination and are incorporated into the NBS framework as a moving target that evolves over time, something that in this chapter is argued as crucial to understanding the development and evolution of the Indian pharmaceutical-sectoral system.

Within NBS, the key characteristics of a business system are its institutionalized arrangements of economic coordination and relationships of authority and types of work systems within a market economy. More specifically, the framework emphasizes the need to understand the nature of the firm as being socially embedded and thus move beyond conventional transaction cost- and resource-based analyses of the firm, solely based on the dichotomy of being organized either through hierarchies or markets, trust-based/loyalty relationships, and modes of economic governance, for instance competition, networks, and alliances (Schaumburg-Müller, 2001).

While the NBS framework establishes more loosely created typologies of 'national business systems' than the dualist VoC approach, it nevertheless focuses on the relationships of socially embedded actors (such as firms) in a similar set of institutional domains, in order to establish typologies. The following five institutional areas make up the proximate social institutions and the characteristics of a given national business system, and can also be applied to create a sectoral-level business system framework:

1. the types of governance arrangements within the business system (trust or contract based)
2. the specific types of work systems that are evident (Taylorist, Fordist, etc.)

3. capital markets and financial flows (external and internal to the system)
4. the type of management and authority relations (e.g., paternal, network, alliance, patriarchal)
5. the role of the state and the state support

In addition to these five proximate social institutions, the NBS framework also incorporates the influential role of background social institutions and the industrial lineage of firms into the analysis. These background institutions add a historical, evolutionary aspect to the framework, which is often overlooked in the VoC approach, and they are important given their influence on the current relationships and interdependencies prevalent in the current institutional system.

While similar to the VoC approach, the NBS framework has, to date, been focused on describing and explaining patterns of economic organization at the national level, i.e., 'national' business systems. Unlike the VoC approach, the quintessential 'international' aspect is given room in the NBS framework. This becomes important when looking at capital, financial, and work systems, as well as at skill sets found within national business systems. For example, with regard to capital, NBS incorporates the possibility for, and importance of, international capital flows to finance economic activities in the business system.

The previous two sections have demonstrated that while a rich literature base has developed with regards to IMNCs, there remains a gaping lacuna with regard to an elaboration of the Indian national- and sectoral production systems, i.e., the socio- and politicoeconomic institutional environments supporting the growth and competitive strength of firms that are specialized in specific sectors (like the Pharmaceutical sector) by providing firms with institutional comparative advantages in a specific sector. Despite recent calls in international business studies to take institutions more seriously, much of this work continues to view institutions as limiting factors to the strategic intent of firms and managers in determining 'strategy'. Thus, little room is allowed for the institutional context to be taken seriously as an integral part of the competitive capabilities of the firm and the specialization patterns that develop in specific sectors within specific countries. It is precisely here where frameworks such as VoC and NBS provide a useful bridge for understanding the institutional foundations of the firm's competitive capabilities and sector-specific institutionally embedded specialization patterns that develop. Individually, these frameworks act as heuristic devices to understand patterns of economic organization and their institutional foundations, and it is these institutional features and their interdependencies that generate the competitive advantages of organizations in specific sector-level institutional contexts.

These differences are largely related to the separate foci of each approach, where international business theories are primarily concerned with elaborating strategies of firms, while VoC and NBS frameworks are interested in describing and explaining patterns of economic organization within capitalist market economies. However, these separate foci are indeed intimately connected if not mutually interdependent: firm strategy influences and is influenced by the institutional context and regime, just as the institutional context and dominant institutional regime influence and are influenced by firm strategy.

In arguing the potential benefits that could be accomplished through combining international business approaches with a more institutional political economy approach, this chapter will make the first inroads into doing so. As such, it takes the empirical phenomena of the rise of IMNCs specifically in the pharmaceutical sector as a starting point. In order to provide a comprehensive understanding of how these firms have grown and are successfully competing in global markets today, it starts off by applying insights from the NBS approach to the historical evolution of the sector. Thus, the unit under analysis is the economic organization of firms at the sector-system level. After developing an account of the historical evolution of the sector, it then turns to providing an initial sketch of the Indian pharmaceutical sectoral system by using the similar set of institutional domains discussed above in both the VoC and NBS frameworks. Given the theme of this edited volume, the following empirical sections will place primary emphasis on the role played by the state and state support in creating, supporting, and hindering the development of the pharmaceutical sector in India, pre- and postliberalization.

The structure of the following section is as follows: it begins by discussing the historical development of the pharmaceutical industry in India and the role of the State during its development. It then moves on to discuss the evolution of the industry and firm internationalization strategies since the liberalization of the Indian economy. The purpose of the section is to provide a historical, socially embedded account of the development of the industry and the evolution of firm strategy and business models. In doing so, it will point out how the rapid and steady internationalization of the Indian pharmaceutical industry post-1990 is in line with the antecedent policies that created the industry, as well as the wider evolution of the global pharmaceutical industry. It concludes by applying insights from the historical evolutionary account to outline the current pharmaceutical sector in India.

6.3 Historical development of domestic industry capacity and the sectoral evolution of firm strategy[2]

The industrial policies of the Indian government from 1947 onward were specifically focused on building up competitive competencies in 'new technology' industries, such as pharmaceuticals. These industries were and continue to be interpreted as the drivers of the Indian economy and of its ability to compete in the global economy. In doing so, and as mentioned by Ozawa in this volume, the state took on both a developmental and regulatory role in the catching-up process of these industries. The problem facing the Indian government in 1947, however, was the lack of necessary institutions, technology, knowledge, and manpower to support growth in these industries. In mediating the situation, from 1947 onward the government became an institutional entrepreneur and institution builder, which is further explained below (Chang, 1995, p. 37). While its entrepreneurial side seemed to weaken in the 1980s due to the political weaknesses of the state as well as issues of growth and competitiveness in the economy, the state's role as an institution builder has barely waned since 1947.

Under British rule, the Indian pharmaceutical industry developed a minimal capacity for the production and manufacturing of antimalarial drugs. During this period, some of the first research institutes were established to manufacture these drugs. Despite this, the industry remained relatively small and virtually nonexistent in terms of the number of domestic firms producing and manufacturing products.

Prior to independence as well as up to and through the first decades after independence, foreign firms largely dominated the Indian pharmaceutical market. They had established a presence in India by exporting formulations from their home countries into the Indian market, at which point small-scale Indian firms took over sales and distribution. Postindependence, large foreign firms began to swarm the market and go beyond exporting, until they dominated the pharmaceutical industrial marketplace: 'They established their units in the country first for the packaging operations of imported formulations, subsequently for the manufacturing of medications with imported ingredients, and later they began the local production of – at least part of – the ingredients they needed' (Balcet and Bruschieri, 2010, p. 116).

Despite the high concentration of, what were then, industry giants in the Indian market, there were little or no spillover effects in terms of increasing the technological capacity and knowledge of domestic firms in the production and manufacturing of pharmaceutical products. Aside from the lack of spillover effects, the price of the drugs produced and sold in India were some of the highest in the world, and were unreasonable for the poverty-stricken domestic economy. This led to a series of policy interventions beginning in 1970 to enhance domestic pharmaceutical production capacities and improve the economic competitiveness of domestic firms and the affordability of their products (see Table 6.1 below). Indeed, confirming Ozawa's findings in this volume, the Indian government took a proactive role in guiding and enacting a series of both general as well as sector-specific policies that in effect nurtured the creation and growth of an indigenous industry and also simultaneously made use of foreign firms and inward foreign direct investment (IFDI) to force technology spillovers in order to encourage the growth of a self-sufficient indigenous industry (Ozawa, pp. 44–46).

The first measure to note is the Drug Price Control Order that began in 1960. However, the most lasting, high-impact policy measure was the Indian Patent Act of 1970, which abolished 'the old British inspired product patent system and deliberately (introduced) a weaker process patent system in 1970 (stimulating) an upsurge in reverse engineering and copying of foreign product patented drugs' (Bruche, 2011, p. 4). This basically meant that the final product itself could not be patented, but rather only the process undertaken to produce the final formulation. As a result, numerous versions of foreign-patented drugs were no longer under patent in the Indian market, meaning the domestic industry could reverse-engineer products to discover the process involved in producing that drug. Once this process had been established, the Indian firm could then patent the process they used, but still could not patent the final product itself. 'Supported by complementary public investments into higher education, public research institutes and state-owned pharmaceutical firms, these

Table 6.1 Key Policy Interventions 1970–2005

Year	Policy
1970	Indian Patent Act
1970	Drug Price Control Order
1973	Foreign Exchange Regulation Act
1978	Drug Policy of 1978
1987	Drug Price Control Order
1995	Drug Price Control Order
2005	The Patents (Amendment) Act
2000–2005	Trade Barrier Changes

Source: Balcet and Bruschieri, 2010, pp.115–118.

changes provided the basis for the rise of India's pharmaceutical industry to become one of the world's major volume players' (Bruche, 2011, p. 4).

The cumulative effect of these policies was the exodus of international pharmaceutical firms from the Indian market. While this exodus happened over time, it was pushed forward faster through a set of policies implemented by the Indian state, which slowly decreased the percentage holdings that foreign firms were allowed to possess in domestic firms. This, combined with the effects of the new patent laws, virtually helped force foreign firms out of the market. The operations of these firms were either shut down completely or sold off to Indian counterparts, thus enabling domestic rivals to obtain 'state-of-the-art factories, laboratories, products, and trained staff which supported their quest for world class quality levels' (Bruche, 2011, p. 4). By 1982, Indian firms had obtained approximately half of the domestic market (Balcet and Bruschieri, 2010). The only way for foreign firms to get access to India's market at this time was then to establish partnerships and joint ventures with Indian firms to license, manufacture, and distribute their products. The effect of this, combined with the changes in the patent law, allowed Indian pharmaceutical firms access to process knowledge and technology held by the major multinationals that had been working in India. They would eventually leverage this knowledge to create cheaper generic brands affordable in the Indian market. After years of building up their generic portfolios and eventually extending into new drug development, Indian pharmaceutical firms were able to create strong portfolios that allowed them not only to go global but also compete with international pharmaceutical companies.

The approach that the Indian government has taken toward developing its strategic industries and in fostering the catching-up process of these industries has utilized a mix of state control, self-control, and cooperation (see Ozawa, pp. 38–39). The model used in the first epoch after Independence (1947–1980s) was primarily state control, whereby if we specifically look at the pharmaceutical sector we find it was a sector reserved for public sector units only and publicly funded research units. A limited amount of licenses were, however, granted to private sector firms. The licensing system that the government set up applied to both the public sector units as well as the few private firms in the market. These licenses governed market entry, bulk drugs, and formulation manufacturing and production, as well as capacity expansions. Moving into the 1980s, the Indian government began to take a mixed model approach in which it slowly began to utilize self-control and cooperation. Thus, after the initial start-up phases of India's strategic industries, barriers preventing foreign firm entry were slowly removed in the 1980s, and policies were created to encourage more private firms to enter the marketplace. By the early 1990s, this helped ensure that strategic sectors became highly competitive and heavily populated. This competitiveness helped in motivating IMNCs to pursue aggressive acquisition strategies abroad.

Liberalization of the economy, and more specifically of industry, began in the 1980s and sped up in the 1990s. These reforms were the result of a consistent 11-year expansion of fiscal deficits, which peaked in 1990–1991. In brief, the depletion of foreign reserves had prevented the Indian government's ability to repay loans and negatively affected its credit rating. This, combined with political instability, galvanized a new era of economic reform. The reforms were aimed at, inter alia, disciplining government spending and alleviating external debt, which had been accrued by the Indian government since 1979. The latter goal was perhaps the most consequential for the creation of IMNCs because it entailed the liberalization of inward FDI in 1991, which was shortly followed by outward OFDI liberalization. Inward FDI liberalization entailed not only opening equity markets up to portfolio investors from abroad, but also correlated with a significant surge in foreign incumbent MNCs setting up shop in India.

During this period, the Indian pharmaceutical firms focused on in this study increasingly started to pursue outward expansion. While the majority of these firms initially focused on exporting into foreign markets in the early/mid-1990s, as capital accounts were liberalized and the OFDI policy regime on foreign exchange limitations was slowly reduced, internationalization strategies based on acquisitions abroad steadily began to increase in the late 1990s, and surged in the first decade of the 21st century. Since the early 2000s, we can note a few substantial changes in the strategy choices of Indian pharmaceutical firms: internationalization through acquisitions first in Europe and North America, more recently in other emerging markets; a substantial increase in partnership agreements accompanied by a leveling out of high-priced acquisition deals since the mid-2000s; and most notably, an increased focus on building competitive strength through concentrating on drug discovery and development capacities at home, as opposed to only concentrating on manufacturing and distribution of molecules and products. This ladder strategy further confirms the type of side-ladder of industrial upgrading (see Ozawa in this volume).

With regards to the increase in partnership agreements, changes to the foreign exchange policies and patent laws, implemented by the state, have played a key role in encouraging the number of partnerships with foreign firms to steadily take off. In the pharmaceutical industry, these partnerships have been crucial in terms of providing many Indian firms with an easier means not only to become involved in the marketing and distribution of drugs but also in new drug development. This was recently evidenced by the three-year agreement between India's Zydus Cadila and Sweden's Karo Bio to cooperate in discovering and developing new molecules to treat inflammatory diseases. These types of partnerships involve out- and in-licensing agreements as well as contract research and manufacturing firms.

Another interesting development in the strategies of Indian pharmaceutical firms post-2000, has been the shift in focus toward drug discovery rather than just manufacturing and distribution. In 2012, Indian firms reinvested roughly $18 million of revenue for research and development (R&D). Many firms have accomplished this by dividing their business segments into separate subsidiary companies at home, specifically focused on discovering new molecules. Examples of these firms include Dr. Reddy's Laboratories and Sun Pharmaceuticals, as well Glenmark. In order to achieve this, these firms have separated their businesses into two separate segments: one segment focused on generic drugs and a second specifically focused on new drug discovery and development. Aside from the large Indian pharmaceutical firms that are not only big enough but also profitable enough to incorporate both segments into one business model, the remainder of the Indian pharmaceutical sector can be divided between the firms that are focused purely on generic drug manufacturing and distribution versus the firms focused solely on new drug discovery and development.

In the generics sector, most firms remain 'pure generics firms', with their primary focus on manufacturing and marketing of active pharmaceutical ingredients (APIs)[3] as well as generic formulations. In order to be successful in this business segment, firms base their competitive strengths on the following features: low-cost manufacturing and supply of APIs (for use in the production of drugs by other companies); efficient and effective generic distribution lines; effective and profitable front-end sales in key generics markets; and intellectual property. In fact, India remains the largest holder of Food and Drug Administration-approved API manufacturing facilities in the world.

On the drug research and discovery side, these firms are solely focused on the property side of the business segment, which includes new molecular entity research and discovery as well as the marketing and distribution of branded products, including branded specialty generics and nongenerics. Key competitive advantages needed to succeed in this line include brand building, successful marketing of novel drugs through key marketing fronts in specific markets, and medical and chemical skills, as well as knowledge and capabilities in intellectual property protection. A common strategy pursued by Indian firms with operations in this segment includes both in-licensing and out-licensing partnership agreements that have steadily increased in connection with changes to the public policy regime. However, another reason for the increase in these types of partnerships has been the extensive costs incurred during clinical trial phases of drug development. As a result, many big pharmaceutical firms in advanced economies have entered into agreements with Indian firms to carry out clinical trials in India. Between 2011 and 2012, the Indian clinical trial industry grew 23 percent, and in 2012, the industry had an estimated net worth of US$ 2.2 billion. Most typically, these out-licensing agreements have also included clauses in which Indian firms maintain marketing rights to the product domestically, and in some cases other emerging markets, while ceding marketing rights abroad to their partners (Grabowski and Vernon, 1994; 2000). In focusing specifically on licensing arrangements related to molecular entity development, Indian firms have successfully managed to be on both sides of the spectrum. A select number of Indian firms have identified and developed new chemical entities (NCE) as attractive candidates to move forward into clinical trials, such as Biocon, Dr. Reddy's Laboratories, and Glenmark, as well as Zydus Cadila. Indeed, the new policy regime in India in the sector has helped support the increased growth in these types of agreements.

Aside from licensing agreements, the change in policy regime has also supported the growth in contract research and manufacturing in the sector. There have also been a growing number of Indian firms that have been contracted to optimize, validate, and screen target molecules developed by other firms. This trend has commonly been described as the rise of contract research in the industry. Essentially, the Indian firm collaborates with a partner firm through an in-licensing agreement in which the Indian firm is granted the right to further develop molecules to move into clinical trials. In these agreements, tasks and time frames are clearly defined and set out through specific milestones for the Indian firm, and collaboration between the two does not include terms that would allude to joint development of the molecule in the future or any subsequent marketing rights for the product should it be approved for market entry. All of the Indian firms under study in this chapter have participated and continue to participate in out-licensing agreements for

NCE development. Today, we find most Indian firms providing the front end of the value chain as well as middle stages of clinical development – 2013 marked the first year an Indian firm, Cadila Healthcare, successfully brought a new chemical entity through the entire development, approval, and marketing process. These developments were indeed supported by the initial establishment and protection of the industry provided by the state, and would not have been possible without changes to the patent and industrial policy regime, postliberalization. Since the mid-2000s, the state has begun to step up its role in fostering innovation. It has introduced numerous policy initiatives, including offering the sector tax breaks and tax deductions for R&D expenditure incurred by firms. The state has also begun a multi-million dollar public private partnership initiative with the aim of turning India into one of the top five global pharmaceutical innovation hubs by 2020. In doing so, the state contributes half of the financing to this initiative.

The above section demonstrated that the Indian pharmaceutical sector has developed from a small, highly competitive yet minimally productive sector into an increasingly innovative[4] and globally competitive sector. This evolution is in large part due to the set of policies that enabled the creation of a domestic industry in the first place. Nevertheless, these policies also helped stunt the development of innovative capacity in the industry from growing further during the 1980s when limited liberalization was initially introduced into the economy. The transformation of the sector and its competitive advantages began to rapidly change and speed up post-1990, due in part to public policy changes, but also and perhaps more importantly due to the outward growth of firms and the transformation of a business strategy focus that was achieved in the domestic market but used to attain global competitive strength in R&D.

6.4 The Indian pharmaceutical sectoral system

The key competitive advantages that the firms in this study have developed include brand building, successful marketing of novel drugs through key marketing fronts in specific markets, and medical and chemical skills, as well as knowledge and capabilities in intellectual property protection and as low-cost manufacturing; supply of APIs (for use in the production of drugs by other companies); efficient and effective generic distribution lines; and effective and profitable front-end sales in key generics markets. In order to understand the development of these competitive advantages, this chapter argues that we need to understand the sectoral

Sector Creation and Evolution: Indian Pharmaceutical Sectoral Business 125

system in which they have evolved. Thus, the following section will focus on applying the insights gained from the previous section's historical account of the creation and evolution of the pharmaceutical sector and the development of firm internationalization strategies to an initial sketch of the Indian pharmaceutical system. This initial sketch is part of a wider research project by the author and will be provided in more detail in future work. However, for the time being and the purposes of this chapter, the following section will focus on detailing three key institutional areas of the pharmaceutical sectoral system in India:

1. corporate governance systems: the types of governance arrangements within the sectoral system, the types of management and authority relations between and within firms
2. the transfer of innovation within the system
3. the role of state support

Each of these three institutional areas irrespectively set out in both the VoC and NBS frameworks discussed earlier in this chapter.

Corporate governance in the Indian pharmaceutical sector is largely based on insider control. Families or individuals who hold the majority of shares in the company mainly govern all IMNCs in this sector. Indeed, dispersed shareholders typically do not dominate IMNCs or capital markets (mutual funds, pension funds, investment banks, hedge funds, etc.). Instead, the largest blocks of equity in the majority of listed firms typically remain in the hands of the founding family or controlling shareholders (Allen et al., 2006, p. 21). A new development in the sector has been the separation of business segments into separate firms divided between a generic focus and a discovery and development focus, as mentioned in the previous section. This result has divided the holdings of the companies, and a growing number of the subsidiaries that are being created with a focus on R&D are increasingly being financed through incubator investment projects and capital from investment banks. While this has meant a change in the reporting systems of firms, it has nevertheless, not changed the fact the majority stakes in the firm continue to be held by the original trustee family or individuals. In sum, strong institutional complementarities between the systems of corporate governance and corporate finance were highly prevalent in many of these companies prior to the separation of segments. These complementarities allowed them to be more flexible in their strategies and investments, as capital market forces restricted them less. However, as the separation of these segments into new businesses has begun to recently develop, it still remains to be seen how this might in turn affect the complementarities of the two areas.

The way in which institutions foster the transfer of innovation throughout the economy is a crucial element enabling technological growth at the firm level. In the late 1960s and early '70s, the Indian government overtly chose to specialize in high-priority industries, and thereafter set up an institutional and regulatory environment that would cater to growth in these industries. At this point, it constructed barriers to entry in these sectors and also set regulations as to how large firms were allowed to become. (Allen et al., 2006, p. 8). A crucial element of this system was the establishment of state research institutes. Many of the current individuals and family heads controlling IMNCs initially started their careers in these institutes. After going on to start their firms in the early 1980s, many of these firms continued to benefit from the network of contacts and financial leverage provided by them.

After the initial start-up phases of the industry, barriers preventing both foreign and domestic firm entry began to be removed, and policies were created to encourage more private firms to enter industry. This has not only helped firms expand abroad, but as mentioned in the last section, two key interrelated developments since liberalization within the Indian pharmaceutical sector have developed: the increased focus of firms on drug discovery R&D and the rise of various forms of collaborative partnerships among firms both at home and abroad. The relations in the sector prior to liberalization were largely highly competitive and network based. These networks include government officials and former state enterprise employees who have created their own spin-off firms. These ties have been extremely useful in terms of providing firms with additional financial leverage as well as the ability to steer domestic public policies in a manner conducive to the needs of each respective firm, as well as the industry as a whole. Furthermore, in the post-FDI liberalization phase, these networks became more active with regard to creating forums and partnerships to support one another, such as the Confederation of Indian Industry, India Brand Equity Foundation, India Partnership Forum, Overseas Indian Facilitation Center, Tamil Nadu Technology Development & Promotion Center, and so forth.

A key development through the rise of these partnerships has been the increase in the amount of cooperative contract-based relations with firms at home, but more specifically with foreign firms. Interesting to note is that at the same time while firms are creating cooperative contract project-based partnerships with foreign firms, they still remain competitors in product markets at home.

This partnership surge and its contribution to the creation of sector competition would likely have been significantly less intense without the signing of the Trade in Intellectual Property Rights (TRIPS) in the World Trade Organization (WTO), between 1995 and 2005. The TRIPS agreements played a major role in changing the Indian patent regime, leading to the introduction of the Patent Amendment Act of 2005, in which product patents were granted for the first time since 1970. Other changes during this period included the reduction over time of price controls; the mandating of good manufacturing practices; the lowering of protective trade barriers; and 'a new attitude from the government towards FDI' (Balcet and Bruschieri, 2010, p. 117).

In conclusion, it is evident that there are strong institutional complementarities between the role of the state and the transformation of innovation in the sector. This is clearly evident in the role that public policy took in creating the sector, but it has also been supported by the aforementioned networks that have helped foster the sector's innovative capacity. While public policy and the state have had less success in directly influencing the technological upgrading of the industry postliberalization, the state still remains a key influential actor. Aside from its policy pursuits like tax breaks and tax deductions, it has also attempted to create various programs and incubation projects to support the transfer of technological upgrading in the sector. One example of this is the aforementioned public private partnership initiative to foster innovation in the sector and turn India into one of the top pharmaceutical innovation hubs by 2020. Another example includes the Drug Development Programme and the Pharmaceuticals Research and Development Support Fund, both of which were specifically developed to encourage new drug discovery and development in the pharmaceutical and biotechnology sectors. Thus, it is not an overstatement to claim that IMNCs' current transformative rise to the multinational stage has been supported by their embeddedness in a policy environment promoting the incubation and development of a select set of industries and firms, and in particular the initial policy of a weak patent system in which reverse engineering was encouraged from 1970–1990 (Goldstein, 2007, p. 95).

Indian public policy has been crucial in helping establish an institutional environment at the sectoral level to support the creation and evolution of the Indian pharmaceutical sector. Despite attempts to build up competitive and innovative industries, such as in pharmaceuticals, the regulatory environment before 1991 hindered inward and outward FDI's ability to encourage innovation through technology transfer. However, it did encourage the creation of a domestic sector with a strong set of skills that have come to be quintessential to the competitive advantages that these firms possess today.

Specifically in creating the sector, the state put in place a set of administrative and policy barriers that not only limited the amount of foreign competition in the Indian market but also forced the initial transfer of knowledge and skill sets in chemical processes and drug manufacturing and production. The liberalization of the Indian economy, which began in the 1980s, but went into full swing (especially for the pharmaceutical sector) post-1990, changed the type of role that the state played in the sector considerably. Indeed, the role of the state in directly supporting the continued growth and development of the sector into a globally competitive force is rather limited. Rather the decline of policies that regulated the outward expansion of firms and the growth of foreign firms competing domestically has most recently been the driving force for significant changes in the competitive advantages and strategies of IMNCs in the sector. However, it continues to play a direct role in regulating competition in the sector domestically, especially with regard to drug pricing and the implementation of new patent laws related to life-threatening diseases that affect the majority of the population, who cannot afford access to treatment.

6.5 Conclusion

In order to grasp how and why IMNCs in the pharmaceutical industry have evolved more completely, this study has argued it is necessary to shed light on the domestic institutional environments before and during the internationalization process of IMNCs. Analyzing these particular national contexts offers a more comprehensive assessment of the possible structural conflicts that may exist on the mesosectoral level, in which firms from their respective national political economies compete on macroglobal economic stages.

This chapter has suggested the need to supplement international business theories with a more comparative political economy institutionalist perspective. In doing so, it has laid the groundwork for developing such a perspective by introducing the reader to the institutional paradigms in political economy and providing their ontological assumptions. Linking two frameworks, it contributed to providing an evolutionary institutional framework of the sectoral system with the capacity to understand the context of firm-level interactions, while simultaneously also grasping sectoral-level evolution. In doing so, this chapter developed a more comprehensive, socially embedded historical account of the development and evolution of the Indian pharmaceutical sector with a specific focus on the role of the state and public policy in supporting this development. Future research will focus on providing a detailed analysis of the pharmaceutical sectoral system and its institutional complementarities. Furthermore, future research could be aimed at elaborating more specifically the extent to which firm strategies are socially embedded and evolve over time with sectoral systems that expand beyond the domestic context, to include the regional, international, and global sectoral system.

Notes

1. See Nölke and Taylor (2010) and Taylor and Nölke (2009; 2010) for more details.
2. Firms studied: Biocon, Dr. Reddy's Laboratories, Glenmark, Ranbaxy, Sun Pharmaceuticals, Zydus Cadila.
3. According to the World Health Organization, Active Pharmaceutical Ingredient (API) is defined as: 'Any substance or combination of substances used in a finished pharmaceutical product (FPP), intended to furnish pharmacological activity or to otherwise have direct effect in the diagnosis, cure, mitigation, treatment or prevention of disease, or to have direct effect in restoring, correcting or modifying physiological functions in human beings'.
4. Measuring innovative output in terms of the number of NCEs discovered *and* developed into final products for marketization, India does not seem so spectacular – as only one firm has successfully achieved this feat (Cadila Healthcare). However, if we redefine innovative output as based on the number of NCEs/NMEs (new chemical entities/new molecular entities) developed by these firms, the picture becomes quite different. For example, in 2014, Glenmark had 7 novel drugs in their pipeline: 1 approved NCE, 3 NCEs and 3 NBEs (New Biological Entities) in clinical development and trials.

7
Financing the Expansion of Brazilian Multinationals into Europe: The Role of the Brazilian Development Bank (BNDES)

Gilmar Masiero, Mario H. Ogasavara, Luiz Caseiro, and Silas Ferreira

7.1 Introduction

The rise of multinational corporations (MNCs) from emerging markets has been a remarkable phenomenon during the last decade (BCG, 2006; 2013; Wright et al., 2005). While total Foreign Direct Investment (FDI) flows grew by 84 percent from 2001 to 2011, those from developing economies grew by 216 percent (UNCTAD, 2013). This is a considerable leap, from 26 percent to 44 percent of the total flows. A series of recent studies have sought to explain the sudden growth of emerging markets MNCs (Brennan, 2011; Sauvant et al., 2010; Ramamurti and Sigh, 2009). To do so, international business scholars have further developed established analytical instruments in order to account for the rise of these multinationals. In some cases, the OLI (Ownership, Location, Internalization) framework (Dunning, 1986), the Uppsala model (Johanson and Vahlne, 1977; 2009), or the product life-cycle model (Vernon, 1966) have been extended (Ramamurti, 2008). In other instances, scholars have contested dominant internationalization theories, insisting on the need for the development of new frameworks (Mathews, 2002a; 2006b).

In a study of multinationals from the Asian Pacific and Latin American regions, Mathews (2002a; 2006b) proposes the 'linkage, leverage and learning' (LLL) framework. He argues that emerging markets MNCs do not depend on the possession of complex ownership advantages to expand internationally, as proposed in Dunning's OLI framework (Dunning, 1986). Instead, these firms use the internationalization process to establish connections with different suppliers, competitors, and customers (linkage), and acquire these advantages (leverage). As a result of repeated linkage and leverage interactions, firms develop learning capabilities, thereby making their operations more effective.

While Matthews (2006) provides important insights into the sudden ascendance of emerging markets MNCs, the framework has some limitations. One of these limitations is the fact that the LLL framework explicitly denies the importance of home-country public policies in fostering the internationalization process. A significant contributing factor for the very existence of emerging markets MNCs is that there have been several cases in which companies from middle-income countries, supported by their home-country governments, acquired large MNCs from high-income countries. In this paper, we seek to focus on this pattern. We believe that the role of national governments in the creation and expansion of emerging markets MNCs needs to be more carefully studied.

Dunning (1993) recognized the importance of governments in shaping the processes of internationalization. He expressed concern that governments aimed to use firms to meet national development goals. However, he did not delve deeper into this phenomenon. As the business and institutional environment in emerging countries is quite different from developed countries, we share the view that scholars aiming to understand the transnational activity of emerging markets MNCs must focus on this lacuna (Goldstein, 2007; Ramamurti, 2008). Among the potential issues, we focus on a closer examination of the role of (partial or full) state ownership of some firms: whether enterprises were formerly state owned or selected to receive direct financial support from (para-)state bodies, such as development banks or pension funds.[1]

To analyze this process, the contextual approach provides an important and missing link to the LLL framework, by calling attention to the social and institutional contexts within which firms' strategies are formed (Pettigrew, 1987; Zutshi and Gibbons, 1998). Within the contextual approach, the choice to internationalize is the key event in companies' strategy, and understanding this strategic change must be based on the analysis of its context, content and process. Focusing specifically on the context of the decision to internationalize, 'context' is divided into two parts: inner and outer context. Outer context refers to the national economic and political environment in which the internationalization decision takes place, whereas inner context refers to internal influences: the firm's capabilities, organizational strategy, management processes, structure, politics, and culture (Pettigrew, 1987).

In this chapter, we combine the LLL framework with the contextual approach to analyze the recent surge of Brazilian firms entering world markets. The contextual approach is an important complement to the LLL framework, in providing insights otherwise rarely available in the international business literature when analyzing emerging markets MNCs. Using this combined approach, we show that in the Brazilian case, the political environment played an instrumental role in fostering the acceleration of Brazilian outward foreign direct investments (OFDI). For this reason, we focus on explaining the contextual factors that contributed significantly to the internationalization of Brazilian corporations.

This chapter has four more sections. Section two provides a brief account of the rise of Brazilian multinationals (BMN) up until the present period, with specific focus on the past decade, in which their overseas investment has increased significantly. Additionally, this section outlines the EU-BRIC investment relations to show the significance of Brazilian investments. Section three explains the recent policies that have been adopted by the Brazilian government through its development bank, the BNDES, which has resulted in a dramatic increase in the provision of financial support for the internationalization of BMNs. Section four presents our preliminary findings on the entry of BMNs into the European Union (EU) this decade and how BNDES has contributed to such expansion. Section five provides a brief summary of our findings and outlines the next stage of research, which should be undertaken to test our hypothesis more robustly.

7.2 The expansion of BMNs and EU-BRIC investment relations

We selected the Brazilian case for several reasons. The majority of new, emerging markets MNCs are from the upcoming frontrunners Brazil, Russia, India, and China – the BRICs (UNCTAD, 2011b). Within these four economies, public policies have been deployed to support OFDI, although with different intensity (Goldstein, 2012). Currently the world's seventh-largest economy, Brazil has experienced an economic resurgence in the past decade. As part of this boom, BMNs have emerged as global players. Although with irregular performance, oscillating along with the performance of the Brazilian economy, pioneering Brazilian companies first entered world markets in the late 1960s (Guimarães, 1986). However, the scale and magnitude of the presence of BMNs in the global arena today is unprecedented.

Recent studies have sought to draw attention to the Brazilian government's role in the growing tide of BMNs in world markets and in particular to the role that is played by the Brazilian Development Bank (BNDES), the main development financing agency (Alem and Cavalcanti, 1995; Valdez, 2011; Masiero and Caseiro, 2012). In earlier periods, this public bank focused on financing the export transactions of national firms, as well as financing their expansion in the domestic market. Since 2005, BNDES has also begun to direct resources to support the creation of overseas subsidiaries of Brazilian firms in the form of greenfield operations or mergers and acquisitions, by providing loans or shareholding participation in BMNs.

Building on this important set of recent studies, our chapter analyzes how BNDES has supported the expansion of BMNs into the EU. The EU has been one of Brazil's most important investment partners for decades, a pattern that is quite distinct when viewed in comparison to the other BRIC economies. Our analysis is based on publicly available data gathered from a variety of sources for the period between 2000 and 2011. We limit our study to Brazilian firms outside the financial sector and exclusively focus on BNDES financing allocated for Brazilian multinationals' growth.[2] Our reason for pursuing this research design is to examine how the development bank has supported or complemented specific industries that have been argued to be crucial for Brazilian development.

As mentioned above, the first Brazilian companies to invest abroad did so in the late 1960s and early 1970s. Detailed data from the Central Bank collected by Guimarães (1986) show that, albeit limited in number, the firms largely responsible for these investments belonged to the oil and banking industries, operating primarily in developed countries. Not coincidentally, both sectors enjoyed state support as the government had to develop policies in response to the challenges brought by the oil crisis.

The banking industry, for example, had its internationalization sponsored by the government in order to take advantage of the funding opportunities in the petrodollar market in Europe. In 1972, Banco do Brasil, a state-owned enterprise (SOE) and the largest Brazilian bank – which already had branch offices in New York and other South American countries – opened its first subsidiary in London. The following year, the bank opened new subsidiaries in Paris and Luxemburg. These European subsidiaries were established with the objective of raising funds to support state-led investments in Brazil. Similarly, the early internationalization of Petrobras, the monopolistic SOE for oil and gas, had the objective of obtaining resources abroad in order to alleviate the restrictions on the balance of payments due to the increasing proportion of oil imports. Petrobras started prospecting operations in Colombia, Madagascar, and Iraq also in 1972. Overall, however, OFDI flows levels were relatively low during the 1970s and even decreased during the early 1980s when the external debt crisis hit the country severely.

In this early phase, outside of the financial BMNs, Rocha (2004) notes that most Brazilian corporations seeking to expand operations abroad were incipient players in terms of the total value of exports and their presence abroad in the early 1980s. Construction and engineering firms predominated, while manufacturers moved at a much slower pace. Manufacturing firms at that time, like Caloi, a bicycle producer, and Gradiente, an electronic appliances producer, had short-lived international operations. Other firms, such as MetalLeve, an auto parts manufacturer, were acquired by multinationals from other countries, while a few like Tigre, a construction materials firm with several plants in South America, are still open.

As illustrated by the numbers for successive periods, shown in Figure 7.1, it was only in the second half of the 1990s, after the economic and financial liberalization, privatization of several SOEs, macroeconomic stabilization of 1994, and further regional integration through the formation of MERCOSUR, that Brazilian investments abroad gained momentum. This momentum, however, was still modest when compared to the surge of OFDI in the 2000s. In part, this is because the economic opening generated contradictory and even negative results in its early phases; it destabilized and led to the downfall of several companies that were not able to raise their low levels of productivity.

Notwithstanding, the surviving companies were forced to quickly and often radically restructure their production and implement advanced management practices. Cost reduction, product differentiation, and

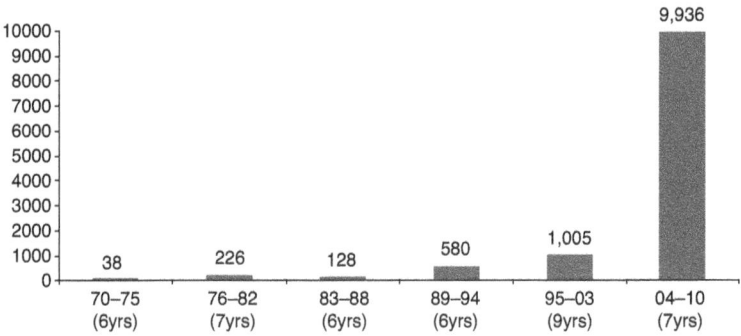

Figure 7.1 Brazilian OFDI, annual average flows per historical period, 1970–2010[3] (US$ million)

Source: Elaborated by authors based on UNCTAD (2012).

internationalization were additional strategies employed to meet the demands of more sophisticated markets and consumers (Arbix and Caseiro, 2011). During this period, several BMNs, especially from engineering services, steel, mechanics, and auto parts, intensified their internationalization (BNDES, 1995; Fleury and Fleury, 2010). It should be noticed that overseas expansions were not supported by any specific governmental policies during this period (Alem and Cavalcanti, 2005).

The take-off stage for overseas expansion began after the mid-2000s. It is during this recent decade that a dramatic surge in international expansion of BMNs took place, in synchrony with emerging markets MNCs from the other BRICs. The most well-known examples of BMNs that are part of this largest wave of internationalization include many firms that benefitted from the privatization policies instituted during the 1990s, which resulted in the formation of large BMNs. These firms include Vale, CSN, and Embraer (Schneider, 2009; Aman, 2009; Finchelstein, 2009), as well as other companies in the petrochemical and steel sectors, such as Braskem, Oxiteno, and Gerdau (Finchelstein, 2009).

These large BMNs are responsible for the increasing Brazilian presence in world markets. But while Brazil lags behind the other BRICs in terms of trade with the EU, the picture is far less gloomy in terms of investments. For this reason, we briefly overview Brazilian-EU investment relations in the following paragraphs. We situate our analysis within a comparative framework, to provide the context in which Brazil finds itself in terms of its importance relative to other emerging economies in a major market like the EU.

Brazil is the top-ranked recipient of FDI from the EU in stock terms. By 2010, these totaled € 188 billion, or 1.8 percent of total EU FDI stocks. Spain is the largest EU investor in Brazil, with investment stock totaling € 53 billion, followed by France (€ 22 billion) and Germany (€ 11 billion). Furthermore, EU investment in Brazil is 150 percent higher than in China and 450 percent higher than in India.

Although Brazil represents the number one recipient of FDI stock among the BRICs, the average growth of the FDI stock is increasing at a slower pace (18 percent) compared to Russia (35 percent), India (28 percent), and China (24 percent). From 2004 to 2008, Russia was the largest destination of EU investments, receiving an amount of € 28 billion in 2008, which represented 3 percent of all EU FDI in the world in that year. However, since 2009, Brazil has risen to become the top destination of EU FDI relative to other BRIC countries, receiving € 21.5 billion in 2010 (5.3 percent of all EU investments), with the largest investments made by Spain and France.

In terms of investments in the EU by the BRICs, Brazil is the largest investor, accounting for € 67.5 billion of FDI stock in 2010 – particularly investing in Spain, Denmark, and Portugal. This amount is almost ten times higher than the accumulated value of China and India. Although it represents only 0.76 percent of all FDI stock in the EU, Brazilian investments in the EU are increasing at high rates. Whereas, in 2002, the EU FDI stock in Brazil was 21.5 times higher than the stock of Brazilian FDI in EU, in 2010, this ratio decreased to only 2.7.

It should be noticed that the 2008 financial crisis did affect Brazilian investment outflows, but OFDI flows have rebounded even in the midst of the global economic slowdown, suggesting that BMNs are pursuing long-term strategies to maintain their growth in foreign markets (Campanario, Stal, and Muniz da Silva, 2012). Brazilian OFDI retracted slightly in 2009. Outflow investment rates quickly recuperated in 2010, a period marked by strong Brazilian domestic economic growth. Indeed Brazilian OFDI reached US$ 11.5 billion in 2010, a level that was the third highest since 1994, only inferior to 2006 and 2008. Furthermore, the 2011 FDC Transnationality Report shows that there were few exits or production shutdowns as a result of the crisis (FDC, 2011).

One of the most striking patterns in the data presented thus far is the rise in Brazilian OFDI flows into the EU. Moreover, the peak in the flow of FDI to the EU from Brazil occurred during a specific period, namely between 2005 and 2008, which is also (as we will detail in the rest of this chapter) the period in which Brazilian public banks initiated a major shift in their policies, by reserving funds to finance the overseas operations of BMNs.

7.3 BNDES and the internationalization of BMNs

As reviewed in section two, there has been a dramatic rise in Brazilian OFDI, with the EU as a prominent recipient. The peak in the FDI flow into the EU from Brazil occurred between 2005 and 2008. Only ten years ago, the Brazilian government, including its agencies and banks, did not have specific policies for supporting the internationalization of Brazilian firms, beyond the financing of regular trade (exports). Things started to change at the turn of the century, when a recently stabilized Brazilian economy allowed policymakers to extend their planning horizons; additionally, globalization was a reality, plunging emerging economies into the global marketplace. And BNDES became one of the main actors in charge of economic planning, due to its experience in dealing with companies and financing industrial policies.

Linked to the federal Ministry of Development, Industry and Foreign Trade by the appointment of its president, BNDES has traditionally played a fundamental role in stimulating the expansion of industry and large-scale infrastructure within Brazil.[4] With over US$ 5 billion in operating income and US$ 334 billion in assets, the institution is a powerful and significant player in the Brazilian economy, and since the mid-2000s, the bank has begun to play an important role in the internationalization of BMNs (Masiero and Caseiro, 2012).

The first remarkable change in public policies toward internationalization took place in 2002, when BNDES modified its statute to allow domestic companies to request credit for the acquisition of productive assets abroad (Law No. 4.418). Such credit was granted under the condition that they were able to prove that they would increase net exports in an equivalent amount to their foreign investments, within a six-year period (Alem and Cavalcanti, 2005). In 2007, the government enacted a new law (Law No. 6.322) that relaxed the referred conditions, by removing the export requirements. The moment for such measures could not be more significant: it took place the year after China's entry into the World Trade Organization (WTO) and the promotion of its aggressive 'go global' strategy. Was it the Brazilian government's attempt to catch up with the Chinese and seize the immense opportunities created by globalization?

The change in policy allowing Brazilian firms to secure loans from the development bank was a major turnaround as the lending rates are much lower than those that would have to be paid by firms seeking to borrow capital in financial markets. BNDES' lending rate is set by the National Monetary Council. The rate was set at 9 percent in early 2006 and decreased by small amounts, reaching a low of 6 percent in June 2009, which is the same rate charged presently.

The Brazilian government also adopted a new industrial policy and increased fund allocations to BNDES. BNDES currently provides support for the internationalization of BMNs by issuing lines of credit for (i) acquisition of foreign assets or greenfield projects; (ii) foreign governments and companies seeking to purchase goods and services sold by BMNs, especially in the engineering services, aviation, and infrastructure industries; and (iii) the consolidation/integration of a specific industry in order to enable these newly formed companies to have the necessary scale and scope to compete locally and globally. The Bank allocates loans to any kind of transnational activity (direct and indirect exports, licensing, representative office and distribution centers, strategic alliances, mergers and acquisitions, and greenfield), and realizes equity investments in the cases of strategic alliances, mergers and acquisitions, and greenfield.

Table 7.1 summarizes the BMNs for which BNDES, or its subsidiary, BNDESPar, is a shareholder. In these cases, BNDES acquired company shares instead of providing loans. Given that the majority of BNDES disbursements for international expansion took place between 2008 and 2010, we report the data for both years. By 2010, BNDES or BNDESPar held shares of 33 companies, and of these, 13 were BMNs distributed in a diverse set of industries, including auto parts, aviation, food and meat processing, energy, pulp and paper manufacturing, petrochemical, steel, transportation, and telecommunications.

The first Brazilian company to use this new BNDES financing program was the meat processing firm JBS. It received US$ 80 million for the US$ 200 million acquisition of the Argentine subsidiary of Swift, an American multinational, in 2005 (Sennes and Mendes, 2009). Two years later, after further relaxation in BNDES internationalization policies, JBS was granted US$ 750 million to purchase Swift's parent company in the United States. Additionally, JBS received another US$ 634 million in 2008 and US$ 1,988 billion in 2009.

Between 2005 and 2011, BNDES disbursements for direct support of internationalization processes totaled approximately US$ 6.8 billion (Guimarães, 2012).[5] In official reports, BNDES executives had stated that the support was provided for projects in 20 countries, concentrated in North America, Latin America, and Europe. In the same period, the net increase in Brazilian OFDI flows to these countries was US$ 39.5 billion (Central Bank of Brazil, 2012). Thus, BNDES participation accounted for 17.3 percent of the total amount of funds invested in this sample of countries by Brazil.[6]

In a few cases, the internationalization of technology-intensive BMNs was partially financed by BNDES. Among these are WEG (electrical equipment) and Bematech and Itautec (both in information technology). However, overall, these technology-intensive firms accounted for only a small fraction of the total disbursements made by the Brazilian development bank between 2005 and 2011 (Masiero and Caseiro, 2012). More than 50 percent of the funding by the bank was directed to supporting a single firm in the Brazilian meat processing industry (US$ 3.652 billion or 50.7 percent for JBS alone). This funding was significantly greater than the credit lines extended to companies in other industries. For example, Itautec, a software and hardware company, received US$ 142 million to acquire Tallard, an American firm, and to capitalize its subsidiaries in the United States (Miami) and Portugal.

Financing the Expansion of Brazilian Multinationals into Europe 139

Table 7.1 BNDES participation in the ownership of BMNs (%)

Company	BNDES Ownership Direct(%), 2008	BNDES Ownership Direct(%), 2010	Date of Information	Operating Revenue (US$ millions)	Number of Employees
AGÊNCIA ESPECIAL DE FINANCIAMENTO INDUSTRIAL-FINAE		100.00	12/2010	n.a	n.a
BNDES LIMITED		WO	07/2011	n.a	n.a
BNDES PARTICIPACOES S.A. BNDESPAR		WO	12/2010	3882.55	n.a
CENTRAIS ELETRICAS BRA SILEIRAS SA -ELET ROBRAS	11.81	21.08	12/2010	15888.07	2576
COMPA NHIA DE Á GUA S DO BRA SIL – CA B AMBIENTAL		33.42	01/2012	1.63	17
COMPA NHIA PARA NA ENSE DE ENER GIA -COPEL		26.41	03/2011	4183.43	9400
COMPA NHIA SIDERURGICA NA CIONAL	3.64	2.18	12/2010	9274.13	19000
CPFL ENER GIA S.A		8.42	09/2011	6866.81	7913
EMBRA ER – EMPRESA BRA SILEIRA DE AERONA UTICA S.A	5.05	5.37	07/2011	5399.73	17265
ENERGISA S.A		0.25	05/2011	1282.85	n.a.
FIBRIA CELULOSE S.A		30.42	05/2011	3207.92	n.a.
GERDA U S.A	3.5	6.60	01/2012	19153.11	45000
IOCHPE MA XION A S		6.77	12/2010	1568.65	5131
JBS		17.54	12/2010	n.a.	n.a
KLA BIN S.A.	20.25	25.94	09/2010	2237.86	8004
LIGHT S.A	33.62	15.02	12/2010	5246.38	4134
LINX			07/2011	n.a	n.a
MET ALFRIO SOLUTIONS S.A.		5.85	11/2010	483.39	n.a
PARANAPANEMA S.A.	17.52	17.23	05/2011	2214.84	2245

Continued

Table 7.1 Continued

Company	BNDES ownership Direct(%), 2008	BNDES ownership Direct(%), 2010	Date of Information	Operating Revenue (US$ millions)	Number of Employees
PETROLEO BRA SILEIRO S.A. -PETROBRA S	7.62		10/2010	132401.02	81918
REDE ENERGIA S.A.	25.3		09/2010	4203.47	7716
SEGURA DORA BRA SILEIRA DE CREDIT O A EXPORTA CA O SA		12.00	07/2011	13.66	n.a
TELEMA R PA RTICIPA COES SA		13.08	03/2011	15920.79	n.a
TUPY S.A.		35.57	07/2011	1175.78	6451
VALE S.A.		6.70	12/2010	59065	77055
VALEPA R S/A.	9.79	11.51	03/2011	n.a	2
AMERICA LATINA LOGISTICA S.A.-ALL	10.61	15.78	03/2010	1719.88	10368
BANCO DO NORDESTE DO BRAZIL S.A.		0.47	12/2011	1753.55	n.a.
BRASILIANA ENERGIA S.A.		53.85	12/2010	3819.5	n.a.
BRASKEM S.A.	5.22	5.30	12/2010	17860.02	n.a.
BRFBRASIL FOODS S.A.		35.09	07/2009	13829.48	120096
CIPHER INFORMÁTICA S.A.		15.50	04/2011	n.a	100
COPEL		23.96	12/2010	1.81	7
GRUPO A EDUCAÇÃ O S/A.			11/2009	41.24	150
INDEPENDENCIA	13.89				
JBS S.A.	13.00	30.40	08/2011	33245.51	n.a.
LDC-SEVBIOENERGIA S/A.			01/2008	971.7	12781
MARFIG	14.66				
NUTRIPLANT INDUSTRIA ECOMERCIO S/A.		10.79	03/2008	23.59	100

Sources: Elaborated by authors based on BNDES and companies' annual reports.

In sum, the comparison of BNDES funding relative to Brazilian OFDI outflows helps put the development bank's role in the internationalization process of BMNs into better perspective. The bank has played an instrumental role in the expansion of key Brazilian companies in targeted economies and in targeted sectors. An understanding of BMN internationalization also underscores the contribution of linkage, leverage (Mathews, 2006b), and outer context factors (Pettigrew, 1987). With the new governmental policy (outer context) to support the international expansion of domestic firms, they were encouraged to look for resources (linkage by acquiring, for instance: knowledge, know-how, or technology) in order to create competitive companies in a specific industry (leverage) in the local and international markets.

It should be noted that firm competitiveness is not only related to the LLL framework but also to the outer context. This means that the government has an essential role in making the LLL strategy possible. However, it also must be emphasized that the bulk of BNDES financial support for Brazilian OFDI was employed within industries of low technological intensity, mostly meat packing. Although some cross-national acquisitions financed by BNDES were channeled through industries of high or medium-high technological intensity (for instance, information technology, pharmaceuticals, and electric motors), the high concentration of BNDES support directed to the internationalization efforts of low-technology industries raises suspicion as to the lack of a coherent strategy to foster Brazilian development through OFDI. In a recent interview, the bank's president, without emphasizing the existence of a new policy, stated that 'the promotion of competitiveness of large Brazilian international companies is an agenda that has been completed' (Landin et al., 2013).

7.4 BMNs in the EU and BNDES

In this section, we focus on the activities of nonfinancial BMNs in the EU and begin a preliminary exploration of how BNDES support may have aided the overseas expansion efforts of these companies into the EU.[7] It should be noted that this data should be viewed as an approximation. Fiscal regulations in Brazil induce investments in tax havens to escape regulations and tax obligations, which may distort official FDI data. As Figure 7.2 shows, from 2000 to 2010, the EU was the second-ranked destination for Brazilian OFDI, after Latin America. During 2004–2010, the EU accounted for 48.1 percent of Brazilian OFDI stocks. Since 2009, the EU has surpassed Latin America as the main recipient region for investments.

Surveys on the degree of internationalization of BMNs, publicly listed, published by the Fundação Dom Cabral, paint a similar picture from a firm perspective (FDC, 2011). In the FDC's latest report, issued in 2011, the EU was the second host region for BMNs. More than one-fifth (21.1 percent in 2010) of the 49 BMNs who responded to the survey were based in the EU.[8] Based on their responses, the FDC estimates that there are at least 26 Brazilian firms operating in 19 countries within the EU.[9]

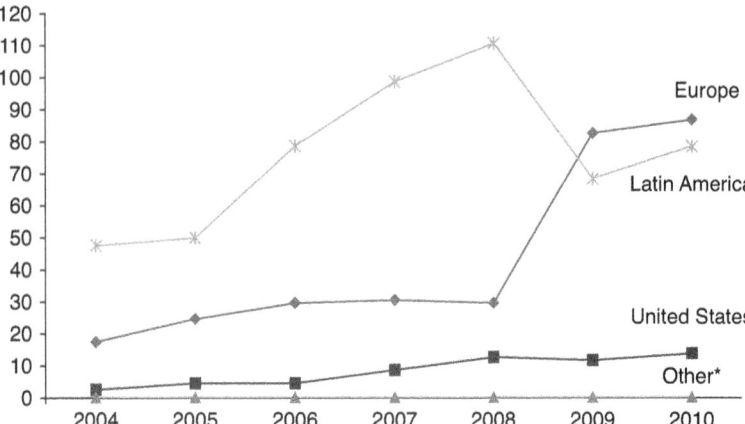

Figure 7.2 Brazilian OFDI stocks in selected regions, 2004–2010, (US$ billions)
Source: Elaborated by authors based on Central Bank of Brazil (2012).
*Other includes Japan, Asia, Oceania and Africa.

A review of the data reported by the United Nations Economic Commission for Latin America and the Caribbean (ECLAC) on the acquisitions completed by Brazilian multinationals that were over R$ 100 million each year from 2007 to 2010 provides information on the largest transactions that were made globally by BMNs.

As Table 7.2 summarizes, 8 of the total 41 acquisitions over US$ 100 million, made by Brazilian companies, took place in Europe. A total of US$ 8.4 billion was invested in the EU, in various industries: banking, manufacturing, food processing, and steel.

Table 7.3 shows all the BMNs with a presence in the EU. The 31 companies operating in Europe present a fair amount of heterogeneity. There are both very large and medium-sized companies, from a diverse range of industries. Based on this sample, we coded firms and assessed the degree of BNDES support for them, based on six criteria: 1) industrial sector, 2) presence in Europe relative to the company's international presence; 3) key EU country for the firm's operations; 4) predominant type of investment in the EU; 5) main activity of the firm in the EU; and, 6) receipt of BNDES support in loans and/or as a shareholder. To code each company, we used BNDES reports and the annual reports of these companies, as well as newspaper articles.

Contrary to the alleged concentration of BMNs in commodities industries and operating mainly in South America (Dunning et al., 2008),

Table 7.3 reveals that BMNs currently operate in a wide range of EU countries in diverse sectors, with a predominance of medium-technology, manufacturing firms.[10] It even includes some manufacturers with large European operations. One prominent example is Romi, an industrial equipment manufacturer that has two of its eleven production plants outside Brazil located in Italy, for the production of plastic injector machines. The firm also has subsidiaries in Germany, Spain, France, and the UK for machine tools sales coordinated by Romi Europa GmbH. Although relatively smaller in size and less common in terms of overall operation, Brazilian software manufacturers are also present in Europe, with Totvs and Stefanini IT Solutions. The first company operates in 10 countries (just one in Europe), while the latter is present in 26 countries (12 in Europe).

Remarkably, the majority of the BMNs (54.8 percent) are undertaking production-related operations in Europe as compared to running sales offices, distribution centers, or research and development (R&D) centers. BMNs operate production plants in Europe from sectors as diverse as petrochemicals, engineering and construction, industrial equipment, steel, automotive parts, and meat processing. Most other Brazilian industrial companies in Europe acquired some laboratory or research centers as part of their mergers and acquisitions (M&A) strategies when entering the European market. In the case of Natura, for example, the cosmetics manufacturer has built laboratories to undertake testing and further R&D of its products.

Almost all European countries host a BMN, but the predominant host markets are Germany, Portugal, UK, France, and Italy. There are some consistent patterns in the location of investments. The case of auto part operations that are concentrated in Germany is illustrative. The most prominent firms in this sector are Sabó, Randon, and Tupy. Tupy only has a representative office. Randon has been engaged in Germany since the early 1990s when it entered a joint venture with JOST-Werke of Germany. Sabó has plants in Austria, Germany, and Hungary, as well as technical offices in France and the United Kingdom.

Most of these cases support the linkage-and-leverage approach to accelerate the internationalization process (Mathews, 2006b). BMNs are establishing partnerships in developed countries in order to gain access to resources (i.e., technology and knowledge) that these companies do not possess. Portugal is the country where the earliest acquisitions of major engineering and construction companies happened about 20 years ago, and in general BMNs in related industries have continued to maintain a strong presence in this economy.

Table 7.2 Acquisitions by BMNs, 2007–2010

BMN	Acquired company	Country	Year	Value of Transaction (US$ million)	Sector
Banco Bradesco	Banco Espirito Santo S.A.	Portugal	2009	132	Financial services
	IBI Mexico	Mexico	2010	164	Financial services
Banco Itau	Banco Itau Europa	Portugal	2009	498	Financial services
Braskem	Sunoco Chemicals Inc.	U.S.	2010	350	Chemicals
Camargo Corrêa	Cimpor Cimentosde Portugal	Portugal	2010	1894	Cement
Gerdau	Chaparral Steel	US	2007	3974	Steel
	Qanex Corporation	US	2007	1458	Metallurgy
	Grupo Industrial Field	Mexico	2007	259	Steel
	Aceros Corsa	Mexico	2007	101	Steel
	Gerdau Macsteel Inc.	US	2008	1458	Metallurgy
	Sidenor	Spain	2008	287	Steel
	Corsa Controladora	Mexico	2008	101	Steel
	Gerdau Ameristeel Inc	Canada	2010	1607	Steel
Gerdau and Kalyiani	SJK	India	2007	170	Steel
GP Investimentos	Drilling Rights and E&P	Argentina, others	2007	1000	Petroleum
JBS Friboi	Swift&Co	US	2007	1400	Metal Processing
	Inalca	Italy	2007	329	Metal Processing
	Smithfield Beef Group Inc	US	2008	565	Food
	Nationa Beef Packing Company, LLC	US	2008	560	Food

Company	Acquisition	Country	Year	Value	Sector
Magnesita	Tasman Group Services	Australia	2008	148	Food Manufacturing
Marfig	LWB Refractories GMbH & Co.K	Germany	2008	952	Food
	Quickfood	Argentina	2007	141	Food
	Moy Park Ltd.; Kitchen RangeFoods Ltd	Ireland, United Kingdom	2008	680	Meat Processing & Food
	Keystone Foods LLC	US	2010	1260	Meat Processing & Food
Prtrobras	El Todillo/La Tapera	Argentina	2007	118	Energy
	Esso Chile Petrolera Ltda	Chile	2008	400	Petroleum
	Pasadena Refining System Inc	US	2010	350	Petroleum
	Devon Energy Corp-Cascade	US	2010	180	Petroleum
Vale	AMCI Auistalia	Australia	2007	786	Mining
	Minade Carón	Colombia	2008	300	Mining
	Rio Tinto (Projeto Potássio Rio Colorado)	Argentina	2009	850	Ore
	Cementos Argos AS Coal Mine	Colombia	2009	373	Ore
	El Hatillo Coal Mining, Cerro Largo Coal				
	Deposit and Fenoco Assets	Colombia	2009	305	Ore
	BSG Resources Guinea Ltd.	United Kingdom	2010	2500	Mining
Votorantim	Acerias Pazdel Rio	Colombia	2007	494	Steel
	US Zinc Corporation	US	2007	295	Recycling
	Cia Minera Atacocha	Peru	2008	145	Mining
	Cementos Avellaneda S.A.	Argentina	2009	202	Cement
	Cimpor Cimentosde Portugual	Portugal	2010	1192	Cement
	Cia Minera Milpo SAA	Peru	2010	419	Mining

Source: Elaborated by authors based on ECLAC (no date).

Table 7.3 The internationalization of BMNs in Europe and BNDES support

Company	Industry	Countries (European/World)	Main Country in the EU*	Company Received BNDES Loan	BNDES holds company shares
Andrade Gutierrez	Engineering &Construction	3/33	Portugal	X	
Banco do Brasil	Banking	7/23	UK		
BR Foods	Food & Beverage	10/20	UK		X
Bradesco	Banking	2/6	UK		
Braskem	Petrochemicals	2/10	Germany	X	X
Camargo Corrêa	Engineering & Construction	5/17	Portugal	X	
Ci&T Software	Software	1/5	UK		
Companhia Siderúrgica Nacional (CSN)	Steel	1/2	Portugal		X
Embraer	Aeronautics	2/5	France	X	
Fibria	Pulp & Paper	2/8	Germany		X
Gerdau	Steel	1/13	Spain		X
Itaú-Unibanco	Banking	5/16	UK		X
JBS-Friboi	Meat processing	1/7	Italy		X
Magnesita	Industrial equipment	6/19	Germany	X	
Marfrig	Meat processing	5/20	UK	X	X
Metalfrio	Refrigeration	2/5	Denmark	X	
Minerva	Meat processing	1/9	Italy		

Company	Industry		Main country	EU*
Natura	Cosmetics	1/8	France	
Odebrecht	Engineering & Construction	3/21	Portugal	X
Oxiteno	Chemicals	1/5	Belgium	
Random	Car parts	1/11	Germany	
Romi	Industrial equipment	5/6	Italy	X
Sabó	Car parts	3/7	Germany	X
Seculus	Wristwatches	1/1	Switzerland	
Stefanini IT Solutions	Software	12/26	UK	X
Suzano	Pulp & Paper	2/5	UK	
Totys	Software	1/10	Portugal	X
Tupy	Steel and car parts	3/7	Germany	X
Vale (CVRD)	Mining	4/37	France	
Votorantim	Cement	11/28	Portugal	
Weg	Industrial equipment	8/22	Portugal	X

Sources: Elaborated by authors based on Fundação Dom Cabral (2011), BNDES, and companies' annual reports.
* Main country in the EU means it has either the company's regional headquarters or the largest production plants.

In Table 7.3, a column was included to summarize the type of investment strategy BMNs adopted to gain access to the EU market. The classification of primary investment strategy is based on information reported in annual company reports. The main mechanism that has allowed BMSs to enter the European market is through M&A. Of the 31 Brazilian firms in Europe, 14 pursued such a strategy to start their activities in Europe.

The second most common strategy is to make greenfield investments. Seven firms are pursuing this strategy, including Embraer, which has established its official headquarters in Villepinte, France, near the Roissy Charles de Gaulle Airport. There are also some companies that have sought to enter by prioritizing the establishment of representative offices to concentrate on sales and marketing activities, as is the case with Tupy, which develops and produces demanding and complex castings for the automotive sector and has maintained a representative office in Germany.

The importance of BNDES for these companies is striking. Leaving out the three banking corporations (Banco do Brasil, Bradesco, and Itaú-Unibanco), 24 BMNs (85.7 percent) operating in Europe have received BNDES support in the form of loans, becoming a shareholder, or both. The development bank can provide loans, capitalize the firm by becoming a shareholder, or do both to help support a Brazilian company seeking to expand its overseas operations. Based on the review of the companies that received either or both types of financial support, it is clear that the state development bank has supported a diverse set of industries and firms.

BNDES holds shares in 13 (46.4 percent) of these 24 companies. The bank has provided loans to 17 of these (60.7 percent) Brazilian companies that are operating in Europe. There are six cases in which the bank has provided loans and also has equities in the companies. At the same time, however, it is also clear that the bank's support is not equal across industries. As noticed by Masiero and Caseiro (2012), a relatively sizeable share of BNDES resources for internationalization has been directed to supporting the meat-processing industry.

In sum, there has been an important evolution in the presence of BMNs in Europe over the last decade. Yet, the level of heterogeneity is also great. There are clearly differences in the complexity and scale of the types of internationalization ventures that have been undertaken by different BMNs in Europe. The fact that such a large share of BMNs also received BNDES support tends to corroborate the hypothesis that the bank's role is quite important. In many cases, the capital necessary for ventures to be undertaken may not have been easily acquired from private lenders, or those costs would be so prohibitive as to make initiatives unviable.

7.5 Concluding remarks and future research

In this chapter, we show that the period in which the flow of FDI to the EU from Brazil peaked, coincided with the years in which Brazilian public banks initiated a major shift in policy, directing resources to finance the overseas operations of BMNs. The share of public resources directed to supporting the expansion of BMNs in key target economies is significant. Indeed, our efforts to quantify these amounts suggest that BNDES funding represented nearly 20 percent of the total amount of resources that were invested in this sample of countries by Brazil in the period between 2005 and 2011. Despite the large magnitude of these resources, the research aimed at better understanding the impact of these flows is only in a preliminary stage. In focusing specifically on the EU, our study confirms that there is a strong correlation between those companies that received BNDES support and those BMNs that were able to expand in Europe.

The marked increase in the participation of the Brazilian government in supporting the internationalization process of BMNs is representative of a larger trend of many rising emerging economies whose states have sought to strengthen their strategic role in driving economic transformations. This interventionism, sometimes called 'state capitalism' or 'governed market' has several aspects: from economic regulations to taxation and financing (Wade, 2004). In addition to state-owned bank financing, which is the subject of our present study, a host of additional policies are usually also employed. We have not focused on analyzing the tax incentives or barriers granted to BMNs by the state, for example. As these are frequently mentioned in the literature as drivers of internationalization of firms, such linkages should be noted.

On a related note, the marked support of BNDES in the internationalization of BMNs, either through loans or subscription of securities (for instance, shares, simple debentures, convertible debentures, subscription bonds, etc.), should be understood in the context of the government's financial management of the Brazilian economy. As a state-owned development bank, BNDES is able to finance companies with the direct capital increases it received from the Brazilian National Treasury, which in turn is fueled by tax revenues (Lacerda et al., 2010). That said, it is important to bear in mind that the Brazilian tax burden is one of the heaviest in the world and the heaviest of the BRICs, with an average taxation of 36 percent of the GDP in the 2000–2010 time span (OECD, 2012). Campanario, Stal, and Muniz da Silva (2012) note that the Brazilian tax system is the main barrier to the FDI flows in and out of Brazil.

Scholars of the internationalization process of firms have struggled to explain how emerging market firms have suddenly become international competitors. Using a combination of an LLL framework and the contextual approach, this study has reviewed the experiences of BMNs. We have shown that an important shift in investment policies (outer context) by the Brazilian state contributed to the internationalization process of Brazilian firms. In particular, the financial support that BMNs received from BNDES for their international expansion helped latecomer firms compensate for their lack of managerial (Bartlett and Ghoshal, 2000) and technological capabilities (Martinez-Noya and Garcia-Canal, 2011).

The influx of capital from the Brazilian development bank provided firms with access to new resources (linkage) and increased their local and international competitiveness (leverage). This influx of funds facilitated the acquisition and development of knowledge (learning), helping companies to adopt a permanent orientation toward internationalization and also toward innovation (Verbeke, 2009). As we have attempted to show in the case of Europe, BNDES played a significant role in encouraging local firms to become global players in specific sectors, focusing on value-added activities that have comparative advantages and lead global value networks (Gereffi et al., 2005).

Finally, while our research underscores that there is a strong correlation between BMNs' presence in Europe and BNDES support for these firms, there are several constraints in the data that limit our ability to further analyze the impact of such assistance. Among them, first, without access to the total amounts of loans and equity investments provided by BNDES and to the earnings from the investments undertaken by companies for specific projects, it is difficult to assess the precise role of the bank's aid in the expansion of the BMNs. Second, a study that seeks to comprehensively assess the effects of BNDES support on the internationalization of companies must necessarily be based on mapping company strategies and operations across several regions and markets.

These issues refer to the inner context, not developed in this chapter, but which certainly needs to be analyzed. Several BMNs that expanded into the EU in the last decade did the same in the Americas. That is, in some cases they sought BNDES's support for acquisitions in other markets and not necessarily directly toward the EU. Future research should be directed toward understanding how the access to credit contributed to the expansion of these BMNs across different markets. Clearly, the Brazilian state bank's support has had dynamic and complex effects and these need to be better explored with more robust hypothesis tests and with company-specific case studies.

Notes

1. For a recent review of the implications of this phenomenon on the global economic order, see Nölke and Taylor (2010) and Nölke (2011b).
2. It should be noted that a sizeable share of BNDES resources are allocated for export assistance. For an excellent summary of BNDES support for Brazilian exports, see Valdez (2011).
3. The selected historical periods correspond to: 1970–1975, first investments of Brazilian Multinationals; 1976–1982, rise in commodities prices, broad government program for domestic investment (II PND), and existence of cheap credit in international markets (petrodollars); 1983–1988, debt crisis in Latin America and high interests rates in international markets; 1989–1994, political democratization, commercial and financial liberalization and privatization; 1995–2003: macroeconomic stabilization (end of hyperinflation), further privatization and regional integration; 2004–2010: boom of commodities prices and financial markets; state support for OFDI, return of Brazilian industrial policies, cheap credit in international financial markets. (For further details on these periods, see Arbix and Caseiro, 2011).
4. The Bank has three subsidiaries: FINAME, BNDESPAR, and BNDES Limited. FINAME is an agency of the Bank that finances large domestic purchases and sales operations, and exports and imports of machinery and equipment. BNDESPAR follows BNDES's plans and policies, capitalizing undertakings of private groups. And BNDES Limited is a new subsidiary opened in London in 2009 that supports BMNs seeking to expand activities in the international market.
5. Between 2008 and 2011, BNDES also lent US$ 9.9 billion to foreign governments and corporations for the procurement of goods and services of Brazilian companies. In such loans, BNDES requires that at least 35 percent of the amount disbursed to the project must be spent on imports of Brazilian products. Of the total amount lent, US$ 5.2 billion (52.5 percent) and US$ 2.1 billion (21.2 percent) were for loans in Latin America and Africa respectively. Europe was the destination of US$ 1.4 billion (14.1 percent) and the United States of US$ 1.1 billion (11.1 percent). Countries from Asia received only US$ 100 million (1 percent). Although such loans cannot be easily linked to specific BMNs, it is clear that the conditionality for receiving such credit includes buying Brazilian goods, and this clearly helps increase the sales of specific firms and industries. Along these lines, Sennes and Mendes (2009) show that the BNDES loans provided to foreign governments strengthened the capacity of companies like Odebrecht, Camargo Corrêa, and Andrade Gutierrez to confront the fierce competition of Chinese contractors in Latin America and Africa. BNDES has also implemented these policies to support foreign purchases of Embraer jets.

6. We should notice that this estimate is an approximation. In interviews conducted by the authors, senior bank officials have stated that the figures released by bank officials in interviews with the press were incorrect. In these interviews, BNDES officials stated that the total amount of disbursements was R$ 9.9 billion (Masiero and Caseiro, 2012). Based on this estimate, the share of BNDES funding is considerably lower.
7. The presence of BMNs in the banking sector in Europe is remarkable. For example, the Itaú-Unibanco Banking Corporation is one of the 15 largest financial institutions of the world with operations concentrated in Latin America, North America, Asia, and Europe. Bradesco Bank is present in Argentina, the Grand Cayman Islands, Japan, Luxembourg, the People's Republic of China (Hong Kong), the United States, and the United Kingdom. Through its activities in Luxembourg, Bradesco conducts operations of Brazilian companies with counterparts in the region.
8. The location index equals the number of countries in a given region, divided by the total number of countries where the company operates.
9. Naturally, BMNs have a stronger presence in South America, given the geographical and cultural proximities Brazil shares with its counterparts in the region, as well as the business opportunities within Mercosur.
10. Surprisingly, there are no Brazilian retail companies operating in Europe. According to FDC (2011), there are eight retail or services franchises in Europe, and due to the relatively low value invested, they were not included in the study. The retail franchises are: three shoe stores (Via Uno, Arezzo, Morana) and four food/restaurant chains (Showcolate, Fábrica di Chocolate, Spoleto and Koni). In services, the only Brazilian franchise in Europe is Linkwell, specializing in graphic services.

Part III
International Institutions

8
How Policies Shape Foreign Direct Investment from Latin America to the European Union

Judith Clifton, Daniel Díaz-Fuentes, and Julio Revuelta

8.1 Introduction

From the 2000s on, foreign direct investment (FDI) from emerging markets has increased significantly: as a consequence, emerging markets multinational corporations (MNC) have come of age. The rise of emerging markets MNC is but one manifestation of the process referred to by Angus Maddison as 'shifting wealth' in the world economy, whereby long-term global imbalances in current and capital accounts have increased the economic muscle and the political stature of a number of emerging countries and regions (OECD, 2010; Quah, 2011).

As a consequence, scholars have turned their attention to seeking to understand the causes and dynamics of this long-term shift. A first 'wave' of literature on the rise of FDI from emerging markets has come from an international business perspective, and has focused on the strategies deployed by firms and governments to promote domestic MNCs abroad, and the determinants of this initial internationalization (see, for example, Goldstein, 2007; Ramamurti and Singh, 2009; Brennan, 2010; Sauvant et al., 2010). Although this literature has been dominated by analysis of Asian multinationals, there has been some attention also to multinationals from Latin America, often referred to as the 'multilatinas' (for instance, CEPAL, 2007; Cuervo-Cazurra, 2008; Inter-American Development Bank, 2008; Casanova, 2009; Fleury and Fleury, 2011). Political economists have also contributed to this first wave, exploring the determinants of outward foreign direct investment (OFDI) from various emerging markets (see Mathews, 2002b; Luo and Tung, 2007; Aulakh, 2007). In a second wave of literature, scholars analyzed OFDI flows from emerging markets in conjunction with the examination of characteristics of host countries including their FDI and FDI-related policies (see, for example, Cuervo-Cazurra and Genc, 2008; Guillén and García-Canal, 2009; Gammeltoft et al., 2010). One of the most intriguing questions raised by scholars is whether and to what extent the rise of MNCs from emerging markets is the result of a new form of 'state capitalism' – that is, an interventionist state that guides select MNCs to venture abroad, or whether emerging markets' success is more due to their following the market-oriented rules set out in the so-called Washington Consensus.

This chapter contributes to this literature on the rise of FDI and MNCs from emerging markets to the European Union (EU) by focusing on understanding how states use FDI policy and the consequences of this for FDI itself, by examining both home (emerging markets) and host (EU member states) countries. Few studies to date have sought to combine an analysis of both the determinants of OFDI and inward foreign direct investment (IFDI) until now. In particular, we contribute to both the first and second wave of literature by focusing on whether and to what extent FDI and FDI-related policies implemented by both home and host countries affect FDI flows from emerging markets to developed ones.

The effect of FDI and FDI-related policies is an important area for study. Governments around the world have undertaken broad measures to open up their FDI policy regime, in particular, from the 1980s on. These policy measures have taken various forms, including numerous bilateral agreements; regional accords that contain investment clauses, such as the North American Free Trade Agreement (NAFTA) and the EU Treaty of Lisbon (Shan and Zhang, 2011); and international trade and investment agreements, such as Trade-Related Investment Measures (TRIMS) and the General Agreement on Trade in Services (GATS). FDI liberalization works in two – often interconnected – directions: removal of obstacles to facilitate investment abroad, or outright promotion, hence encouraging more OFDI and rendering the country as host more attractive for potential investors, in a bid to increase IFDI. International organizations such as the Organization for Economic Cooperation and Development (OECD) and the United Nations Committee on Trade and Development (UNCTAD), encourage governments to further liberalize FDI policy, arguing that increasing FDI usually leads to economic growth and development (OECD, 2002), although historical reasons for which a government might restrict FDI include national strategic interests, protection of local industrial groups, or a loss of sovereignty on economic issues. A general move worldwide toward greater FDI policy liberalization has been accompanied by an FDI boom (UNCTAD, 2011a).

Despite this general trend toward liberalization, all governments retain some forms of FDI restrictions, and significant differences remain at the country level. Additionally, FDI policy liberalization is not a 'one-way street': governments can, and do, reverse liberalization by introducing new forms of restrictions, for a variety of reasons. Studies including Javalgi, Griffith, and White (2003) and Clifton, Díaz-Fuentes and Revuelta (2010) have found that regulation, among other factors, may act as a significant factor in determining patterns of international investment.

To sharpen the analysis, we focus in particular on FDI from Latin America to the EU. Our hypotheses are guided by mainstream economic theory, which would generally expect greater FDI policy liberalization to lead to greater FDI. So, as regards OFDI, we would expect that, in those Latin American economies where FDI liberalization has progressed most, OFDI will be greater, all other things being equal. Secondly, and similarly, we would expect those EU host countries with greater liberalization to attract most IFDI, again, controlling for other factors. In particular, we will seek to establish how EU member states have reacted to the dilemma presented by increased FDI from emerging markets, and whether they have veered toward protectionism, to shelter privileged interests, or whether, in contrast, they are working harder to attract much-needed investment in times of austerity.

We find that both the major Latin American and EU countries progressively liberalized their FDI regimes from the late 1990s to 2010. Further liberalization in the EU is likely to occur as competence to design the FDI regime is gradually transferred to the European Community (EC) as agreed in the Treaty of Lisbon. So, in broad contrast to governments' protectionist reactions in the 1930s, the Great Recession made EU political leaders more open to available sources of FDI, at least, until 2010, in those countries and sectors under analysis. Moreover, liberalization policies favored an increase of IFDI and OFDI between the regions. So, FDI liberalization policy is found to be a clear determinant of FDI. However, despite an increase, OFDI from Latin America remained below its potential. Interestingly, the relationship between the two regions has become concentrated between Brazil and Spain. This is not the whole story, however. Some governments introduced restrictive policies that reduced investment. In particular, we found that protectionist policies implemented by EU member states disproportionately reduced investment levels from Latin America more than from the other countries in the sample.

The rest of the chapter is organized as follows. The second section sketches the recent move toward FDI liberalization as pursued by states around the world, and also explains why states may also chose to restrict FDI. The third part focuses on the evolution of FDI from Latin America to the EU. Sections four and five set out the methodology and the empirical results, respectively. Conclusions follow with implications for public policy.

8.2 The worldwide move toward FDI liberalization

It is widely accepted that IFDI may have both advantages and disadvantages, although mainstream approaches argue the advantages usually outweigh the disadvantages (OECD, 2002). In sum, while IFDI is thought to stimulate economic growth and improve productivity, the disadvantages include a possible reduction in national economic and political sovereignty. Among empirical studies on IFDI, the evidence on economic growth and productivity is more mixed than is often assumed. Because a comprehensive overview of the theory and evidence is beyond the aims of this chapter, a brief discussion must suffice. Aitken and Harrison (1999) find that the net effect of FDI on productivity is quite small, while Borensztein et al. (1998) and Carkovic and Levine (2005) find that FDI does not have an unmitigated and positive effect on economic growth. Blomström et al. (1994) and Alfaro et al. (2004) point out that FDI *can* increase the rate of growth in the host economy through technology transfer, depending on the host country's absorptive capacity and human capital, but this is usually only the case in developed countries. As regards the disadvantages of IFDI, in addition to findings that it may not augment economic growth and productivity, as mentioned above, there are questions as to the government's loss of control over 'strategic' sectors for national development, particularly acute when a large asymmetry between host and home exists (UNCTAD, 2011b) IFDI could also reduce national income and increase the risk of offshore outsourcing (Olsen, 2006; Bhagwati ., 2004; Falk and Wolfmayer, 2008).

In practice, across the last two decades, governments have broadly moved toward more open FDI regimes as regards their opening of their economies to IFDI, as well as the promotion of OFDI using a multitude of instruments including tax breaks, subsidies, and so on. It should not be forgotten, however, that FDI policy is subject to reversals and backtracking (UNCTAD, 2011a). Governments may seek to use policy to restrict FDI for similar reasons that they seek to restrict trade. Hence, they may look to protect particular sectors, infant industries, or national champions, for political, economic, or ideological reasons, or decide that a sector previously open to IFDI is strategic and should be protected, as occurred in sectors including ports, energy, and infrastructure (Clifton and Díaz-Fuentes, 2010a; 2010b). As the financial crisis broke out, the UNCTAD (2008) warned countries of growing pressures to restrict, or even reverse, FDI liberalization. In the face of shifting wealth, countries in the north may be tempted to react, perhaps in the form of greater FDI protectionism. FDI restriction policies include issues such as foreign equity restrictions, screening and prior approval requirements of foreign investors, restrictions on foreign key personnel, and various other measures, such as limits on the purchase of land or on repatriation of profits and capital.

The policy dilemma is to balance the management of potentially contradictory objectives of FDI and industrial policy, while simultaneously coordinating these policies in the international arena to preserve global conformity to trading and investment rules. In the context of the ongoing financial and economic crisis, governments in the EU are striving to find a balance between the need to attract IFDI to their ailing economy and to introduce IFDI restrictions where distressed sectors are calling for protection.

IFDI can be limited by a set of direct and indirect techniques. Red tape can come in a multitude of forms. For instance, national legislation on the composition of firms' boards is not, strictly speaking, directly related to IFDI, although an obligation to include a quota of native executives may well affect the investment decision. In the face of this complexity, the OECD has advanced furthest in developing a sophisticated methodology in order to quantify the extent to which governments may restrict IFDI. The OECD (2013) classifies restrictions into four overall groups: 1) restrictions on foreign equity; 2) screening and prior approval requirements applicable to foreign investors; 3) restrictions on foreigners in key personnel positions, such as directors and managers; 4) other operational restrictions on the operation of foreign companies, including limits on the purchase of land, the establishment of branches, or on repatriation of profits and capital (Golub, 2003; 2009; Koyama and Golub, 2006; Kalinova et al., 2010). The OECD's restriction classifications do not include, therefore, 'natural' barriers to IFDI, such as market size, the degree of existing integration with neighboring countries, or entry barriers due to public ownership of strategic sectors, and they do take into account questions pertaining to the actual enforcement of statutory restrictions, in other words, the implementation of FDI policy and its institutional quality.

Applying these criteria, the OECD (2013) quantifies FDI restrictions applied by governments in its 'FDI Regulatory Restrictiveness Index' (henceforth, *FDIrest*). The OECD (2013) includes data on 55 countries, including all 34 OECD and G20 Members, in addition to signatories of the OECD Declaration on International Investment and Multinational Enterprise, including Argentina, Brazil, Colombia, Egypt, Latvia, Lithuania, Morocco, Peru, and Romania, as well as other non-OECD countries, including China, India, Indonesia, Jordan, Kazakhstan, Kyrgyz Republic, Mongolia, Russia, Saudi Arabia, South Africa, Tunisia, and Ukraine. *FDIrest* measures restrictions across 22 major industrial and service sectors. There are six years available: 1997, 2003, 2006, 2010, 2011, and 2012. After quantifying the four indicators mentioned above, *FDIrest* estimates a given country's restrictiveness with a score ranging from '1', meaning full FDI restrictions for this indicator, to '0', meaning an absence of FDI restrictions in this indicator, that is, wholly liberalized. On this basis, an overview of governments' FDI and FDI-related policies are shown in Figure 8.1. A general trend is clear whereby governments eliminated many restrictions to FDI between 1997 and 2010. However, the OECD has noticed that FDI restrictions tend to arise mostly in primary sectors such as mining, fishing, and agriculture, but also in media and transport.

Looking first at the EU, at the internationally comparative level, we can see how the EU has one of the most open FDI regimes in the world, similar to the United States, and more open than that of Canada or Japan. Traditionally, EU member states were largely responsible for their own FDI regime, in sharp contrast to trade policy, which was established as a common policy from the outset, in the Treaty of Rome. This meant that member states could exercise some discretion in the design of their FDI regime. However, in recent years, there has been an upward delegation of responsibility for FDI policy to the supranational level. This culminated in the Treaty of Lisbon, when significant responsibility for FDI policy was merged with the EU's common commercial policy (Shan and Zhang, 2011). The Treaty authorizes the EC to sign international investment agreements on behalf of the members. Among the main stated aims of this new policy are to ensure better market access for OFDI from the EU and gradually replace the web of bilateral investment treaties with an overarching EU framework (European Commission, 2010). It is to be expected that, as this policy evolves, EU member states will have less room to turn toward protectionism. However, it is also likely that there will be a transition period whereby member states continue to exercise at least some discretion as regards FDI policy, although this is

How Policies Shape Foreign Direct Investment 161

constrained by new EC rules. So, differences among FDI regimes in the EU are likely to continue for some years ahead. Differences among the EU member states can be observed in OECD data, as seen in Figure 8.1. The EU is also far more open than most of the emerging markets. Within the EU, in the same period, FDI policy has converged between the old (EU-15) and the new members at a level of 0.04 in the *FDIrest*. Differences among EU member states are apparent: Portugal, Slovenia, Netherlands, Finland, and Spain have the most open FDI regimes. Data on 2010 indicates that EU members, despite the outbreak of the financial crisis in 2008, continued to liberalize their FDI regimes. Since then, no further restriction or change has been noted during 2011 and 2012 in the EU.

Turning to Latin America, we already know that many restrictions to FDI regimes were eliminated across the region as part of the requirements of the so-called Washington Consensus, since capital access was a condition of receiving loans from the international financial organizations (Williamson, 2003; Arestis, 2004). OECD (2013) includes data for the period 1997–2010 on: Brazil, Mexico, Argentina, and Chile, and data for 2010 on Colombia and Peru. Mexico maintains, by far, the greatest protection against FDI, although liberalization has increased over the period. In 2010, levels of protection in Mexico were higher than those in Russia, for instance. Figure 8.1 shows that Brazil has done much to dismantle FDI restrictions, although some reversal toward more protectionism occurred between 2006 and 2010 in the agriculture

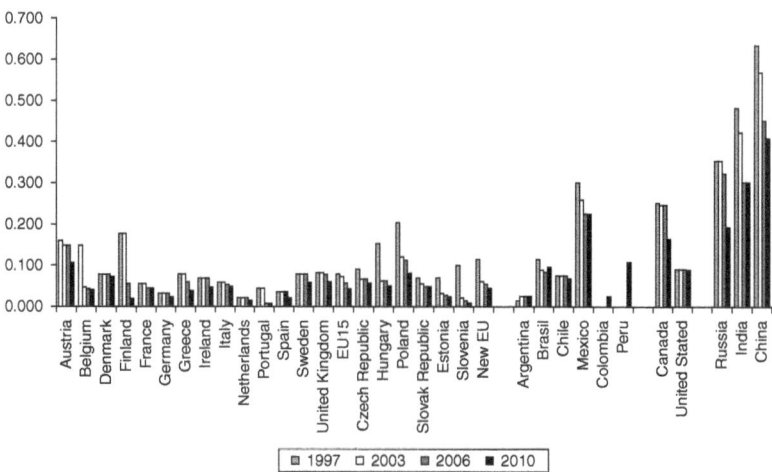

Figure 8.1 FDI restrictiveness index, selected countries 1997–2010
Source: Compiled by authors using OECD (2013).

and forestry subsectors (in terms of 2) screening and approval mechanisms and 4 (operational restrictions on capital repatriation and land ownership). However, from 2010 to 2012, FDI restrictions were reduced in the media sector. Chile and Peru have intermediate positions, while the least protection is offered by Colombia and Argentina. In the case of the latter, a minimal reversal was also noticed in the agriculture and forestry subsector between 2010 and 2012.

8.3 FDI from Latin America to the European Union from an international perspective

The concentration of FDI among developed countries during the 1980s was referred to in the UNCTAD (1991) report as the FDI 'Triad'. The metaphor of the Triad has now been replaced with that of 'Shifting Wealth' (OECD, 2010d) as economic power moves away from the United States-Japan-European Union nexus and toward the East and the South. The crisis has acted as an accelerator of this shift. Many emerging markets have proved resilient to the ongoing crisis, so that FDI among emerging markets and from emerging to developed markets is becoming increasingly important, and is growing faster – or declining more slowly – than flows between many developed markets (UNCTAD, 2011b). Of world IFDI between 1990 and 2010, the share directed toward developed economies peaked between 1996 and 2000, comprising nearly three-quarters of all world IFDI; however, by the end of the 2000s, specifically between 2009 and 2010, this share fell to under one-half of world IFDI. So, by the end of the 2000s, IFDI in emerging and transition countries actually *overtook* that in developed ones (UNCTAD, 2011a). IFDI toward emerging and transition markets broadly rose across the two decades, from US$ 72.5 billion between 1990 and 1995 to US$ 612 between 2009 and 2010.

Importantly, emerging and transition countries have also increased their role in OFDI, from US$ 32.2 billion between 1990 and 1995 to US$ 353.8 billion between 2009 and 2010. Although Asia – particularly China – dominates these trends, Latin America has also increased its overall importance in the world economy over the last decade (CEPAL, 2010). Here, effects of the international financial crisis were largely diluted, thanks to unprecedented financial support and adherence to solid macroeconomic policies (Izquierdo and Talvi, 2010). Latin America made up one-quarter of all IFDI going to emerging and transition countries between 1990 and 1995, increasing to one-third at the end of the 1990s. The EU was the leading investor in Latin America during the

1990s: IFDI from the EU to the region was strongest in Southern America, particularly, Brazil, Argentina, Colombia, and Chile. IFDI from the EU to Mexico and Central America was unstable and less significant. EU-Latin American IFDI falls into two categories: the first category is investment in the service sectors, particularly in Southern America, and the second category is in the manufacturing sector in Mexico and Central America. Looking now at the individual member-state level, IFDI from Spain was considerable, due to the interest of Spanish multinationals in the service sectors, which took advantage of the deregulation of utilities to acquire shares in telecoms, energy, and water providers (Clifton, Lanthier and Schroeter, 2011). Meanwhile, IFDI from Germany, the United Kingdom, and the Netherlands was primarily directed to the manufacturing sector, particularly, in Brazil, Mexico, and Argentina. During the 2000s, IFDI to the region continued to grow. In this decade, Brazil, Mexico, Chile, and Colombia dominated inflows. By the end of the 2000s, IFDI to Latin America made up nearly 8 percent of the world total. Across the two decades, the EU was the most important investor in Latin America, constituting nearly 40 percent of total IFDI to that region.

Emerging and transition countries have, in recent years, become more important sources of OFDI. OFDI from Latin America grew throughout the two decades, from US$ 3 billion in 1990–1995 to US$ 40.3 billion between 2009 and 2010. Brazil and Mexico dominated OFDI flows from the region, with strong growth in the second half of the 2000s, although Chile and Colombia also increased their shares. The bulk of this OFDI from Latin America was destined for other countries in the region: most multilatinas are, therefore, regional in nature (CEPAL, 2011; 2012). However, some multilatinas – especially those based in Brazil and Mexico – have ventured further, to the EU, Canada, and the United States (Fleury and Fleury, 2011; Masiero et al., in this volume). Casanova (2009) labeled these the 'Global Latinas'. At the end of the 2000s, OFDI from Latin America represented over 3 percent of the world total. Although these results from Latin America might be considered transitory, due to the effects of the crisis in developed countries, we argue that they represent an important moment for emerging countries in the region.

We now take a closer look at OFDI from Latin America to the EU. Table 8.1 shows Latin American stock in the EU in 2005 and 2010. OFDI flows to the EU climbed, peaking at € 29.1 billion in 2007. This data is asymmetrical in that, while it represents an important achievement for Latin American investment, it represents only a small percentage as seen from the EU, at less than 4 percent of the total non-EU IFDI in 2010.

Table 8.1 Latin American FDI stock in the EU

	€ million		% from Latin America	
	2005	2010	2005	2010
Brazil	8,119	67,575	26.1	64.0
Mexico	9,131	10,284	29.4	9.7
Uruguay	802	5,076	2.6	4.8
Venezuela	1,989	3,740	6.4	3.5
Colombia	330	1,956	1.1	1.9
Argentina	1,969	1,772	6.3	1.7
Chile	774	1,663	2.5	1.6

Source: Elaborated by the authors based on Eurostat (2013).

Spain, by far, outstripped any other EU member state as regards attracting Latin American OFDI, accounting for two-thirds of all flows across the two decades. After Spain, Denmark attracted around 12 percent of flows, followed by France (8.9 percent), Sweden (6.7 percent), Portugal (5.4 percent), and Italy (4.5 percent). Interestingly, the origins of this investment changed somewhat: until 2005, Mexico and Brazil roughly shared OFDI volumes to the EU (together making up over 50 percent of all flows from the region to the EU); however, in the second half of the 2000s, Brazil's share grew rapidly, making up nearly two-thirds of all OFDI stock from the region by 2010 (see Masiero et al., in this volume). Mexico followed in second place, with only 9.7 percent, followed by Uruguay, Venezuela, Colombia, Argentina, and Chile.

So, by 2010, Latin American OFDI to the EU was heavily dominated by the Brazil-Spain nexus. The majority of Brazilian investments were in the service sectors, particularly in Spain, Denmark, Portugal, Belgium, Italy, and Sweden, but Brazil was also active in the manufacturing sector, most prominently in Spain, Sweden, and Italy. Mexico, the second most important investment in the EU, focused on Spain, France, and Germany, and largely on the service sectors, although it made inroads into manufacturing, particularly in Spain and the Netherlands. Argentinean OFDI was largely directed to the service sector in Spain, Denmark, and Italy, and to the Italian manufacturing sector. Finally, Uruguayan OFDI was destined for services in Spain and Italy, while Colombian and Venezuelan outflows were mainly destined for the Spanish service sector. With this sketch of FDI flows between Latin America and the EU complete, we now turn to analyzing whether and to what extent policy shaped these trends.

8.4 Methodology and data

Our purpose is to ascertain to what extent FDI and FDI-related policy toward liberalization or protectionism shaped FDI from Latin America to the EU. Therefore, we start by estimating cross-section regressions for OLS using FDI stock from the home/investor country (*j*) in the EU host country (*i*) as a dependent variable. The main independent variables of the analysis are *FDIrest* of the host EU country and an interaction effect between this and a dummy variable valued at '1' when the home country is a Latin American one, and '0' when it is not. We also use a vector of control variables in the regression. Our selection of control variables that potentially explain IFDI stock is based on the traditional empirical FDI literature. As mentioned earlier, Javalgi et al. (2003) and Clifton, Díaz-Fuentes and Revuelta (2010) have shown that regulation may help determine FDI. According to Li and Guisinger (1992), Kolstad and Villanger (2008), and Ramasamy and Yeung (2010), economic conditions of the host country are important determinants of FDI. Dunning (1981), using investment development path theory, showed how the economic conditions of the home country also determine IFDI. Li and Guisinger (1992) and Cuervo-Cazurra (2008) show that cultural proximity is a potential factor favoring IFDI. The vector of control variables is composed of explanatory variables including, for the home country, the gross domestic product, or GDP, (*GDPi*); GDP per capita (*GDPpci*); GDP per capita growth (*GDPpcgrowthi*); and the investment rate of the EU host country (*Investmentratei*), and for the host country, GDP (*GDPj*); GDP per capita (*GDPpcj*); GDP per capita growth (*GDPpcgrowthj*); and a dummy variable valued at '1' if a language is shared as a common, official language in both host and home country, and '0' if it is not (*Language*).

Because *FDIrest* does not include annual data until 2010, we cannot conduct a dynamic analysis using a panel. Hence, our research design is to conduct a cross-section regression of the years 1997, 2003, 2006, and 2010, years for which data on the dependent variable and *FDIrest* are available. Likewise, limited data on the independent variable restricts the geographical scope of this study. The sample of countries considered in the empirical analysis comprises 52 countries, including 24 EU member states (Austria, Belgium, the Czech Republic, Denmark, Estonia, Finland, France, Germany, Greece, Hungary, Ireland, Italy, Latvia, Lithuania, Luxembourg, the Netherlands, Poland, Portugal, Romania, Slovakia, Slovenia, Spain, Sweden, and the United Kingdom), and 28 non-EU countries (Argentina, Australia, Brazil, Canada, Chile, China,

Colombia, Egypt, Iceland, India, Indonesia, Israel, Japan, Kazakhstan, Mexico, Morocco, New Zealand, Norway, Peru, Russia, Saudi Arabia, South Africa, South Korea, Switzerland, Tunisia, Turkey, Ukraine, and the United States). Data was sourced using Eurostat (2013) for *FDIstockij*; the OECD (2013) for *FDIresti* and *FDIrestj*; and the World Bank (2013) for *GDPi, GDPpci, GDPpcgrowthi, Investmentratei, GDPj, GDPpcj*, and *GDPpcgrowthj*.

8.5 Results

Our results map out the relationship between FDI liberalization in home and host country and their effect on IFDI to the EU. Results are presented in Table 8.2, corresponding to the years 1997, 2003, 2006, and 2010. Starting in 1997, we can see that greater FDI liberalization by both the home and host country had a positive effect on IFDI to the EU, although the effects of liberalization were particularly important for the host country. The 'cost' of restricting FDI can be expressed quantitatively: for every 0.1 point an EU member state increased its score on *FDIrest*, its IFDI stock fell around € 1.2 billion for all countries. Size

Table 8.2 EU IFDI stock regression analysis for selected control variables and FDI restrictions, 1997–2010

Dep. Var: FDIstockij	1997	2003	2006	2010
Constant	−71401.7***	−125469.9***	−194796.7***	−110941.5***
FDIresti	−11915.2*	−42257.0***	−48102.1***	−30535.1*
FDIrestj	−7991.0***	−21743.6***	−30091.8***	−25466.2***
LnGDPi	1275.8***	2307.5***	4253.3***	2917.8***
LnGDPpci	9.6	339.7	346.6	−1515.1
GDPpcgrowthi	309.2*	689.5***	992.4***	231
Investmentratei	23.9	−225.7	−41.8	−264.7*
LnGDPj	1469.2***	2347.3***	2577.0***	1786.0***
LnGDPpcj	158.3	1377.6**	2055.1***	1769.8***
GDPpcgrowthj	163.9	425.5**	397.5*	−91.7
Language	6872.0***	12018.2***	13404.6***	18135.9***
Latin America*FDIresti	−16541.3	−33316	−59784.8*	−56884.0*
N	410	744	836	961
R^2	0.25	0.24	0.22	0.22
F	12.18***	21.42***	21.63***	24.93***

Source: Elaborated by authors based on EUROSTAT (2013), OECD (2013) and World Bank (2013). * Significance level at 10%, ** significance level at 5%, *** significance level at 1%.

mattered: home countries with larger GDPs had bigger FDI stocks in the EU. Additionally, host countries with larger GDP and higher rates of economic growth attracted more IFDI.

Six years later, in 2003, the same factors that had positively influenced greater IFDI stock in the EU in 1997 remained the same. Key factors included having an open FDI regime; a strong economic base in the home country; and a strong economic position in the EU host country. Two new factors positively influencing IFDI to the EU emerged: growth rates in home economies and purchasing power per capita. The 'cost' of restricting IFDI in the EU rose: increasing a country's score on *FDIrest* by 0.1 points resulted in a smaller stock to the tune of € 4.2 billion.

Again in 2006, a more liberalized FDI regime and high GDP positively influenced EU IFDI, as did the growth of GDP per capita in the host country. GDP per capita in the home country figures as a clear positive determinant, but economic growth in the home country was only weakly significant. The 'cost' of not liberalizing remained high: for every increase of 0.1 points in the *FDIrest* index, EU countries reduced IFDI stock € 4.8 billion. In this year, we also observe the negative effect of FDI restrictive policies, which is more significant where the home/investor country is Latin American, when compared to the other countries in the sample. Although this effect had not featured in a pronounced way previously, it seems that, once FDI from Latin America really took off, more restrictive regulation by EU member states became particularly damaging to FDI from Latin America.

In the final year under analysis, 2010, FDI liberalization, as well as home and host country GDP, continued to positively influence IFDI to the EU. However, growth in the host or home country did not determine IFDI during this year. Given the context of the ongoing crisis, which particularly damaged growth in the EU, this result appears logical. Nevertheless, the 'cost' of restricting FDI fell: an increase of 0.1 points in the *FDIrest* index resulted in a fall in IFDI stock of 'only' € 3 billion. Again in this period, IFDI from Latin America to the EU is disproportionately negatively affected when EU member states increase levels of FDI protection, as compared to other countries in the sample.

8.6 Conclusions

The aim of this chapter was to contribute to better understanding the ways in which FDI policy as implemented by states from emerging and developed markets helped shape investment patterns between the regions. Our specific focus was directed to examining FDI from Latin

168 *Judith Clifton, Daniel Díaz-Fuentes, and Julio Revuelta*

America to the EU. Using data constructed by the OECD that quantified the regulatory regime around FDI as applied by governments, as well as other data, on FDI stock, GDP, and so on, we sought to understand whether and to what extent FDI policy shaped FDI patterns. Years for which data was available were 1997, 2003, 2006, and 2010.

Our paper has three main findings. First, despite the crisis, most states decided to continue liberalizing FDI regimes. In the case of the EU, although the rise of FDI from emerging markets could be seen as a double-edged sword, for the most part, pressures toward protectionism were resisted, at least, for the sectors and time periods studied here. Second, this broad trend toward policy liberalization was accompanied by an overall rise in FDI volumes. FDI policy as implemented by states did indeed help determine IFDI in the EU. Specifically, the liberalization of FDI by both home and host country positively influenced EU IFDI stock, while restrictive policies negatively affected stock, which we quantified for each year. We also saw how the IFDI stock from Latin America in the EU became quite heavily focused in the Brazil-Spain nexus. Finally, we noted that when EU member states did augment their efforts to restrict IFDI, it was the Latin American markets that suffered disproportionately from this policy, since OFDI to the EU dropped more significantly than it did in the rest of the countries in the sample.

Final conclusions can be drawn from this chapter in relation to the overall theme of this volume. This chapter used an indicator constructed by the OECD to analyze to what extent states liberalized or protected FDI. It is probable that not all efforts to restrict or promote FDI are captured by this single indicator. Although the OECD indicator is probably the most sophisticated available at the international level, it is not sophisticated enough to reflect the nature and quality of FDI policy implemented by states. It does not help us ascertain whether FDI policy by the emerging markets is different, somehow, from that implemented by developed ones, as the thesis of 'state capitalism 3.0' might argue. So, further research must be undertaken in order to uncover qualitative differences when seeking to compare policy implemented by Latin American and EU states, if any exist. Intriguingly, restrictive FDI policy by EU states caused more relative damage to FDI from Latin America than the other country samples. The reasons for this are not obvious when looking at the OECD indicator: we propose to examine this in future research by combining a qualitative analysis of FDI policy with the quantitative approach adopted here.

9
The Action-Reaction in the Global Trade: Comparing the Cases of the Brazilian Chicken and the Thai Tuna Industries

Suthikorn Kingkaew

9.1 Introduction, literature review, and research methodology

Institutional factors are widely recognized as the underlying force that has shaped the development of various industries and their firms. Institutional factors such as trade policy, banking practice, law and regulation, the political and economic background of a country, labor regulation, national culture, and tax policy have shaped the contours of international trade. Several of these institutional factors are the result of either direct or indirect support by the government. Various national governments have taken a proactive role in promoting and nurturing their own national champions in selected industries in order to create spillover benefits to the economy (Scott, 1995; Peng et al., 2008; Oliver, 1997; Nölke and Taylor, 2010; Nölke, 2011a; Bhalla, 1977).

Many studies have been conducted based on the growing influence of large corporations and their increasingly dominant role in the global business arena (Chang, 2002; 2008; Wade, 2003; 2004; Nolan et al., 2008; Amsden, 2001; 2008; Chandler et al., 1997; Chandler, 2004; Dicken, 2007; Porter, 1990; Howes and Singh, 2000). In fact, the influence of big businesses has long been recognized. Marx (1990) and Marshall (1920) addressed the significant scale advantage of large corporations over their smaller rivals. Berle and Means (1932) reemphasized this trend of concentrated capital. They observed that the US economy at the beginning of the 20th century was no longer driven by small, owner-operated businesses, but had transformed into a situation whereby large corporations, under the management of salaried professionals rather than their equity owners, were the core driver of the economy (Teece et al., 1997 Schumpeter, 1950; Schmitz, 1993; Marx, 1990; Marshall, 1920; Berle and Means, 1932).

Based on studies by Chandler et al. (1997), Chandler (2004), Amsden (2001), Chang (1994; 2002), Wade (2004), and Dicken (2007) on industrial development and the industrial structure of the major advanced economies and successful late industrialized economies, it can be concluded that big businesses have been the core driver of our modern economy; they have played an active role in the economic transformation of many nation-states and in continuously shaping the face of the global economy. The United States, Germany, and other industrial countries have long implemented varied forms of industrial development policy. As a result, numerous big businesses have been established and have succeeded in becoming the core economic drivers of their respective countries, for example, General Electric and Boeing in the United States; Siemens and Volkswagen in Germany; and Toyota and Nippon Steel in Japan. Moreover, several late industrialized countries, such as Taiwan and South Korea, have followed this path. Using industrial policy, they have successfully nurtured and subsequently established their own national giants, such as Samsung in South Korea, and Acer in Taiwan.

Despite such benefits, various other studies have widely criticized this unfair support by different governments. Nölke (2011a) and Nölke and Taylor (2010) have observed various tensions between existing multinational corporations (MNCs) from developed countries and newcomer MNCs from developing countries. They also expect rising conflicts among MNCs from developed and developing countries. In particular, Nölke (2011a) and Nölke and Taylor (2010) conclude that when comparing MNCs from developed with those from developing countries, the governments in developing countries have established closer collaboration with their selected local firms in specific industries in order to nurture and foster them to become global giants. Although a preliminary review has acknowledged the strong involvement of governments of developing countries, this paper would argue that such observed involvement is an active response by developing countries to the strong support provided by developed countries' governments in protecting and nurturing *their* local industries. This paper pays particular attention to the actions of developed countries to protect their local industries and firms, and the responses by developing countries to overcome these trade restrictions. It focuses on the agrofood industry, employing the cases of the global chicken and canned tuna markets to illustrate the actions of developed countries and the reactions of developing countries.

The global agrofood industry was selected based on its status as a highly protected industry in which various developed and developing countries have created measures to protect and nurture their local industries. Based on the total 436 World Trade Organization (WTO) trade disputes – from the first case, filed on January 10, 1995, to the most recent case, filed on April 12, 2012 – the agrofood sector accounted for 134 cases, approximately one-third of all the cases. Despite this, the agrofood trade accounted for merely 5 percent of the US$ 15.775 trillion global trade in 2008. This reflects the enormous tensions in the global agrofood industry (Cramer, 2003; Donovan et al., 2001; Gehlhar and Regmi, 2005; WTO, 2009; 2012a).

Although major importing countries have undertaken various measures that have shaped the structure of the global agrofood market, this article is unable to examine all of these factors. In this article, certain important protective measures by developed countries will be investigated in detail. These measures are classified into two categories: 1) trade barriers on agrofood products and 2) various standards imposed on imported agrofood products that represent imperative factors hindering agrofood trade around the world.

Case studies are the ideal methodology for conducting such a broad and in-depth investigation. This study uses an institutional framework to examine the correlation between the levels of restriction imposed by major developed countries and the rise of firms from developing countries. Tariff and nontariff barriers are underlying institutional factors that are considered in this article. This study collected primary data through semistructured interviews with key actors, including top executives in various food companies and senior government officials, as well as secondary data from the public domain, such as the Agricultural Market Access Database (AMAD).

This study focuses on Brasil Foods in the chicken industry and Thai Union Frozen (TUF) in the canned tuna industry. These companies are at the apex of the industries' development with dominating positions as the largest global exporters. These firms from developing countries have defied the restrictions on global agrofood trade and successfully penetrated into developed countries' markets. Although they have succeeded in becoming the leaders in their relevant industries, the underlying factors behind their success are different. The success of Brasil Foods is the result of strong support by the Brazilian government, while there is no direct support for TUF from the local government. This difference provides a solid ground for examining a contemporary issue in international business, the role of developing countries' governments in supporting their local companies.

9.2 Action from developed countries: Barriers to global agrofood trade

The formation of the General Agreement on Trade and Tariff (GATT), which later became the WTO, has led to a considerable reduction in various trade barriers and the expansion of global trade. In particular, under the WTO, agricultural protection has gradually been reduced; this has led to the rising value of global agrofood trade over the past decade, from approximately US$ 300 billion in 1999 to US$ 797 billion in 2008 (UN Comtrade, 2011; WTO, 2010). Tariffs on agricultural products are traditionally set at a higher rate than on other products as many countries seek to protect their local farming sector and implement a self-sufficiency policy toward food production.

The trade barriers for chicken and canned tuna products in the United States and the EU are outlined in the following paragraphs. These markets were examined as they together account for a third of global chicken consumption and more than half of global canned tuna imports. A summary of tariff barriers for imported chicken products can be seen in Table 9.1. The breakdown analysis will be given as follows.

The United States and the EU devised a similar pattern of import tariff rates, setting higher tariff rates on processed products. The EU provides a low-tariff quota for chicken exports from different countries. On average, the products within the quota are charged around half of the normal tariff rates. For example, in 2010, Thai chicken imports were subjected to an additional charge of up to 1,024 € per ton when exceeding the

Table 9.1 Import tariffs of major markets for chicken products

Major imported destination	Global Chicken Market		
	Whole Chicken	Cut Chicken meat	Processed products
US	8.8 US cents per kg	17.6 US cents per kg	6.40% of price
EU	26.2–32.5 Euro cents per kg	26.9–102.4 Euro cents per kg	10.90% of price

Source: Elaborated by author based on WTO (2011).

160,033 tons of export quota to EU. This practice has limited the ability of Thai chicken processors to expand their market share in the EU (CPF, 2011; WTO, 2011; Rural Payment Agency, 2011).

Table 9.2 outlines tariff rates on canned tuna imports to the major importing countries. These rates indicate that all of these countries implement tariff escalation, devising progressive tariff rates on whole tuna, loin, and canned tuna imports. This measure has been set in order to protect the local canned tuna processing industry.

Besides the normal tariff barrier, the US authority set a favorable tariff rate for imported canned tuna from specific countries within a set quota. Each country is assigned a quota in accordance with its existing share in the US canned tuna market. The tariff rates are set according to the level of economic development: less developed countries receive lower rates than more developed countries. The United States also provides a zero tariff rate for canned tuna products from its unincorporated territories such as American Samoa, as well as from member countries of the Central America Free Trade Agreement (CAFTA). As a result, many canned tuna processing facilities were established in these locations to take advantage of tariff-free trade (OECD, 2010b).

The difference in effective tariff rates between whole tuna and processed tuna products may help support local processing plants by providing low-cost raw materials as well as protecting them from cheaper imported processed products. This zero tariff is also set in concordance with the aim of encouraging the import of whole tuna in order to substitute the declining activity of the local tuna fishing industry (FAO, 2009; EU TRADE, 2010; EU, 2000; Josupeit, 2010; Miyake et al., 2010).

Despite various agreements under the WTO to promote the free trade of agricultural products, developed countries are permitted to retain various measures to protect their local agrofood industries. They have employed different tariff tactics such as megatariffs and tariff escalation

Table 9.2 Import tariffs of major markets for tuna and canned tuna products

Major imported destination	Global Canned Tuna Market (Rate as percentage of price)		
	Whole Tuna	Loin	Canned Tuna
US	0%	6% (0% in quota)	12.50% (6% in quota)
EU	18% (Effective 0%)	24%	24%

Source: Elaborated by author based on WTO (2011) and OECD (2010b).

as well as nontariff measures such as agricultural subsidies, high standards of product and antidumping duties (Burfisher, 2001; AMAD, 2007; WTO, 2010).

Megatariffs are a practice that sets very high tariffs to effectively limit all imports above the minimum access amount that has been agreed under the WTO's agreements on agricultural products. The application of extremely high tariffs on a few product categories allows the imposing country to selectively protect key local industries. Tariff escalation is a practice to protect local industries whereby a higher tariff is levied on processed goods than on intermediate goods. By value, the majority of global food trade, more than 60 percent, is traded as processed products; therefore, the practice of tariff escalation produces a considerable effect on the agrofood trade. The lower tariff rate on raw materials provides low-cost supplies for local food processors. And at the same time, tariff escalation also allows local food processors to compete with imported processed products that are subjected to high tariff rates. Cramer (2003) observed that the major markets, including the United States and the EU, raise their tariff barriers along with increasing the level of processing. For instance, the EU on average levies a 13 percent tariff rate on agricultural commodities, while fully processed agricultural products are subjected to a 31 percent tariff rate (Burfisher, 2001; AMAD, 2007; WTO, 2010; Cramer, 1999; 2003).

Despite WTO agreements on the reduction of subsidies, the level of agricultural subsidy in many developed countries remains higher than developing countries. The subsidies have been used to reduce production costs, making the cost of various products artificially low and negatively affecting the agrofood trade. The subsidy has made it difficult for imported products to compete with locally subsidized products. Moreover, several developed countries have implemented export subsidies in order to promote the exporting of an excess supply of local agricultural products; this puts enormous pressure on exports from developing countries (Laird, 1997; WTO, 2010; 2011).

The United States and the EU have maintained subsidies for agricultural production, including chicken products. Starmer et al. (2006) found that these measures have resulted in monetary benefits for the US chicken processing industry, on average US$ 1.25 billion per year between 1997 and 2005 (Starmer et al., 2006; USDA, 2008). Similarly, the EU has introduced the Common Agricultural Policy (CAP) to provide EU-wide support for the agricultural industry. In particular, it provides direct export subsidies for various chicken products (Rural Payment Agency, 2011). It is estimated that approximately 40 percent of the EU common budget is spent on agriculture; however, this sector generates less than 2 percent of gross domestic product (GDP) and employs less than 5 percent of the workforce (Charlemagne, 2012).

Another important nontariff barrier is antidumping duty, which can be used to further enhance protection. Several countries have used antidumping duty to ward off cheaper imported products without sufficient proof of any misconduct by the exporting companies. This has resulted in several ongoing trade disputes among countries, including the recent application of an antidumping duty by the Chinese authorities on imported chicken products from the United States (WTO, 2010; Laird, 1997).

Various types of preferential treatment, such as reduced tariff quotas and the generalized system of preferences GSP, are set by importing countries according to specific products and the different exporting countries. The unequal tariff rates have played an important role in shaping the structure of agrofood trade and subsequently the structure of the industries. Many firms have responded to these preferences by acquiring production facilities in countries that can export to important markets at lower tariff rates, enabling them to compete effectively in these markets.

To maintain good public health, various countries have imposed different hygienic standards on imported food products. These standards are being applied to globally traded food products and thus affect the flow of trade. To prevent importing countries from using these standards as a nontariff barrier, the WTO has derived the Agreement on Sanitary and Phytosanitary Measures, the Agreements on Technical Barriers to Trade, and the Agreement on Rules of Origin as general guidelines for international food trade. Furthermore, two main organizations have been set up to oversee standards for global food trade. These include the World Organization for Animal Health (OIE) for regulations on animal health and disease, and the CODEX Alimentarius Commission for regulations on food safety (Vogel, 1995; OECD, 2010b; Blaha, 2011; Ahmed, 2006).

Despite these measures, however, the WTO agreements permit importing countries to impose their own specific measures outside the recognized international standards. These measures must be based on scientific studies as well as be essential for the protection of humans, animals, or plants. As a result, exporting firms are still obliged to follow several sets of complicated rules, specified by different importing destinations. These imposing standards thus remain an imperative factor that affects global food trade. In particular, firms from developing countries may find it difficult to meet all the certification requirements due to the relatively high cost of the process and the lack of institutional capabilities. The impact is beyond the scope of the food processing companies, however, as it extends to other activities throughout the value chain. All of these factors have made international standards an important institutional factor that prevents developing countries' firms from exporting their food products to the global market. Consequently, this inherently affects the ability of firms from developing countries to move up the value chain and become global players (Blaha, 2011; OECD, 2010b; Codex Alimentarius Commission, 2007; Vogel, 1995; Ahmed, 2006).

To comply with these standards, both government authorities and private entities within exporting countries are assuming a tremendous task: they are implementing various measures to overcome this issue. This study examines the sanitary standard as one aspect of an important trade-restricted standard that is being widely imposed on chicken and canned tuna products by major importing markets, the United States and the EU.

The regulation of food safety is an important public policy as food safety can impact directly the well-being of every citizen. Countries are therefore enforcing various standards on imported food products to ensure the health and safety of their citizens (Christopher and Vogel, 2005). Despite the original aim of protecting the health and safety of citizens, however, the imposed sanitary standards have a profound influence on the global agrofood trade. The sanitary standards that are being applied to chicken and canned tuna products are outlined as follows.

The United States and the EU are implementing various sets of standards for their imported chicken products. The United States has set a very restrictive rule based on its own Hazard Analysis, Critical Control Points and Good Manufacturing Practice assessments of the whole production chain. Based on this restrictive measure, the United States allows only a few selected countries to export chicken products to its market. These include Australia, Canada, Chile, France, the United Kingdom, Mexico, and New Zealand. The lack of eligible exporting countries is due to the fact that the US authority requests foreign countries' inspection systems to undergo a comprehensive and recurring auditing process. In addition, the eligible countries must be free from Exotic New Castle Disease, which is commonly found in major chicken-exporting countries. Consequently, the extensive standards have allowed the United States to restrict the importation of chicken products, as can be seen from the fact that very few eligible countries are major exporters of these products (USDA, 2011a; Josling et al., 2001).

The EU also enforces a restrictive set of sanitary regulations for imported chicken products, as evidenced by the small number of export-eligible countries. These 11 countries include Argentina, Brazil, Canada, Chile, China, Croatia, Iceland, Israel, Thailand, Uruguay, and the United States (USDA, 2011b; EU Directorate-General for Health and Consumers, 2011c; EU Directorate-General for Health and Consumers, 2011b).

The huge surplus in the US and EU chicken production and their position in the top five global chicken-producing countries and the top three global chicken-exporting countries may be the underlying factors behind the highly restrictive US and EU chicken markets.

Unlike US meat and poultry imports, which are regulated by the Food Safety and Inspection Service, canned tuna products, as well as other foods and drugs, are under the supervision of the Food and Drug Administration (FDA). Although lacking the 'export-eligible countries' scheme seen in the chicken market, canned tuna processors are still subjected to rigorous assessment by approved local inspection authorities. The entire value chain of canned tuna products is subjected to a vigorous monitoring process by both local authorities and the FDA (FDA, 2011a; 2011b; 2011c).

Similar to the regulation on imported chicken, the EU's control of imported canned tuna products is based on the certification of all actors in the production chain by an approved local inspection authority. A country is eligible to export its products to the EU after proving the competency of its local inspection authority. The competent authority is required to continue working with experts from the EU Food and Veterinary Office as well as investing in up-to-date equipment and staff training. There are currently approximately 100 countries that are approved for exporting fishery products to the EU. This contrasts greatly with the 11 eligible countries that can export chicken products to the EU (Blaha, 2011; EU Directorate-General for Health and Consumers, 2011a).

The major difference between the sanitary requirements for exporting chicken and canned tuna products is the use of the export-eligible scheme by major importing countries. On the one hand, there are only a few countries that can export chicken products to the US and EU markets. On the other hand, the United States omits this restrictive scheme for its imports of canned tuna, and the EU broadly grants the export right to approximately 100 countries. The varied requirements may exist because the United States and the EU seek to protect their own local chicken industries, while the insufficient local supply may force them to import low-priced, canned tuna products from overseas producers.

Compliance with, and understanding of, the complicated import-standard systems is not only a problem for local authorities but is also a paramount task for exporting companies. Besides the cost of the ongoing certification process, they are required to continuously invest a part of their profit to support certain infrastructure, such as large information technology (IT) systems for traceability data management, up-to-date scientific equipment, and ongoing personnel trainings. From interviews, several companies have recognized this issue as an important hurdle to their growth. The ongoing certification processes require continuous investment and the diversion of resources from necessary operations. The increasing requirements are evidently adding to the costs within the production chain, and, as a result, companies are operating with decreasing profitability. The increasing requirements have hindered their profitability and consequently reduced their ability to expand and move up the value chains. All of this may necessitate their mergers and acquisitions (M&A) moves – carried out in order to obtain larger scale for continuing necessary investment. Moreover, the acquisition of brand owners and food processors in major imported markets can be seen as a mechanism to bypass various tariff and nontariff barriers.

Due to the underlying differences in the method of raw material production between the two value chains, the welfare of farmed chicken will be considered in relation to the global chicken market, and the environmental regulation on canned tuna products will be considered in relation to the global canned tuna market. The important requirements set by the major import markets, including the United States and the EU, will be outlined as follows.

To a certain extent, maintaining animal welfare is an essential step toward efficient production. However, there are aspects of animal welfare, such as an animal's behavioral needs, pain, and fear, which are outside the purpose of maintaining high productivity. The consideration of animal welfare in any society would entail not only the biological and psychological components of the animal but also various aspects of the society in general. These social aspects, such as ethical concerns, moral values, and economic development, vary from country to country. As a result, animal welfare is perceived differently in various countries. To mediate the variation, the WTO has recommended a guideline for the global trade of animal and animal products in compliance with welfare standards set by the World OIE. For the welfare of chickens, it set out several rules as part of its recent 2011 Terrestrial Animal Health Code. These include mainly the transport and slaughter processes (OIE, 2011; Appleby and Sandoe, 2002; Broom and Johnson, 1993; Carenzi and Verga, 2009; Bowles et al., 2005).

Despite the internationally recognized code of practice for chicken welfare, there exists variation in welfare standards among major importing countries. In particular, the EU has clearly announced its intention to increase its welfare requirements for domestic and imported chicken products. The new directive implemented in 2010 has increased several welfare standards. For example, a farm is required to comply with the maximum density limit at 33 kg per m^2; otherwise, it needs to report to the authorities and follow a special protocol. The EU further establishes a maximum limit for temperature, hum idity, and level of ammonia and carbon dioxide in the farming environment, as well as prohibits all surgical interventions beyond therapeutic and diagnostic purposes (EU, 2007; Horne and Achterbosch, 2008).

The impact of these changes on the global chicken value chain can be observed as exporting countries and their respective chicken companies are realigning their production chains in compliance with the newly introduced legislation. This study found that in order to comply with the new rules, Thai chicken exporters together with various government agencies have spent considerable resources in transforming their production chains. A similar study by Bowles et al. (2005) found that Argentinean and Thai companies had transformed their chicken production chains in response to changing animal welfare standards required by the EU. Another radical approach was also observed: some companies, rather than transforming the whole production, designate a separate production chain for products bound for the EU market. This strategy is intended to save costs by the certification of only certain production chains instead of the whole operation (EU, 2007; Horne and Achterbosch, 2008; Avec, 2011).

The dolphin-safe standard is another example of the effect of standards imposed by developed countries on the canned tuna industries in developing countries. The regulation was introduced to prohibit dolphin-unsafe tuna products from being marketed in the United States. This has resulted in the relocation of most of the US tuna fleets from the Eastern Pacific Ocean, where dolphins and yellowfin tuna associate with each other, to the Western and Central Pacific Ocean, where they do not. This implemented standard also led to a trade embargo of tuna products from countries such as Mexico, Panama, and Venezuela that catch tuna in the Eastern Pacific Ocean. This strongly affected tuna fishing and the processing industries in these countries. Subsequently, in 1991 Mexico challenged this regulation and asked for a GATT dispute resolution panel to examine the matter. The panel ruled in favor of Mexico as 'GATT rules did not allow one country to take trade action for the purpose of attempting to enforce its own domestic laws in another country even to protect animal health or exhaustible natural resources' (WTO, 1991). In 1992, the International Dolphin Conservation Act was implemented by ten major tuna-fishing countries to create regulations for the protection of dolphins in tuna fishing. Five years after the international dolphin protection agreement and following various discussions and confrontations, the United States lifted this embargo in 1997. Although the regulation was lifted, however, the United States still enforced a requirement that is stricter than the international standard for its 'dolphin-safe' label. This practice has continued to have an impact on global tuna trading. This dispute has continued until the present day. Recently, in January 2012, the WTO ruled in favor of Mexico that the US regulation to protect dolphins is more restrictive than necessary (Gosliner, 1999; WTO, 1991; 2012b; Joseph, 1994).

The restrictions in the global agrofood trade imposed by various tariff and nontariff barriers created by developed countries have significantly reduced the competitiveness of firms from developing countries. For example, under the quota restriction, it may not be economical for developing countries and their firms to produce agrofood products for exporting to developed markets beyond the quota level, as they have to endure the extra cost. This in turn limits the ability of these firms to expand and attain economies of scale for competing with larger firms in developed markets. Moreover, without economies of scale, these firms always have lower bargaining power than other actors in the value chain, especially major retailers in developed countries. All of these factors form a solid foundation for governments from developing countries to justify various measures for supporting their firms.

The protection and the subsidizing of local chicken industries by the United States and the EU not only restricts the exports from developing countries and the expansion of their firms but also destroys the industries and the farming households in several countries, particularly low-income countries in Africa. Following trade liberalization under the WTO in the late 1990s, these countries have imported an excess supply of chicken parts such as drumsticks and wings from the United States and EU at extremely low prices. Several African countries have faced a rapid rise of chicken imports from the United States and the EU, and consequently the destruction of local chicken farming industries. In Senegal, imports increased 200-fold from 1998 to 2004, and as a result, 70 percent of chicken farms were forced out of business (Sharma et al., 2005). A similar phenomenon also occurred in other African countries (ACDIC, 2007). This necessitates a response by these countries to protect their local chicken industries. However, these low-income developing countries were unable to respond effectively as they are dependent on aid from developed countries and international organizations that enforce market liberalization upon them (Atarah, 2005; Johnson, 2009).

9.3 The responses from developing countries to support local industries

The growth of M&As can be observed in the cases of major chicken and canned tuna companies from developing countries, including 1) TUF, which acquired Chicken of the Sea in the United States and MW Brands in Europe; 2) Dongwon from South Korea, which acquired Starkist, the largest US canned tuna company; 3) JBS, which acquired Smithfield and Pilgrim's Pride, the leading beef and chicken producers in the United States; and 4) Brasil Foods, which was created by a merger between Sadia and Perdigao, two major chicken producers in Brazil. This paper compares the rise of the largest players in both the chicken and the canned tuna industries in order to demonstrate that the different levels of support by governments in developing countries is caused by varying degrees of trade restriction in these two industries.

In the case of Brazil, the largest exporter and the third-largest producer of chicken, its leading position is a result of lower production cost and an abundance of cheap corn and soybean supplies for feed production. Yet despite lower production cost, it still has difficulties exporting to the EU. Brazil has continued its negotiations with the EU for an increase in import quota and reduced limitations on various chicken exports. The US chicken market is even more restrictive than the European market, and several major chicken producers, such as Brazil and Thailand, are unable to export any products to the United States as it enforces highly restrictive rules and limits access to its market to only eight export-eligible countries (Dorémus-Mege et al., 2004; Merco Press, 2012; USDA, 2011a).

Brasil Foods is a result of the merger between the two largest chicken producers in Brazil. The newly created company has acquired the status of the largest Brazilian food company, the largest poultry exporter in the world, and the world's second-largest exporter of meat. This newly created company is poised to dominate the global poultry trade by producing approximately half of Brazil's 3.6 million tons of total chicken export. It also shares 40 percent of total Brazilian pork exports. This merged company has created greater bargaining power through its enormous scale of procurements. In 2008, Sadia/Perdigao together bought

12.5 percent of 58 million tons of total Brazilian corn production and approximately 20 percent of the 24 million tons of national soy production (Samora, 2009; Brasil Foods, 2010).

The merger exhibited the Brazilian government's intention to support industrial consolidation. The government used Perdigao, which is indirectly owned by various government pension funds, to initiate the merger with Sadia, which was suffering from a major operating loss at the time. Furthermore Brazil's state development bank took a leading role by providing financial support to Perdigao in this merger. As mentioned by the bank's president, Luciano Coutinho, the bank intends to drive consolidations in meat processing and other industries in order to create national champions that can compete head-to-head with global giants. The deal is part of US$ 58 billion in lending proposed by this state-owned bank in 2009 to support the consolidation and restructuring of Brazilian industries (Caminada, 2009; Moura and Marcelino, 2009).

The Brazilian government went further in assisting in the expansion of its local meat processing industry. In 2009, it provided a loan to JBS, its leading meat processor, to acquire Pilgrim's Pride, the second-largest chicken processor in the United States. The acquisition of Pilgrim's Pride was partially funded by the Brazilian development bank through the US$ 2 billion purchase of JBS bonds. The acquisition of this US company allows JBS to gain access to the highly restricted US chicken market. JBS is one of the world's largest producers of meat products; it is the world largest producer of beef products, and the third-largest producer in the US pork market. JBS itself is a product of aggressive M&As in the past – approximately 30 acquisitions in the past 15 years, including Smithfield, the leading pork and beef producer in the US market. The company is the second-largest player in the US beef and chicken markets. JBS has become internationalized, with more than 70 percent of its sales coming from the US market. By the end of 2009, JBS had become the world's largest beef producer and exporter, with a combined capacity to process 90,290 cattle per day. It is also one of the world's largest chicken producers, with operations in the United States, Mexico, and Puerto Rico, and a combined capacity to process 7.6 million chickens per day (Spector et al., 2009; Moura and Marcelino, 2009; Moura and Kassai, 2010; Kassai, 2010; JBS, 2010; Caminada and Marcelino, 2009; Blankfeld, 2011; Andrejczak, 2009).

In the past, the major players in the global canned tuna industry were from developed countries, particularly those in the United States, the EU, and Japan, where the majority of global demand is coming from. Due to rising production costs, these countries have lost their competitiveness in canned tuna production, and as a result, production facilities have been moved to developing countries. Many firms from developing countries are operating as small original equipment manufacturers (OEM) for international brands. With minimal trade restriction, some of these firms have expanded and attained economies of scale and subsequently moved up the value chain to higher value-added activities such as branding and distribution. TUF is an important example of a firm that has successfully followed this developmental path.

TUF, a leading seafood processor and brand owner, is currently one of the most successful Thai companies. It is an export-oriented company, of which more than 90 percent of its revenue is generated from its international operations. Its major overseas markets include the United States (50 percent), Japan (30 percent), and Europe (20 percent). In 2010, the company employed more than 12,000 workers and generated THB 71.5 billion or approximately US$ 2.26 billion in revenue (based on 2010 average exchange rate at 31.7 THB/US$). The company is the world's largest supplier of canned tuna. and currently controls approximately 25 percent of the global canned tuna market.

TUF has expanded from being a small contract manufacturer with revenue of approximately US$ 10 million in 1990 to becoming a major supplier for leading brands in major markets around the world, before acquiring Chicken of the Sea in 1997 (Pederson, 1999; PR Newswire, 2000). It also merged with several local canned tuna processors in Thailand, which included Songkla Canning in 1998. TUF also merged with another canned tuna processor, Thai Ruamsin Pattana, in 1999. These mergers enabled TUF to expand its processing capacity, revenue, and profit by around 30 percent. These events exhibited the company's intention to expand aggressively through consolidating its position in the local industry. In 2003, TUF expanded further by acquiring Empress International, a major seafood distributor in the United States. Through this acquisition, the company established the Xcellent brand for its business-to-business market. Empress currently supplies its seafood products to leading restaurant chains in the US market. In July 2010, the company reached another important milestone when it acquired MW Brands, one of the largest seafood processors in Europe (Kultawanich 2010).

The MW Brands group is a result of several M&As in the past. The company was part of the food giant Heinz until 2006, when it was packaged and sold for US$ 522 million to Trilantic, a private equity arm of the now-bankrupt Lehman Brothers. Trilantic was later taken over by its management in 2009. TUF succeeded in bidding for MW Brands (Ficai, 2010; Kate and Webb, 2010; TUF, 2010a; 2010b) whose vertically integrated business operates its own fishing fleet and production facilities that are located in four different countries. MW Brands' primary processing facilities are located in Ghana and the Seychelles in order to take advantage of low operating costs and close proximity to raw material supply. The company also has further processing facilities in France and Portugal to take advantage of the close proximity to major European markets. The company has its own distribution channels and leading brands in the European market (Kate and Webb, 2010; TUF, 2010a; 2010b).

This acquisition marks a significant breakthrough for the TUF in the European seafood market. It has complemented TUF's strong position in the United States, and resulted in TUF's becoming one of the largest seafood companies in the world. The company has achieved greater economies of scale and scope as well as better negotiating power with suppliers, which has resulted in improved profitability. The addition of high value-added businesses, in particular strong European brands, to TUF operations would certainly improve the company's future operating margin. Since the integration, the sales of its own branded products have risen from less than 50 percent to 61 percent of its total sales. Moreover, by exporting from MW Brands's processing plants in Ghana and the Seychelles, TUF can gain a significant advantage from lower import duty to the European market (Bangkok Post, 2010; Ficai, 2010; Kate and Webb, 2010; TUF, 2010a; 2010b; 2011).

Through the acquisition of MW Brands, the company gained membership in EUROTHON (European Tropical Tuna Trade and Industry Committee), a powerful, exclusive lobby group intended to protect the economic interests of the various stakeholders in European canned tuna industries. The membership of TUF has diverted the attention of EUROTHON away from the competitive threat from processors based in Southeast Asia. Its membership should also fragment the political coherence of the EU tuna lobby group on various trade restriction issues (Hamilton et al., 2011).

The success of TUF is largely due to its own efforts, devising and implementing appropriate strategies at the right time. The Thai government has not provided any specific support to the firm. The government simply devised generic measures to support the internationalization of local firms, such as tax incentives and lower borrowing costs. Moreover, the lack of coordination and unified direction among various government authorities has diluted the efforts and reduced the effectiveness of these generic measures. In particular, there are several Thai government agencies that have similar or intersecting roles with other agencies. The lack of tax-sparing measures for double taxation also discourages local firms from expanding overseas.

9.4 Discussion and Conclusion: Comparing the actions and reactions

The difference in restriction of international trade between canned tuna and chicken products may be the reason behind the variation in market concentration between these two industries that can be observed. This difference may play an important role in forging the developmental path for large global players in both industries. The variation in protection levels between these two industries has also resulted in different responses by governments and firms in developing countries (Table 9.3).

The ascension of TUF, the world's largest canned tuna company from Thailand, was not a result of direct support from the government. It is, rather, based on the success of the company in moving up the value chain in the less restrictive global trading environment, from simple OEM manufacturer for global brands and global retailers through to the setting up of distribution channels and the acquisition of global brands. This is in contrast to the rise of Brasil Foods to become the largest

Table 9.3 A global and local overview of the chicken and canned tuna industries

Industry	International Trade	Restriction in major developed countries (the US and the EU)	Response from governments in developing country
Chicken	Restrictive trade, trade is around 11% of global production	These countries devise various measure to protect and nurture their local industries and firms	They come up with various responsive and nurturing measures to offset the difficulties
Canned Tuna	Relatively relaxed global trading regime, around 65% of global production	Less restrictive due to insufficient local supply of canned tuna products in developed countries' markets	Less reactive and relying more on private response

Table 9.4 The different paths in becoming the largest exporters in chicken and canned tuna

The largest exporter	Industry	International Trade	Support in becoming the largest player
Brasil Foods	Chicken	Restrictive trade	The merger was funded by government banks with support from government pension funds as a major shareholder
TUF	Canned Tuna	Relatively relaxed	No direct or specific support

chicken exporter in the world. The latter company has received direct financial support from the state-owned bank as well as indirect support from government pension funds, the major shareholder of the acquiring company, Perdigao. Table 9.4 compares the rise of the largest chicken and canned tuna exporting companies.

The diversity within these two value chains represents the nature of international trade, in which the varied actions by major importing countries can produce different responses by exporting countries in creating global giants. The Brazilian government has been directly involved in promoting its national champions (in particular, Brasil Foods, which has become the world's largest chicken exporter), while the rise of TUF was not the result of specific support from the Thai government.

In conclusion, this study highlights the direct correlation between the level of import restriction for certain agrofood products in developed markets, including the United States and the EU, and subsequent reactions by developing country governments in supporting and nurturing their firms.

Conclusion: State Support for Emerging Market Multinationals
Andreas Nölke

The contributions to this volume demonstrate in ample ways that home state support measures are crucial for the outward expansion of emerging market multinationals. Some of these support measures are very obvious, like the Brazilian National Developing Bank (BNDES) financial support for the acquisitions of Brazilian multinational corporations (MNCs) (Masiero et al.), while others are subtler, such as the various informal *guanxi* links between Chinese businessmen and state representatives (Nölke). Interestingly, state support within the international regulatory environment also appears to matter a lot with regard to emerging market MNC activity, as demonstrated for the cases of foreign direct investment (FDI) regulation (Clifton et al.) and trade (Kingkaew). This conclusion chapter maps the various measures in a systematic way. It also highlights commonalities and differences among multinationals based in established and emerging countries (Mikler; Ozawa). Within this context, it will not only be based on the contributions to the volume (references in brackets without year of publication) but will also embed their findings in the existing literature on the topic (for instance, Goldstein, 2007; 2013; Nölke, 2013). Finally it will highlight some conclusions for further research as well as for policymakers.

Basically, there are two broad types of state support for MNCs based in emerging economies within this specific type of state capitalism. On the one hand, we are witnessing domestic measures that support the growth of these companies in their home economies, for example, by direct financial support, or regulatory measures that are geared toward the particular requirements of these companies. On the other hand, the focus is on state support during the process of outward extension of these companies, for example, taking the form of diplomatic support for the access to natural resources in other countries or by negotiating bilateral or multilateral agreements.

1 Domestic support measures for home MNCs in emerging markets

For analyzing the role of domestic support measures, I am using the well-established heuristics of the comparative capitalism research program, as inter alia developed within the varieties of capitalism (VoC) approach (Hall and Soskice, 2001a). Although this approach has been explicitly developed in opposition to the very state-orientated neocorporatist theories of the 1970s and 1980s, its distinction between various institutional spheres and complementarities still allows for a good overview of state support measures for large companies from emerging economies (Mikler). Five institutional spheres are typical for VoC studies: corporate finance, corporate governance, industrial relations, education and training, and the transfer of innovation within the economy (Jackson and Deeg, 2006). As shall be demonstrated below, these five categories do not exhaust the range of state support measures from multinational companies in emerging markets, and thus will be complemented by factors such as sector-specific regulatory policies (Ozawa). The focus, however, is on specific support measures, thereby excluding overall coordination mechanisms such as close, formal or informal interpersonal networks between major corporations and public officials (Nölke).

Corporate finance: State subsidies: In contrast to companies based in liberal market economies as well as to an increasing number of large companies based in coordinated market economies, successful multinational companies from emerging markets are less dependent on finances raised on international capital markets (Jeong; Nölke; Grätz). Although many of these companies feature a listing at the New York or London stock exchange, the resources derived from these listings are of limited importance for company finances, in particular in comparison to internally generated resources and lending from national banks. The most important effect of this particular structure of corporate finance is that the expansion of MNCs from emerging markets is limited in its exposure toward short-term shareholder value maximization. This does not only allow for very long-term strategies of global market share expansion but also for the accumulation of a financial cushion. The latter proved to be particularly helpful during the most recent global financial crisis (Nölke). Typically these companies may also use direct or indirect public subsidies, including tax incentives, financial guarantees, and credit provided by state banks or state-controlled pension funds (Goldstein, 2007, p. 98). This access to public resources is also responsible for providing these companies more profitable financial conditions than many Western competitors. Of particular prominence are the activities of the BNDES that set up a special line of credit in 2002 in order to support outward foreign direct investment (OFDI) by Brazilian multinationals. Although the allocation of those credits is somewhat controversial, it has led to a series of acquisitions of foreign companies by Brazilian multinationals (Masiero et al.; Kingkaew).

Corporate governance: State ownership and state control: Business finance in emerging market MNCs is closely connected to the dominating form of corporate governance. These companies are usually not dominated by atomized minority shareholders or institutional investors on the global capital markets, but by their founding families or by the state (Grätz; Jeong; Taylor). Correspondingly, 'companies from these states are not subject to the discipline of the market for corporate control' (Goldstein, 2013, p. 162). Again, the absence of an open market for corporate control allows companies to avoid the short-term requirements of global capital markets – a management that does not have to fear an unfriendly takeover can more easily ignore comments of financial analysts than the management of companies without 'block holders'. An obvious contrast furthermore stems from the existence of a large number of companies that are owned by the state or are under state control. Many of these companies are under the radar of Western media such as the Financial Times listing, since this listing only contains companies with a minimum share of 15 percent of minority shareholders. State-controlled companies are of course particularly relevant in China, but also in Russia and generally in natural resource industries (Wooldridge, 2012). The extent of the state control over these companies is usually underestimated, given that most surveys only look at the share of public ownership. Particularly in Brazil, the state – as well as the families cooperating with the state – succeed with a number of stock pyramids as well as by using the support of state-dominated pension funds in order to dominate many companies in spite of a nominally rather limited ownership of shares (Abu-El-Haj, 2007, p. 106). However, even the systematic reconstruction of those legal agreements – in the sense of an identification of the finally dominating shareholder – would underestimate the degree of state control over many large corporations in emerging markets, given that this exercise would still not cover the close informal networks between business and public authorities (Grätz; Nölke; Grätz, 2013b).

Industrial relations, education, and training: Tolerance toward selective implementations of labor rights and provision of a large number of university graduates: A formal study of labor law in large emerging markets might lead to the somewhat misleading conclusion that this legal framework contains a number of highly important protection measures. However, this finding would stand in clear contrast to the observation that many of these companies owe their excellent competitiveness both on domestic and international markets to a strategy of low labor costs (Nölke). We may solve the tension between these observations by differentiating the core staff of large companies that are being protected by labor laws and organized by unions on the one side and the large majority of neither organized nor protected workers in highly flexible labor or even in the informal sector on the other (Phillips, 2004, pp. 161–164). State support here is highly relevant since the state is keeping an eye shut regarding comprehensive enforcement of labor laws. In addition, the education and training system in large emerging markets is dominated and organized by the state, in contrast to frequently private education institutions in liberal market economies and to a tight cooperation between business labor unions and the state for educational training in the coordinated market economy of Germany. Even if the qualification profiles of these graduates do not provide what is needed for all kinds of companies, state institutions still support emerging market multinationals by qualifying a very large number of students, thereby supporting the strategy of these companies to be competitive by having access to cheap labor, particularly in comparison to MNCs based in the traditional centers of the global economy (Ramamurti, 2008). Correspondingly, the success of the pharmaceutical industry in India is unthinkable without the large number of engineers recruited from Indian universities who are getting paid comparatively low salaries (Taylor).

Transfer of innovation: Selective protection of intellectual property and promotion of 'national champions': State support measures play an important role in the acquisition of innovative technologies by emerging market MNCs (Ozawa; Masiero et al.). Of particular importance are policies with regard to intellectual property rights and to competition policy. At least during the first phase of catch-up, companies from emerging markets depend on access to the intellectual property rights of companies from the center of the world economy, particularly in the context of joint ventures and other forms of business cooperation (Goldstein, 2007, p. 119). The role of the state is primarily important for avoiding an enforcement of global intellectual property regulations in too strict and comprehensive a manner (Taylor). During the later phases, this form of innovation transfer will be complemented by the acquisition of companies in Western Europe, Japan, or the United States, and finally also by indigenous innovation. In particular in China, companies are responsible for a permanently increasing the number of global patent applications (Seiser, 2012; Goldstein, 2013, p. 166). The tolerant attitude of public authorities in large emerging economies with regard to the enforcement of global rules in the field of intellectual property rights is therefore not something that is necessarily permanent. It could also give way to an increasing motivation of emerging markets MNCs to enforce their own intellectual property rights. However, during recent decades, most emerging market MNCs demonstrated an interest in a rather weak form of protection of these rights in order to allow 'reverse engineering'. Correspondingly, the US government is still quite unhappy about the state of affairs: 'While the BRIC countries have taken significant steps towards improving the letter of their intellectual property laws, and initiatives have occurred to enforce these laws, widespread enforcement of intellectual property rights against local piracy and counterfeiting continues to be insufficient' (Bird, 2006, p. 362).

The prerogatives of a belated integration into the global economy are also highly important for the design of competition policies in large emerging economies (Goldstein, 2007, pp. 99–102). In order for the companies of these economies to be able to compete with companies from developed economies, we are witnessing – similar to the traditional French industrial policy – the creation of so-called 'national champions' (Ozawa; Grätz; Masiero et al.; Kingkaew). Typical considerations of competition policies in the European Union (EU) and the United States such as the protection of consumer prices are frequently neglected in order to support the expansion strategy of emerging market multinationals. An archetypical case of this kind of strategy is the telecommunication empire of the Mexican Carlos Slim Helú, who not only received preferable conditions during the privatization of the Mexican telecommunication sector but also held a temporary monopoly on the Mexican market in order to accumulate sufficient resources to buy telecommunication companies in other Latin American states and more recently in the EU.

Particularities of the regulatory context in emerging markets: Not all public support measures for emerging market MNCs can be identified by using the categories of comparative capitalism, given that the latter has been developed for the case of companies from the established center of the global economy. An important exception relates to an experience with a particular institutional context of privatization processes that has benefited Latin American multinationals (Goldstein, 2007, p. 69). During the last decades many sectors in Latin America have been partially or completely privatized. This has led to particular competitive advantages for those companies that have established themselves during or after the wave of privatizations. Correspondingly, 'multilatinas' have learned the rules of the privatization game earlier than many Western companies (for instance, related to the design of private-public partnerships), thereby supporting these companies during later rounds of privatization. Regarding the regulatory context, other particularities are the stark differentiation between sectors in China, where some sectors are deeply liberalized and others remain protected (Nölke), or the importance of sector-specific regulations in India (Taylor).

In conclusion, state domestic support measures are an important explanatory factor for the rise of emerging market MNCs, even as in most of these countries – except in China – the largest parts of these companies are not owned by public authorities anymore. Theories for explaining the rise of these companies as well as their transnational expansion therefore need to be enlarged by specific state support factors, requiring a combination of concepts derived from international business and political science. The established heuristics of comparative capitalism can serve as an overall structure for this enterprise, but has to be complemented by specific factors, such as experience in a postprivatization regulatory environment. Another even more important complement exists with regard to the transnational dimension of capitalism: public support measures are not only necessary for the domestic rise of these companies but also for their cross-border activities. Here we need to complement concepts from comparative capitalism and international business with those from international political economy (Nölke, 2011a).

2 Support of emerging market MNCs in international politics

The close cooperation between emerging markets' MNCs and home state institutions is not limited to domestic issues. This cooperation has been complemented by collaboration with regard to transnational politics. The latter mainly pertains to activities that directly support access to markets or resources for these companies (including OFDI support, access to natural resources, and creation of regional markets). After describing these, I will deal with activities that support the expansion of these companies by more indirect activities (negotiation of global economic norms, selective implementation of such norms).

OFDI support policies: Somewhat in-between national measures for company support and transnational measures are programs for the support of outward direct investment (Buckley et al., 2010, pp. 252–272; Mirza, et al., 2011, pp. 30–32). On the one hand we find rather indirect measures that do not necessarily focus on the support of OFDI. These include several aspects of general economic liberalization such as the abolition of government capital controls or licensing permits. On the other hand we also find a number of measures that are directly meant for the stimulation of OFDI, not only direct OFDI-related subsidies but also tax rebates, investment insurance, and the creation of agencies for the support of FDI (Nölke; Taylor; Masiero et al.; Clifton et al.). In the context of the liberalization of the Indian economy, these measures included the relaxation of OFDI restrictions with regard to specific sectors, target countries, and ownership shares (Taylor and Nölke, 2010, p. 157). A particular advantage of multinational differences stemming from large emerging markets is the strong weight that their governments are able to mobilize within corresponding negotiations (van Tulder, 2010, pp. 63–65). In contrast to smaller emerging markets or developing countries, these governments can design OFDI regimes that are very helpful for domestic MNCs, by enabling simple access to host economies and restricting access from multinationals from established economies to their home markets.

Collaboration for the access to natural resources: A particular intensive form of cooperation between governments and large companies from emerging markets is to be found in the field of access to natural resources in foreign economies. Natural resources traditionally are more strongly controlled by state authorities than most other economic sectors, since their exploitation does not only follow economic but also political prerogatives. Correspondingly, companies from emerging markets make use of their close collaboration with home governments in order to get access to resources in other countries (Goldstein, 2007, pp. 105–116; ten Brink, 2011, pp. 7–9, pp. 12–14). This is particularly well known for the case of China, given that the Chinese government frequently utilizes its diplomacy for the access of Chinese companies to natural resources in other countries, for example, in the oil sector, including countries that are avoided by Western companies, particularly due to concerns regarding human rights (Nölke). A typical measure includes the linkage of funds for the economic system to the utilization of goods and services of multinational companies based in the home country, or the linkage of assistance to the granting of access to domestic markets for these companies (Buckley et al., 2010, p. 289; Konijn and van Tulder, forthcoming).

Just as prominent is the close cooperation between public authorities and companies from oil, gas, uranium mining, and aluminum in the case of Russia (Grätz; Grätz, 2013b, 2013c).

Negotiation of bilateral and regional trade and investment agreements: Multinational companies are among the most important driving forces of the establishment of bi- and multilateral trade and investment agreements and double tax agreements (Jeong; Clifton et al.; Kingkaew). These agreements do not only support multinational companies by granting access to foreign markets but also the transnational integration of emerging market companies in global value-added chains, in particular if those are linked with elements of deep integration, for example, the abolition of behind-the-border barriers (Claar and Nölke, 2012). Where the process of trade liberalization on the global level has been stagnant for many years now, the negotiation of bilateral and regional trade and investment agreements is very active (Solis et al. 2009). MNCs from emerging markets are particularly dependent on these agreements, given that their domestic markets are less deep than those of the EU or the United States. The close collaboration between those companies and their government is focused on maintaining their comparative advantages with regard to the established economies, for example, with regard to avoiding strict labor norms or the powerful enforcement of intellectual property rights. At the same time they are striving for the establishment of larger markets via South-South cooperation, for example, via the establishment of Mercosur in Latin America as a domain of Brazilian multinationals (Flynn, 2007). These activities, however, are also not uncontroversial, as Brazilian companies and the Mexican telecommunication company América Móvil now sometimes take on a position of dominance in some small Latin American economies that is comparable to the traditional role of US multinationals (Clifton et al., 2007, p. 17).

Representation of the preferences of MNCs in international institutions: The discussion of public support measures for the support of emerging markets multinationals has already indicated that some of these measures are potentially in conflict with the still-dominating institutions of the liberal global economic order (Nölke and Taylor, 2010, pp. 170–173; Nölke, 2011b, pp. 283–287). These potential conflicts include regulations of intellectual property rights as put down in the agreement on Trade-Related Intellectual Property Rights (TRIPS) of the World Trade Organization (WTO). They also relate to the attempt by some Western economies to use the WTO or the International Labour Organisation in order to establish basic labor or social rights, thereby threatening the competitive advantages of multinationals based in large emerging markets. However, single emerging markets are not necessarily alone in their opposition to specific Western norms: 'Despite their differences, big BRIC businesses and multinational corporations have common interests and are likely to find common ground to influence global trade and investment rules' (Goldstein, 2013, p. 162; see also Armijo and Katada, forthcoming). Due to the close cooperation between state and large emerging economies, as well as the size of these economies generally, they have been able to prevent further liberalization measures or the forceful implementation of these measures within international institutions in recent years (van Tulder, 2010, p. 68). However, this success is still in the balance. If the United States succeeds in pushing through its trade and investment agenda via the negotiation of the Trans-Pacific Partnership Agreement (TPP) and the Transatlantic Trade and Investment Partnership (TTIP), this would go much further than the blocked Doha agenda.[1]

On closer examination, the behavior of emerging market MNCs demonstrates that they tend to be less relevant as direct transnational political actors in comparison to multinational companies from the United States and the EU. Whereas the latter tend to act as independent lobbying institutions at international conferences or collaborate with other companies as well as with nongovernmental organizations in the context of transnational governance, MNCs from emerging markets tend to rely on the representation of their interests via their national government (Nölke, 2011b, pp. 280–282). An important exception to this rule relates to the activities of Brazilian companies in the field of corporate social responsibility, given that the latter are quite active participants in these activities (Pena, forthcoming), as they are in other fields, such as trade regulation (Hopewell, 2013). However, taking into account that rules of corporate social responsibility are only related to a small share of companies in the emerging markets (including multinationals in Brazil), this exception still confirms the general rule.

Support via less stringent implementation of international norms: Emerging market MNCs do not necessarily have to mobilize against global institutions that are threatening their business conduct, since they are also supported by their national governments through the selective implementation of these norms. This not only refers to the sometimes somewhat haphazard outcome of the TRIPS agreement, but also to Organization for Economic Cooperation and Development (OECD) guidelines in the field of corporate governance. The focus of these guidelines is on the protection of minority shareholders and institutional investors, which contradicts the practices of MNCs from large emerging markets. However, given that these OECD guidelines are not binding, conflicts of interest can be solved by simply not implementing these norms in a comprehensive manner. Similarly, accounting regulations set by the International Accounting Standards Board (IASB) appeal to the transparency requirements of Western investors on international capital markets, something that is not on the priority list of many emerging market MNCs. Still, usually they are not being challenged head-on, but their implementation is less stringent than might be desirable from the perspective of the IASB. A third example relates to the implementation of WTO norms, for example, with regard to public subsidies for emerging markets corporations via public development banks. The deviating practice of the Brazilian BNDES has come to light in the context of the trade conflict between Airbus versus Canada, given that the BNDES support for research and development of Embraer has earned a charge of unfair competition with regard to the Canadian company Bombardier (Flynn, 2007, p. 19).

3 Implications

The contributions to this volume have demonstrated that the home state still matters a lot for MNCs, not only for those from emerging markets (Mikler, Ozawa). This goes against claims from both orthodox liberals and orthodox Marxists that assume that in the context of advanced globalization, MNCs are increasingly footloose. Instead, we may conclude that the close collaboration between emerging market MNCs and their home governments amount to something that may be considered a new form of state capitalism. In contrast to previous waves of state capitalism, however, state capitalism 3.0 is neither generally protectionist (1.0), nor centrally directed (2.0), but rather based on a variety of formal and informal cooperative relationships between public authorities and individual companies. The sophisticated management of both inward and outward foreign direct investments plays a central role within this new wave of state capitalism, based on circumstances that were hardly available during previous waves, that is, an intensively globalized economic system. Domestic elites face the need for national development on the one hand, and want to retain national control on the other hand – a tension that frequently is solved by the protection of domestic capital and the initiation of diverse policies in order to build up national champions.[2]

Our findings have implications for different strands of theorizing. Not only established theories on multinational corporations such as the eclectic paradigm (Dunning, 1986) or the product cycle model (Wells, 1983) need to be modified in order to take the specific circumstances of emerging market MNCs into account but also those theories that have specifically been developed to take into account these companies, such as the Linking, Leverage, Learning-approach (Mathews, 2002a,b, 2006a,b), need to be further developed (Masiero et al.). Based on concepts derived from comparative capitalism and international political economy, but mainly based on empirical studies, the contributions to this volume may provide a starting point for the necessary theoretical revisions. Further theory development, however, is not only necessary on the side of students of international business but also on the side of development studies. While our notion of state capitalism fits well with earlier debates in this discipline (Johnson, 1982; Wade, 2004; Bresser-Pereira, 2010), it also contains important modifications. Our notion of state capitalism 3.0 is clearly different from earlier thinking on the developmental state. In fact, it is difficult to imagine a state that still has the capacity for coherent, centrally directed industrial planning during the current phase of global liberal capitalism, certainly in the case of large emerging economies. At the same time, our observations clearly contradict (neo-)liberal notions of the thorough economic openness that is assumed to go hand in hand with increasing amounts of FDI, but also dependency theorists' assumptions that that FDI necessarily is a force for evil.

Finally, our results should be relevant for policymakers as well. Over the last years, the rise of emerging market multinationals has increasingly led to concerns about unfair competition and undue (foreign) state influence upon business, as, for example, recently demonstrated by a report to the US Congress (Martin, 2012). These concerns carry considerable conflict potential, particularly in the case of China: 'The Chinese model of state support for outward FDI is partly explained by skepticism regarding western ideas about relying on the market, which prompts authorities to see the world in terms of brutal competition for limited resources and therefore to seek ownership rather than long-term, arm's length contracts. In the west, in turn, many consider Chinese corporate strategies as part of a wider plot to control the world's economy' (Goldstein, 2013, p. 167). Correspondingly, it seems highly important to spread some understanding of the rationality behind these different strategies, in order to prevent unnecessary conflicts, bilaterally and at the level of multilateral institutions. After all, the political fragmentation that is going hand in hand with the evolution of state capitalism 3.0 makes it difficult to identify a single source of political authority suitable to be a competent partner for negotiating the rules of capitalism in the context of the rise of emerging market multinationals – but it also decreases the need to be afraid of some kind of new directorate for the world economy.

Notes

1. I owe this point to an anonymous reviewer.
2. I am grateful to Jonas Grätz for highlighting this point.

Bibliography

Abu-El- Haj, J. (2007) 'From Interdependence to Neo-Mercantilism: Brazilian Capitalism in the Age of Globalization', *Latin American Perspectives*, 34(5), 92–114.
ACDIC (2007) *No More Chicken, Please* (Yaoundé: Association Citoyenne de Défense des Intérêts Collectifs).
Aden, A. H. (2001) *The Rise of the Rest: Challenges to the West from Late-Industrialized Economies* (New York: OxfordUniversity Press).
Ahmed, M. (2006) *Market Access and Trade Liberalisation in Fisheries* (Geneva: International Centre for Trade and Sustainable DevelopmentICTSD).
Aitken, B. J. and A. E. Harrison (1999) 'Do domestic firms benefit from foreign direct investment? Evidence from Venezuela', *American Economic Review*, 89, 605–618.
Alem, A. and C. Cavalcanti (2005) 'O BNDES e o apoio à internacionalização das empresas brasileiras: algumas reflexões', *Revista do BNDES*, 12(24), 43–76.
Alfaro, L., A. Chanda, S. Kalemli-Ozcan and S. Sayek (2004) 'FDI and economic growth: The role of local financial markets', *Journal of International Economics*, 64, 89–112.
Allen, F., R. Chakrabarti, S. De, J. Qian and M. Qian (2006) 'Financing Firms in India',*University of Pennsylvania, Wharton Financial Institutions Center Working Paper*, 06–08.
AMAD (2007) Agricultural Market Access Database, http://www.amad.org/co untrylist/0,3349,en_35049325_35049378_35118135_1_1_1_1,00.html, date accessed August 20, 2011.
Aman, E. (2009) 'Technology, Public Policy and the Emergence of Brazilian Multinationals', in L. Brainard and L. Martinez-Diaz (eds) *Brazil as an Economic Superpower? Understanding Brazil's Changing Role in the Global Economy* (Washington, DC: Brookings Institution Press).
Amihud, Y. and B. Lev (1981) 'Risk Reduction as a Managerial Motive for Conglomerate Mergers', *Bell Journal of Economics*, 12(2), 605–617.
Amihud, Y. and B. Lev (1999) 'Does Corporate Ownership Structure Affect Its Strategy toward Diversification?', *Strategic Management Journal*, 20(11), 1063–1069.
Amsden, A. H. (1989) *Asia's Next Giant: South Korea and Late Industrialization* (Oxford: Oxford University Press).
Amsden, A. H. (1997) 'South Korea: Enterprising Groups and Entrepreneurial Government', in A. D. Chandler, F. Amatori and T. Hikino (eds)*Big Business and the Wealth of Nations* (Cambridge: Cambridge University Press).
Amsden, A. H. (2001) *The Rise of 'The Rest'– Challenges To the West From Late-Industrializing Economies* (Oxford: Oxford University Press).
Amsden, A. H. (2008) 'The Wild Ones: Industrial Policies in Developing Countries', in N. Serra and J. Stiglitz (eds) *The Washington Consensus Reconsidered: Towards a New Global Governance* (Oxford: Oxford University Press).

Amsden, A. H. (2012) 'National Companies or Foreign Affiliates: Whose Contribution to Growth is Greater?'*Columbia FDI Perspectives*, No. 60.

Anderson, J. (2007) 'The HUMINT Offensive from Putin's Chekist State', *International Journal of Intelligence and CounterIntelligence*, 20(2), 258–316.

Andreff, W. (2003) 'The New Transnational Corporations: Outward Foreign Direct Investment from Post-Communist Economies in Transition', *Transnational Corporations*, 12(2), 73–118.

Andreff, W. (2013) 'Maturing Strategies of Russian Multinational Companies: Comparison with Chinese Multinationals', in D. Dyker (ed.) *Foreign Investment, The World Scientific Reference on Globalisation in Eurasia and the Pacific Rim* (London: Imperial College Press).

Andrejczak, M. (2009) 'Brazil's JBS to Acquire 64% Stake in Bankrupt Pilgrim's Pride', *MarketWatch The Wall Street Journal*, September 16, 2009.

Annushkina, O. and R. T Colonel (2013) 'Foreign Market Selection by Russian MNEs –Beyond a Binary Approach?', *Critical Perspectives on International Business*, 9(1/2), 58–87.

Aoki, M., G. Jackson and H. Miyajima (2007) *Corporate Governance in Japan: Institutional Change and Organizational Diversity* (Oxford: Oxford University Press).

Appleby, M. C. and P. Sandoe. (2002) 'Philosophical Debate on the Nature of Well-Being: Implications for Animal Welfare', *Animal Welfare*, 11, 283–294.

Arbix, G. and L. Caseiro (2011) 'Destination and Strategy of Brazilian Multinationals', *Economics, Management and Financial Markets*, 6(1), 207–238.

Arestis, P. (2004) 'Washington Consensus and Financial Liberalisation', *Journal of Post Keynesian Economics*, 27(2), 251–271.

Armijo, L. E. and S. Katada (2014, forthcoming) *Global Rebalancing and Financial Statecraft* (Basingstoke: Palgrave MacMillan).

Åslund, A. (2007) *Russia's Capitalist Revolution: Why Market Reforms Succeeded and Democracy Failed?* (Washington, DC: Petersen Institute).

Åslund, A. (2012) 'The Enigmatic Russian Banking System: An Introduction', *Eurasian Geography and Economics*, 53(2), 244–249.

Atarah, L. (2005) *Playing Chicken: Ghana vs. the IMF* (San Francisco: CorpWatch).

Aulakh, P. S. (2007) 'Emerging multinationals from developing economies: Motivations, paths and performance', *Journal of International Management*, 13, 235–240.

AVEC (2011) *AVEC Annual Report 2010* (Brussels: Association of Poultry Processors and Poultry Trade in the EU Countries AVEC).

Balcet, G. and S. Bruschieri (2010) 'Acquisition of Technologies and Multinational Enterprise Growth in the Automotive and the Pharmaceutical Industries: Drivers and Strategies', in K. P. Sauvantand J. P. Pradhan (eds) *The Rise of Indian Multinationals: Perspectives on Indian Outward Foreign Direct Investment* (New York: Palgrave Macmillan).

Baldwin, D. A. (1985) *Economic Statecraft* (Princeton: Princeton University Press).

Balzer, H. (2005) 'The Putin Thesis and Russian Energy Policy', *Post Soviet Affairs*, 21(3), 210–225.

Bangkok Post (2010) 'TUF Bids for French Firm US Track Record Points to Success', *Bangkok Post*, June 12, 2010.

Bank of Korea (2012) 'Impact and Implication of Expanding Overseas Production by Korean Companies', *Bank of Korea Economic Review*, No. 2012–2014.

Bardhan, A. and D. Jaffee (2005) 'On Intra-Firm Trade and Manufacturing Outsourcing and Offshoring', in E. M. Graham (ed.) *Multinationals and Foreign Investment in Economic Development* (Basingstoke: Palgrave Macmillan).
Bartlett, C. A. and Ghoshal, S. 'Going Global: Lessons from LateMovers.'*Harvard Business Review* 78 (2), 132–142.
Basu, A. K. and U. Grote (2006) 'China as Standard-Setter: The Examples of GM-Cotton and Ecological and Food Safety Standards', *The Seventh Annual Global Development Conference Pre-Conference Workshop on Asian and Other Drivers of Global Change*. St. Petersburg, January 18–19, 2006.
BCG (2006) *The BCG 100 New Global Challengers: How Top Firms from Rapidly Developing Economies are Changing the World* (Boston: The Boston Consulting Group).
BCG (2013) *Allies and Adversaries: 2013 BCG Global Challengers* (Boston: The Boston Consulting Group).
Bell, S. (2011) 'Do We Really Need a New "Constructivist Institutionalism" to Explain Institutional Change?', *British Journal of Political Science*, 41(4), 883–906.
Bergman, A. (2006) 'FDI and Spillover Effects in the Indian Pharmaceutical Industry', *Research and Information System for Developing Countries, RIS Discussion Papers*, 113.
Berle, A. A. and G. C. Means (1932) *The Modern Corporation and Private Property* (New York: Macmillan).
Bhagwati, J. (2004) *In Defense of Globalization* (Oxford: Oxford University Press).
Bhagwati J., A. Panagariya and T.N. Srinivasan, (2004) 'The muddles over outsourcing', *Journal of Economic Perspectives*, 18(4) 93–114.
Bhalla, S. (1977) 'Agricultural Growth: Role of Institutional and Infrastructural Factors', *Economic and Political Weekly*, 12, 1898–1905.
Bird, R. C. (2006), 'Defending Intellectual Property Rights in the BRIC Economies', *American Business Law Journal*, 43(2), 317–363.
BIS (2012) Annual Report 2011, Czech Intelligence Agency, http://www.bis.cz/n/ar2011en.pdf, date accessed June 16, 2013.
Black, B. S., B. Metzger, T. O'Brien and Y. M. Shin (2001) 'Corporate Governance in Korea at the Millennium – Enhancing International Competitiveness. Final Report and Legal Reform Recommendations to the Ministry of Justice of the Republic of Korea', *Journal of Corporation Law*, 26(3), 537–608.
Blaha, F. (2011) *EU Market Access & Eco-Labelling for Fishery and Aquaculture Products* (Zurich: Swiss Import Promotion Programme SIPPO).
Blankfeld, K. (2011) 'JBS: The Story behind the World's Biggest Meat Producer', *Forbes*, April 21, 2011.
Blomström, M., R. E. Lipsey and M. Zejan (1994) 'What explains developing country growth?' in W. Baumol, R. Nelson and E. Wolf (eds.) *Convergence and Productivity: Gross-National Studies and Historical Evidence* (Oxford: Oxford University Press).
BMI (2013) Verfassungsschutzbericht 2012 Vorabfassung, Bundesministerium des Innern, http://www.verfassungsschutz.de/embed/vsbericht-2012-vorabfassung.pdf, dateaccessed June 16, 2013.
BNDES (1995) *Caracterização do processo de internacionalização de grupos econômicos privados brasileiros* (Rio de Janeiro: Banco Nacional de Desenvolvimento Econômico e Social).

Bonturi, M. and K. Fukasaku (1993) 'Globalisation and Intra-firm Trade: An Empirical Note', *OECD Economic Studies*, 20(Spring), 145–159.

Borensztein, E., J. De Gregorio and J. W. Lee (1998) 'How does foreign direct investment affect economic growth?', *Journal of International Economics*, 45, 115–35.

Bowles, D., R. Paskin, M. Gutierrez and A. Kasterine (2005) 'Animal Welfare and Developing Countries: Opportunities for Trade in High-Welfare Products from Developing Countries', *Revue Scientifique et Technique*, 24(2), 783–790.

Braithwaite, J. (2008) *Regulatory Capitalism: How It Works, Ideas for Making It Work Better* (Cheltenham: Edward Elgar).

Brasil Foods (2010) Annual and Sustainability Report 2009 (Sao Paulo: Brasil Foods).

Bremmer, I. (2009) 'State Capitalism Comes of Age', *Foreign Affairs*, 88(3), 40–55.

Bremmer, I. (2012) 'Are State-led Economies Better?', *Reuters Magazine*, July 3, 2012.

Brennan, L. (ed.) (2010) *The Emergence of Southern Multinationals. Their Impact on Europe* (London: Palgrave Macmillan).

Brennan, L. (2011) *The Emergence of Southern Multinationals: Their Impact on Europe* (London and New York: Palgrave Macmillan).

Brennan, L. (2013) 'Europe's Response to New Sources of Foreign Direct Investment', in L. Brennan (ed.) *Enacting Globalization: Multi-Disciplinary Perspectives on International Integration* (London and New York: Palgrave Macmillan)

Breslin, S. (2012) 'Government-Industry Relations in China: A Review of the Art of the State', in A. Walter and X. Zhang (eds) *East Asian Capitalism: Diversity, Continuity, and Change* (Oxford: Oxford University Press).

Bresser-Pereira, L. C. (2010) *Globalization and Competition: Why Some Emerging Countries Succeed While Others Fall Behind* (Cambridge: Cambridge University Press).

Broom, D. M. and K. G. Johnson (1993) *Stress and Animal Welfare* (London: Chapman and Hall).

Bruche, G. (2011) 'Emerging Indian Pharma Multinationals: Latecomer Catch-up Strategies in a Globalised High Tech Industry', *European Journal of Management*, 6(3), 300–322.

Bruff, I. (2011) 'What About the Elephant in the Room? Varieties of Capitalism, Varieties in Capitalism', *New Political Economy*, 16(4), 481–500.

Bryant, R. L. and S. Bailey (1997) *Third World Political Ecology* (London: Routledge).

Buckley, P. J., J. L. Clegg, A. R. Cross and H. Voss (2010) 'What Can Emerging Markets Learn from the Outward Direct Investment Policies of Advanced Countries?', in K. Sauvant, G. McAllister with M. Maschek (eds) *Foreign Direct Investments from Emerging Markets* (Houndmills and New York: Palgrave Macmillan).

Burfisher, M. E. (ed.) (2001) *The Road Ahead: Agricultural Policy Reform in the WTO-Summary Report* (Washington, DC: United States Department of Agriculture).

Caminada, C. (2009) 'Brazilian Poultry Processor Perdigao Takes Over Sadia', *Bloomberg*, May 19, 2009.

Caminada, C. and F. Marcelino (2009) 'JBS Said to Be Near Buying Bankrupt Pilgrim's Pride', *Bloomberg*, September 17, 2009.

Campanario, M., E. Stal and M. Muniz da Silva (2012) *Outward FDI from Brazil and Its Policy Context: Columbia FDI Profiles* (New York: Columbia University), http://www.vcc.columbia.edu/files/vale/documents/Profile-_Brazil_OFDI_10_May_2012_-_FINAL.pdf, date accessed August 12, 2013.

Carenzi, C. and M. Verga (2009) 'Animal Welfare: Review of the Scientific Concept and Definition', *Italian Journal of Animal Science*, 8(1), 21–30.

Carkovic, M. and Levine, R. (2005) 'Does foreign direct investment accelerate economic growth?' in E. M. Graham, T. H. Moran and M. Blomström (eds.) *Does Foreign Direct Investment Promote Development: New Methods, Outcomes and Policy Approaches*, (Washington D.C.: Institute for International Economics Press).

Casanova, L. (2009) *Global Latinas* (London: Palgrave Macmillan).

CBR (2010) 'Russian Federation: Outward Foreign Direct Investments of Nonbanking Corporations, by Country, 2007–2009, the Q1-Q2 of 2010', http://cbr.ru/eng/statistics/print.aspx?file=credit_statistics/inv_out-country_E.htm, date accessed January 10, 2011.

CBR (2012) Russian Federation: Outward Foreign Direct Investment Positions by Geographical Allocation in 2009–2011, http://cbr.ru/eng/statistics/print.aspx?file=credit_statistics/dir-inv_out_country_E.htm&pid=svs&sid=ITM_586, date accessedJune 10, 2013.

Čečel', A. and E. Pis'mennaja (2010) 'Poraotdavat' [Time to give away], *Vedomosti*, May 28, 2010.

Central Bank of Brazil (2012) *Capitais Brasileiros no Exterior* (Brasilia: Central Bank of Brazil).

CEPAL (2007) *Foreign Direct Investment in Latin America and the Caribbean 2006*, (Santiago: CEPAL-ECLAC).

CEPAL (2010) *The Reactions of the Governments of the Americas to the International Crisis: An Overview of Policy Measures*. (Santiago: CEPAL-ECLAC).

CEPAL (2011) *Foreign Direct Investment in Latin America and the Caribbean 2010*, (Santiago: CEPAL-ECLAC).

CEPAL(2012) *Foreign Direct Investment in Latin America and the Caribbean 2011*, (Santiago: CEPAL-ECLAC).

Chadha, A. (2005) 'Trips and Patenting Activity: Evidence from the Indian Pharmaceutical Industry', *National University of Singapore, Department of Economics Working Papers*, 0512.

Chandler, A. (2004) *Scale and Scope: The Dynamics of Industrial Capitalism* (Cambridge: Harvard University Press).

Chandler, A., J. Amatori and T. Hikino (1997) 'The Large Industrial Enterprise and the Dynamics of Modern Economic Growth', in A. Chandler, J. Amatory and T. Hikino (eds) *Big Business and the Wealth of Nations* (Cambridge: Cambridge University Press).

Chang, H.-J. (1994) *The Political Economy of Industrial Policy* (New York: St. Martin's Press).

Chang, H.-J. (1995) 'Entrepreneurship and Conflict Management', in H. J. Chang and R. Rowthorn (eds) *The Role of the State in Economic Change* (Oxford: Clarendon Press).

Chang, H.-J. (1998) 'Korea – The Misunderstood Crisis', *World Development*, 26(8), 1555–1561.

Chang, H.-J. (2000) 'The Hazard of Moral Hazard: Untangling the Asian Crisis', *World Development*, 28(4), 775–788.

Chang, H.-J. (2002) *Kicking Away the Ladder: Development Strategy in Historical Perspective* (London: Anthem Press).
Chang, H.-J. (2006) *The East Asian Development Experience: The Miracle, The Crisis and The Future* (London: Zed Books).
Chang, H.-J. (2008) *Bad Samaritans: The Myth of Free Trade and the Secret History of Capitalism* (New York: Bloomsbury Press).
Charlemagne (2012) 'Milking the Budget: Even in Times of Austerity, Europe Spends Too Much Subsidising Rich Farmers', *The Economist*, November 24, 2012.
Cho, H.-K. and T. Kalinowski (2010) 'Bank Nationalization, Restructuring and Re-Privatization: The Case of Korea since the Asian Financial Crisis', *Korea Observer*, 41(1), 1–30.
Cho, L.-J. S. Seong, and S.-H. Lee (eds) (2007) *Institutional and Policy Reforms to Enhance Corporate Efficiency in Korea* (Seoul: KDI).
Choi, J.-P. (1999) *End of the Chaebol Era* (Seoul: Gowon).
Christopher, A. and D. Vogel (2005) 'Conclusions', in A. Christopher and D. Vogel (eds) *What's the Beef? The Contested Governance of European Food Safety* (Cambridge: The MIT Press).
Claar, S. and A. Nölke (eds) (2012),'Tiefe Integration in den Nord-Süd-Beziehungen', *Journal für Entwicklungspolitik*, 28(2), special issue.
Claessens, S., S. Djankov and L. H. P. Lang (1998) 'Corporate Growth, Financing, and Risks in the Decade before East Asia's Financial Crisis', *The World Bank Policy Research Working Paper*, No. 2017.
Claessens, S., S. Djankov, and L. H. P. Lang (2000) 'East Asian Corporations: Heroes or Villains?', *World Bank Discussion Paper*, No. 409.
Clark, I. (1999) *Globalization and International Relations Theory* (Oxford: Oxford University Press).
Clark, K. B. and T. Fujimoto (1991) *Product Development Performance – Strategy, Organization, and Management in the World Auto Industry* (Cambridge: Harvard Business School Press).
Clifton, J., F. Comin and D. Diaz Fuentes (2007) 'Transforming Network Services in Europe and the Americas: From Ugly Ducklings to Swans?', in J. Clifton, F. Comin and D. Diaz Fuentes (eds) *Transforming Public Enterprises in Europe and North America* (Houndmills and New York: Palgrave Macmillan).
Clifton, J. and D. Díaz-Fuentes (2010a) 'Is the European Union ready for FDI from Emerging Markets?' in K. Sauvant, W. A. Maschek and G. McAllister (eds.) *Foreign Direct Investment from Emerging Markets: The Challenges Ahead*, (London: Palgrave Macmillan).
Clifton, J. and D. Díaz-Fuentes (2010b) 'The European Union, Southern Multinationals and the question of the Strategic Industries', in L. Brennan (ed.) *The Emergence of Southern Multinationals. Their Impact on Europe* (London: Palgrave Macmillan).
Clifton, J., D. Díaz-Fuentes and J. Revuelta (2010) 'The Political Economy of Telecoms and Electricity Internationalization in the Single Market', *Journal of European Public Policy*, 17(7), 988–1006.
Clifton, J., P. Lanthierand H. Schroeter (2011) 'Regulating and Deregulating the Public Utilities 1830–2010', *Business History*, 53(5), 659–672.
Codex Alimentarius Commission (2007) *The Report of the 30th Session of the Codex Alimentarius Commission* (Geneva: Codex Alimentarius Commission).

Corsetti, G., P. Pesenti and N. Roubini (1998a) *What Caused the Asian Currency and Financial Crisis?* mimeo(Yale University).
Corsetti, G., P. Pesenti and N. Roubini (1998b) 'PaperTigers? A Model of the Asian Crisis', *NBER Working Paper*, No. 6783.
CPF (2011) *Annual Report 2010* (Bangkok: Charoen Pokphand Food CPF).
Cramer, C. (1999) 'Can Africa Industrialize by Processing Primary Commodities? The Case of Mozambican Cashew Nuts', *World Development*, 27(7), 1247–1266.
Cramer, C. (2003) 'Should Developing Country Industrialisation Policies Encourage Processing of Primary Commodities?', *The Courier: The Magazine of ACP-EU Development Cooperation*, 196, 30–32.
CRISIL (2006) *Creating the Indian MNC* (Delhi: CRISIL Center for Economic Research).
Crossland, D. (2013) 'Europe Goes Cold on Shale Deposits', *The National*, March 21, 2013.
Cuervo-Cazurra, A. (2008) 'The multinationalization of developing country MNEs: The case of multilatinas', *Journal of International Management*, 14, 138–154.
Cuervo-Cazurra, A. and M. Genc (2008) 'Transforming disadvantages into advantages: developing-country MNEs in the least developed countries', *Journal of International Business Studies*, 39, 957–979.
Das, N. (2007) 'The Emergence of Indian Multinationals in the New Global Order', *International Journal of Indian Culture and Business Management*, 1(1/2), 36–150.
Dicken, P. (2007) *Global Shift: Mapping the Changing Contours of the World Economy* (London: SAGE Publications).
Donovan, J. A., A. J. Caswelland E. Salay (2001) 'The Effect of Stricter Foreign Regulations on Food Safety Levels in Developing Countries: A Study of Brazil', *Review of Agricultural Economics*, 23(1), 163–175.
Dore, R. (2000a) 'Will Global Capitalism be Anglo-Saxon Capitalism?', *New Left Review*, 6, 101–119.
Dore, R. (2000b) *Stock Market Capitalism: Welfare Capitalism: Japan and Germany versus the Anglo Saxons* (Oxford: Oxford University Press).
Dore, R., W. Lazonick and M. O'Sullivan (1999) 'Varieties of Capitalism in the Twentieth Century', *Oxford Review of Economic Policy*, 15(4), 102–120.
Doremus, P. N., W. W. Keller, L. W. Pauly and S. Reich (1999) *The Myth of the Global Corporation* (Princeton: Princeton University Press).
Dorémus-Miege, C., C. Gaudard, D. Horman, B. Hermelin and J.-J. Grodent (2004) *Chicken Exports: Europe Plucks Africa! A Campaign for the Right to Protect Agricultural Markets* (Paris: AgirIci).
Dornbusch, R. (1997) 'Financial Crisis in East Asia and the Prospects for Recovery', *A Special Lecture at the Korea Institute of Finance*, Seoul, December 1997.
Drezner, D. W. (2007) *All Politics Is Global: Explaining International Regulatory Regimes* (Princeton: Princeton University Press).
Duanmu, J.-L. (2012) 'Firm Heterogeneity and Location Choice of Chinese Multinational Enterprises (MNEs)', *Journal of World Business*, 47(1), 64–72.
Dunning, J. H. (1981) 'Explaining the international direct investment position of countries towards a dynamic or developmental approach', *Weltwirtschaftliches Archiv*, 117(1), 30–64.
Dunning, J. (1986) 'The Investment Development and Third World Multinationals', in K. M. Khan (ed.) *Multinationals of the South: New Actors in the International Economy* (London and New York: Palgrave Macmillan).

Dunning, J. (1993) *The Globalization of Business* (London and New York: Routledge).
Dunning, J., C. Kim and D. Park (2008) 'Old Wine in New Bottles: A Comparison of Emerging-Market TNCs Today and Developed-Country TNCs Thirty Years Ago', in K. Sauvant (ed.) *The Rise of Transnational Corporations from Emerging Markets: Threat or Opportunity?* (Cheltenham: Edward Elgar).
Durnev, A. (2010) 'Comment: Do We Need a New Theory to Explain Emerging Market Multinational Enterprises?', in K. P. Sauvant, G. McAllister and W. A. Maschek (eds) *Foreign Direct Investments from the Emerging Markets* (Basingstoke: Palgrave Macmillan).
Džumajlo, A. (2012) '"TMK dotjanulas" do Persidskogozaliva', *Kommersant*, December 4, 2012.
Easter, G. (2008) 'The Russian State in the Time of Putin', *Post Soviet Affairs*, 24(3), 199–230.
Eatwell, J. (1982) *Whatever Happened to Britain? The Economics of Decline* (London: Duckworth).
The Economist (2011) 'The Dwindling Allure of Building Factories Offshore', May 12, http://www.economist.com/node/18682182?story_id=18682182, date accessed May 25, 2011.
The Economist (2012a) 'The Rise of State Capitalism', *The Economist*, January 21, 2012.
The Economist (2012b) 'Who's Afraid of Huawei?', *The Economist*, August 4, 2012.
ECLAC (no date) *Various Years Foreign Direct Investment in Latin America and the Caribbean* (Santiago de Chile: Economic Commission for Latin America and the Caribbean).
Ėkspert (2012) 'RejtingkrupnejšichkompanijRossiipoob"emu realizaciiprodukcii' [Rating of the largest Russian companies according to the amount of revenues], *Ėkspert*, October 1, 2012.
EU (2000) *Partnership Agreement between the Members of the African Caribbean and Pacific Group of States of the One Part, and The European Community and its Member States, of the Other Part*, signed in Cotonou, Benin, on June 23, 2000 (Brussels: European Commission).
EU (2007) 'Council Directive 2007/43/EC of 28 June 2007 Laying Down Minimum Rules for the Protection of Chickens Kept for Meat Production', *Official Journal of the European Union*, 182, 19–28.
EU Directorate-General for Health and Consumers (2011a) *EU Import Conditions for Seafood and other Fishery Products* (Brussels: EU Directorate-General for Health and Consumers).
EU Directorate-General for Health and Consumers (2011b) *European Union Import Conditions for Poultry and Poultry Products* (Brussels: EU Directorate-General for Health and Consumers).
EU Directorate-General for Health and Consumers (2011c) *Third Country Establishments List per Sector* (Brussels: EU Directorate-General for Health and Consumers).
European Commission (2010) *Towards a comprehensive European international investment policy*. (European Commission: Brussels).
Eurostat (2013) *Statistics Database*, http://epp.eurostat.ec.europa.eu/portal/page/portal/statistics/search_database.

EU TRADE (2010) *Overview of EPA* (Brussels, EU TRADE).
Falk, M. and Y. Wolfmayer (2008) 'Services and Materials Outsourcing to low-wage countries and employment: Empirical evidence from EU countries',*Structural Change and Economic Dynamics*, 19, 38–52.
Fallows, J. (1995) *Looking at the Sun: The Rise of the New East Asian Economic and Political System* (New York: Vintage Books).
FAO (2009) *Tuna Report Thailand – June 2009* (Rome: FAO GLOBEFISH).
FDA (2011a) 'Fish and Fishery Product Imports: Affirmative Steps: Lists of Foreign Processors Approved by Their Governments', http://www.fda.gov/Food/FoodSafety/Product-SpecificInformation/Seafood/SeafoodHACCP/ucm118763.htm, date accessed August 23, 2011.
FDA (2011b) *Fish and Fishery Products Hazards and Controls Guidance*, 4th ed. (New Hampshire: Food and Drug Administration).
FDA (2011c) 'The Imported Seafood Safety Program', http://www.fda.gov/Food/FoodSafety/Product-SpecificInformation/Seafood/ImportsExports/ucm248706.htm, date accessed August 23, 2011.
FDC (2011) *Transnationality Ranking of Brazilian Companies*, 6th ed. (Belo Horizonte: Fundação Dom Cabral).
Ficai, F. (2010) 'Deal of the Day: Thailand's TUF Gobbles Up European Seafood Icons', *Financial Times*, July 28, 2010.
Finchelstein, D. (2009) Different States, Different Internationalizations: A Comparative Analysis of the Process of Firms' Internationalization in Latin America, *28th Lasa International Congress*. Rio de Janeiro, June 10–15, 2009.
Fischer, S. (1998) 'The Asian Crisis: A View from the IMF', address by Stanley Fischer, first deputy managing director of the International Monetary Fund, *Midwinter Conference of the Bankers' Association for Foreign Trade*, Washington DC, January 22, 1998.
Fleury, M. T. and A. Fleury (2010) 'Gestao estrategica de competencias para a internacionalizacao das empresas brasileiras', in A. Fleury (ed.) *Gestao empresarial para internacionalizacao das empresas brasileiras* (Sao Paulo: Editora Atlas).
Fleury A. and M. T. L. Fleury (2011) *Brazilian Multinationals* (Cambridge: Cambridge University Press).
Flynn, M. (2007) 'Between Subimperialism and Globalization: A Case Study on the Internationalization of Brazilian Capital', *Latin American Perspectives*, 34(6), 9–27.
Friedman, T. (2000) *The Lexus and the Olive Tree*, revised ed. (London: Harper Collins).
Fuchs, D. (2007) *Business Power in Global Governance* (Boulder: Lynne Rienner Publishers).
Fukuyama, F. (1992) *The End of History and the Last Man* (New York: Avon Books).
Furman, J. and J. E. Stiglitz (1998) 'Economic Crises: Evidence and Insights from East Asia', *Brookings Papers on Economic Activity*, 2, 1–135.
Gaddy, C. G. and A. C. Kuchins (2008) 'Putin's Plan: The Future of "Russia Inc."', *The Washington Quarterly*, 31(2), 117–129.
Gammeltoft, P., H. Barnard and A. Madhok (2010) 'Emerging multinationals, emerging theory: Macro- and micro-level perspectives', *Journal of International Management*, 16, 95–101.
Gehlhar, M. and A. Regmi (2005) *New Directions in Global Food Markets* (Washington, DC: United States Department of Agriculture).

Gereffi, G., J. Humphrey and T. Sturgeon (2005) 'The Governance of Global Value Chains', *Review of International Political Economy*, 12(1), 78–104.
Gerschenkron, A. (1962) *Economic Backwardness in Historical Perspective* (Cambridge: Harvard University Press).
Gill, S. (1991) *American Hegemony and the Trilateral Commission* (Cambridge: Cambridge University Press).
Goldstein, A. (2007) *Multinational Companies from Emerging Economies: Composition, Conceptualization and Direction in the Global Economy* (Houndsmills: Palgrave Macmillan).
Goldstein, A. (2012) Big Business in BRIC, *3rd Copenhagen Business School OFDI Conference*. Copenhagen, October 25, 2012.
Goldstein, A. (2013) 'The Political Economy of Global Business: The Case of the BRICs', *Global Policy*, 4(1), 162–172.
Goldstein, A. and F. Pusterla (2008) '"Emerging Economies" Multinationals: General Features and Specificities of the Brazilian and Chinese Cases', *CESPRI Working Paper*, No. 223.
Golub, S. S. (2003) 'Measures of Restrictions on Inward Foreign Direct Investment for OECD Countries', *OECD Economic Studies*, No. 36.
Golub, S. S. (2009) 'Openness to Foreign Direct Investment in Services: An International Comparative Analysis', *The World Economy*, 32(8), 1245–1268.
Guillén, M. and E. García-Canal (2009) 'The American model of the multinational firm and the new multinationals from emerging economies', *Academy of Management Perspectives*, 23(2), 23–35.
Gosliner, M. L. (1999) 'The Tuna-Dolphin Controversy', in J. R. Twiss and R. R. Reeves (eds) *Conservation and Management of Marine Mammals* (Washington, DC: Smithsonian Institution Press).
Grabowski, H. K. and J. M. Vernon (1994) 'Return to R&D in New Drug Introductions in the '80s', *Journal of Health Economics*, 13(4), 383–406.
Grabowski, H. K. and J. M. Vernon (2000) 'The Determinants of Pharmaceutical Research and Development Expenditures', *Journal of Evolutionary Economics*, 10(1–2), 201–215.
Grätz, J. (2013a) 'Home-Country Specific Advantages and Foreign Investment of Russian Oil and Gas Companies: A Network Approach', *International Journal of Technological Learning,Innovation and Development*, 6(1/2), 62–87.
Grätz, J. (2013b) *Russland als globaler Wirtschaftsakteur: Handlungsressourcen und Strategien der Öl- und Gaskonzerne* [Russiaasglobal economicactor: resourcesandstrategiesofoil- andgascompanies] (Munich: Oldenbourg).
Grätz, J. (2013c) Russian Multinationals from the Ferrous and Non-Ferrous Metals Industries, Zurich, mimeo.
Graz, J.-C. (2003), 'How Powerful Are Transnational Elite Clubs? The Social Myth of the World Economic Forum', *New Political Economy*, 8(3), 321–340.
Graz, J.-C. and A. Nölke (eds) (2008) *Transnational Private Governance and its Limits* (London: Routledge).
Greenspan, A. (1998) 'Testimony of Chairman Alan Greenspan, Before the Committee on Banking and Financial Services', U.S. House of Representatives, January 30, 1998, http://www.federalreserve.gov/boarddocs/testimony/1998/19980130.htm, date accessed July 17, 2013.
Guimarães, E. (1986) 'The Activities of Brazilian Firms Abroad', in C. Oman (ed.)*New Forms of Overseas Investment by Developing Countries: The Case of*

India, Korea and Brazil (Paris: Organization for Economic Cooperation and Development).
Guimarães, S. (2012). 'Pronto para investir', *Revista França Brasil*, 305 (France Brazil Chamber of Commerce).
Gupta, A. (2006) 'Emergence of Indian Multinationals', *Technology Exports*, 8(3), 1–12.
Gupta, V. K. (2006) '"Inventor" Productivity in a Publicly Funded R&D Agency – the Case of CSIR in India', *World Patent Information*, 26(3), 235–238.
Haggard, S., W. Lim and E. Kim (eds) (2003) *Economic Crisis and Corporate Restructuring in Korea: Reforming the Chaebol* (Cambridge: Cambridge University Press).
Hahm, J.-H. and F. S. Mishkin (2000) 'Causes of the Korean Financial Crisis: Lessons for Policy', in I. S. Shin (ed.)*The Korean Crisis: Before and After* (Seoul: KDI).
Haley, W. and G. Haley (2013) *Subsidies to Chinese Industry: State Capitalism, Business Strategy, and Trade Policy* (Oxford: Oxford University Press).
Hall, P. A. (2013) 'Brother, Can You Paradigm?', *Governance*, 26(2), 189–192.
Hall, P. A. and D. Soskice (2001a) 'An Introduction to Varieties of Capitalism', in P. A. Hall and D. Soskice (eds) *Varieties of Capitalism: The Institutional Foundations of Comparative Advantage* (Oxford: Oxford University Press), 1–70.
Hall, P. A. and D. Soskice (eds) (2001b) *Varieties of Capitalism: The Institutional Foundations of Comparative Advantage* (Oxford: Oxford University Press).
Hall, P.A. and D. Soskice (2003) 'Varieties of Capitalism and Institutional Change: A Response to Three Critics', *Comparative European Politics*, 1(2), 241–250
Hall, P.A. (2007), "The Evolution of Varieties of Capitalism in Europe", in B. Hancke, M. Rhodes. and M. Thatcher (eds.), *Beyond Varieties of Capitalism: Contradictions, Complementarities and Change* (Oxford: Oxford University Press)
Hall, P. A. and D. W. Gingerich (2009) 'Varieties of Capitalism and Institutional Complementarities in the Political Economy', *British Journal of Political Science*, 39(3), 449–482.
Hall, P. A. and K. Thelen (2009) 'Institutional Change in Varieties of Capitalism', *Socio-Economic Review*, 7(1), 7–34.
Hamilton, A., A. Lewis, M. McCoy, E. Havice and L. Campling (2011) *Market and Industry Dynamics in the Global Tuna Supply Chain* (Honiara: Pacific Islands Forum Fisheries Agency).
Hancke, B. (ed.) (2009) *Debating Varieties of Capitalism: A Reader* (Oxford: Oxford University Press).
Hanemann, T. and D. Rosen (2012) *China Invests in Europe: Patterns, Impact and Policy Implications* (New York: Rhodium Group).
Hanson, P. (2010) 'Russia's Inward and Outward Foreign Direct Investment: Insights into the Economy', *Eurasian Geography and Economics*, 51(5), 632–652.
Harrod, J. (2006) 'The Century of the Corporation', in C. May (ed.) *Global Corporate Power* (Boulder: Lynne Rienner Publishers).
Headey, D. (2009) 'Appraising a Post-Washington Paradigm: What Professor Rodrik Means by Policy Reform', *Review of International Political Economy*, 16(4), 698–728.
Heidenreich, M. (2012) 'The Social Embeddedness of Multinational Companies: A Literature Review', *Socio-Economic Review*, 10(3), 549–579.
Hirsch, S. (2012) 'Nation States and Nationality of MNEs', *Columbia FDI Perspectives*, No. 57.

Hirschman, A. O. (1945) *National Power and the Structure of Foreign Trade* (Berkeley: University of California Press).
Hollingsworth, J. R. and R. Boyer (eds) (1997) *Contemporary Capitalism: The Embeddedness of Institutions* (Cambridge: Cambridge University Press).
Holmström, M. (2001) 'Business Systems in India', in G. Jakobsen and J. E. Torp (eds) *Understanding Business Systems in Developing Countries* (London: Sage).
Horne, P. V. and T. Achterbosch (2008) 'Animal Welfare in Poultry Production Systems: Impact of EU Standards on World Trade', *World Poultry Science*, 64(1), 40–52.
Hopewell, K. (2013) 'New Protagonists in Global Economic Governance: Brazilian Agribusiness at the WTO', *New Political Economy*, 18(4), 603–623.
Howell, C. (2003) 'Varieties of Capitalism: And Then There Was One?', *Comparative Politics*, 36(1), 103–124.
Howes, C. and A. Singh (eds) (2000) *Competitiveness Matters: Industry and Economic Performance in the U.S.* (Ann Arbor: The University of Michigan Press).
Hsueh, R. (2011) *China's Regulatory State: A New Strategy for Globalization* (Ithaca and London: Cornell University Press).
Hsueh, R. (2012) 'China and India in the Age of Globalisation: Sectoral Variation in Postliberalization Reregulation', *Comparative Political Studies*, 45(1), 32–61.
Hymer, S. H. (1976) *The International Operations of National Firms: A Study of Direct Foreign Investment* (Cambridge: The MIT Press).
Illarionov, A. (2006) 'Russia Inc.', *New York Times*, February 4, 2006.
IMEMO/Vale (2013) *Global Expansion of Russian Multinationals after the Crisis: Results of 2011* (Moscow and New York: Institute of World Economy and International Relations and Vale Columbia Center on Sustainable International Investment).
IMF (2011) *World Economic Outlook Database: April 2011 Edition*, http://www.imf.org/external/pubs/ft/weo/2011/01/weodata/index.aspx, date accessed May 10, 2011.
Inter-American Development Bank (2008) *From Multilatinas to Global Latinas: The New Latin American Multinationals* (Washington, D. C.: Inter-American Development Bank).
Izquierdo, A. and E. Talvi (2010) *The Aftermath of the Crisis: Policy Lessons and Challenges Ahead for Latin America and the Caribbean* (Washington, D. C.: Inter-American Development Bank).
Jackson, G. and R. Deeg (2006) 'How Many Varieties of Capitalism? Comparing the Comparative Institutional Analyses of Capitalist Diversity', *Max Planck Institute for the Social Sciences, MPIfG Discussion Paper*, 06/02.
Jackson, G. and R. Deeg (2008) 'Comparing Capitalisms: Understanding Institutional Diversity and Its Implications for International Business', *Journal of International Business Studies*, 39(4), 540–561.
Jang, H.-S. (2001) 'Corporate Governance and Economic Development: The Korean Experience', in F. Iqbal and J.-I. You (eds) *Democracy, Market Economics, and Development: An Asian Perspective* (Washington, DC: The World Bank).
Javalgi, R. G., D. A. Griffith and D. S. White (2003) 'An empirical examination of factors influencing the internationalization of service firms', *Journal of Services Marketing*, 17(2), 185–201.
JBS (2010) *Annual Report 2009* (Sao Paulo: Brazil).
Jeong, S.-I. (2004) *Crisis and Restructuring in East Asia – The Case of the Korean Chaebol and the Automotive Industry* (London and New York: Palgrave Macmillan).

Jeong, S.-I. (2005) 'Innovation-Friendly Corporate Governance Structure and Financial System – Their Korean Form', *Research Report of STEPI*, No. 2005–12.
Jeong, S.-I. (ed.) (2007) 'Effects of Regulations on the Firm's Technological Innovation', *Research Report of STEPI*, No. 2007–13.
Jiang, W. (2010) 'Chinese Industry and Foreign Economic Policy: Lessons from Canada', *Canadian International Council China Paper*, No. 14.
Johanson, J. and J. Vahlne (1977) 'The Internationalization Process of the Firm: A Model of Knowledge Development and Increasing Foreign Market Commitments', *Journal of International Business Studies*, 8(1), 23–32.
Johanson, J. and J. Vahlne (2009) 'The Uppsala Internationalization Process Model Revisited: From Liability of Foreignness to Liability of Outsidership', *Journal of International Business Studies*, 40(9), 1411–1431.
Johnson, C. (1982) *MITI and the Japanese Miracle: The Growth of Industrial Policy, 1925–1975* (Stanford: Stanford University Press).
Johnson, M. C. (2009) 'Why Did the Chicken Cross the Border? An Investigation of Government Responses to Import Surges in Senegal, Cameroon and Ghana', *Annual Meeting of the American Political Science Association*. Toronto, September 3–6, 2009.
Jones, R. W. (2000) *Globalization and the Theory of Input Trade* (Cambridge: MIT Press).
Jordana, J. and D. Levi-Faur (eds) (2004) *The Politics of Regulation: Institutions and Regulatory Reforms for the Age of Governance* (Cheltenham: Edward Elgar).
Joseph, J. (1994) 'The Tuna-Dolphin Controversy in the Eastern Pacific Ocean: Biological, Economic, and Political Impacts', *Ocean Development and International Law*, 25(1), 1–30.
Josling, T., D. Orden and D. Roberts (2001) 'Technical Barrier in Global Poultry Market: A Search for "Missing Trade"', *The Annual Meetings of the International Agricultural Trade Research Consortium (LATRC)*. Auckland, January 18–19, 2001.
Jost, T. (2012) 'Much Ado about Nothing? State-Controlled Entities and the Change in German Investment Law', *Columbia FDI Perspectives*, No. 71.
Josupeit, H. (2010) 'World Tuna Trade Challenges and Opportunities', *Seychelle Tuna Conference*. Mahé, February 4–6, 2010.
Jwa, S.-H. and I.-K. Lee (eds) (2000) *Korean Chaebol in Transition: Road Ahead and Agenda* (Seoul: Korea Economic Research Institute).
Kahancová, M. (2007) 'Corporate Values in Local Contexts: Work Systems and Workers' Welfare in Western and Eastern Europe', Max Planck Institute for the Study of Societies, MPIfG Working Paper 07/1.
Kalinova, B., A. Palerm and S. Thomsen (2010) 'OECD's FDI Restrictiveness Index: 2010 Update', *OECD Working Papers on International Investment*, 2010/3.
Kalotay, K. (2002) 'Outward Foreign Direct Investment and Governments in Central and Eastern Europe: The Cases of Russian Federation, Hungary and Slovenia', *Journal of World Investment*, 3(2), 267–287.
Kalotay, K. (2008) 'Russian Transnationals and International Investment Paradigms', *Research in International Business and Finance*, 22(2), 85–107.
Kalotay, K. and A. Sulstarova (2010) 'Modelling Russian Outward FDI', *Journal of International Management*, 16(1), 131–142.
Kalyuzhnova, Y. and C. Nygaard (2008) 'State Governance Evolution in Resource-Rich Transition Economies: An Application to Russia and Kazakhstan', *Energy Policy*, 36(6), 1829–1842.

Kang, C.-K., J.-P. Choe and J.-S. Chang (1991) *Chaebol –The Leader of Growth or the Incarnation of Greed?* (Seoul: Bibong Books).

Kang, N. and J. Moon (2012) 'Institutional Complementarity between Corporate Governance and Corporate Social Responsibility: A Comparative Institutional Analysis of Three Capitalisms', *Socio-Economic Review*, 10(1), 85–108.

Kaplinsky, R. and D. Messner (2008) 'Introduction: The Impact of Asian Drivers on the Developing World', *World Development*, 36(2), 197–209.

Kassai, L. (2010) 'JBS Weighs Merging U.S. Unit into Pilgrim's Pride to Limit BNDES Influence', *Bloomberg*, July 28, 2010.

Khanna, T. and K. Palepu (2006) 'Emerging Giants: Building World-Class Companies in Developing Countries', *Harvard Business Review*, 84(10), 60–70.

Kim, H.-W. and H.-S. Shin (eds) (2006) *Adopting the New Basel Accord: Impact and Policy Responses of Asia-Pacific Developing Countries* (Seoul: Korea Development Institute).

Kim, K.-P. and G.-S. Park (2008) 'Financial Crisis and Minority Shareholders' Movement in Korea: The Unfolding and Social Consequences of the Movement', *Korea Sociology*, 42(8), 59–76.

Kim, S.-H. (ed.) (2012) '2012 Study on Indicators of Science, Technology, and Innovation',*Research Report of STEPI*, No. 2012–15–1.

Kim, S.-J. (2002) 'Financial Sector Reform in Korea: A Dilemma Between Bank-Based and Market-Based Systems', *Korea Journal*, 42(1), 42–73.

Kim, W.-K. (2004) 'Innovation-Driven Economy and Total Factor Productivity', *KIET Industrial Economic Review*, 9(5), 21–27.

Klotz, A. (2008) 'Case Selection', in A. Klotz and D. Prakash (eds) *Qualitative Methods in International Relations* (Basingstoke: Palgrave Macmillan).

Kogut, B. (2005) 'Learning, or the Importance of Being Inert: Country Imprinting and International Competition', in S. Ghoshal and D. E. Westney (eds) *Organization Theory and the Multinational Corporation*, 2nd ed. (Basingstoke: Palgrave Macmillan).

Kolstad, I. and E. Villanger (2008) 'Determinants of foreign direct investment in services', *European Journal of Political Economy*, 24, 518–533

Kolstad, I. and A. Wiig (2012) 'What Determines Chinese Outward FDI?', *Journal of World Business*, 47(1), 26–34.

Konijn, P. and R. van Tulder (forthcoming) 'Resources-for-Infrastructure (R4I) Swaps: A New Model of a Successful Internationalisation Strategies of Rising Power Firms', *Critical Perspectives on International Business*, 10.

Koyama, T. and S. Golub (2006) 'OECD's FDI Regulatory Restrictiveness Index: Revision and extension to more economies', *OECD Economics Department Working Paper*, No. 525 (Paris: OECD).

Kremlin.ru (2012) 'Interv'jutelekanalu Russia Today' [Interview to the TV channel Russia Today], http://kremlin.ru/transcripts/16393, date accessed June 16, 2013.

Krugman, P. (1994) 'The Myth of Asia's Miracle', *Foreign Affairs*, 73(6), 62–78.

Krugman, P. (1997) 'What Ever Happened to the Asian Miracle?'*Fortune*, 136(4), 26–29.

Kultawanich, A. (2010) 'Thai Tuna Firm TUF Hooks Big One with MW Brands Buy', *Thomson Reuters*, July 28, 2013.

Kurlantzick, J. (2013) 'The Rise of Innovative State Capitalism', *Businessweek*, June 28, 2013.
Kuznetsov, A. V. (2007a) 'StrukturaRossijskichprjamychkapitalovloženij' [Structure of Russian FDI], *Mirovajaėkonomikaimeždunarodnyeotnošenija*, April 4, 2007.
Kuznetsov, A. V. (2007b) 'Prospects of various types of Russian transnational corporations (TNCs)', *Electronic Publications of Pan-European Institute*, October 2007.
Kuznetsov, A. V. (2010) 'Urgent Tasks for Research on Russian TNCs', *Transnational Corporations*, 19(3), 81–96.
Kuznetsov, A. V. (2011) 'Outward FDI from Russia and Its Policy Context, Update 2011, Columbia FDI Profiles', http://www.vcc.columbia.edu/files/vale/documents/Profile_Russia_OFDI_-_2_August_2011_FINAL.pdf, date accessed June 10, 2013.
Kwon, J.-J. (2004) 'Financial Reform in Korea: Unfinished Agenda', *Seoul Journal of Economics*, 17(3), 403–437.
Lacerda, A., J. Bocchi, J. Rego, M. Borges and R. Marques (2010) *Economia brasileira* (São Paulo: Editora Saraiva).
Laird, S. (1997) *WTO Rules and Good Practice on Export Policy* (Geneva: World Trade Organisation).
Landin, R., R. Leopoldo and I. Tereza (2013) 'BNDES decide abandonar a política de criação de "campeãs nacionais"'. *Estadão*, April 22, http://economia.estadao.com.br/noticias/economia-geral,bndes-decide-abandonar-a-politica-de-criacao-de-campeas-nacionais,151356,0.htm, date accessed June 1, 2013.
Lee, Y.-K. and Y.-J. Lim (2000) 'In Search of Korea's New Corporate Governance System', in K. L. Judd and Y. K. Lee (eds) *An Agenda for Economic Reform in Korea: International Perspective* (Seoul: KDI).
Li, J. and S. Guisinger (1992) 'The globalization of service multinationals in the "triad" regions: Japan, Western Europe and North America', *Journal of International Business Studies*, 23, 675–696.
Liang, X, X. Lu and L. Wang (2012) 'Outward Internationalization of Private Enterprises in China: The Effect of Competitive Advantages and Disadvantages Compared to Home Market Rivals', *Journal of World Business*, 47(1), 134–144.
Lin, J. Y. (2012) *New Structural Economics: A Framework for Rethinking Development and Policy* (Washington DC: World Bank).
Lin, L.-W. and C. Milhaupt (2013) 'We Are the (National) Champions: Understanding the Mechanisms of State Capitalism in China', *Stanford Law Review*, 65(4), 697–759.
Lin, X. (2010) 'State versus Private MNCs from China: Initial Conceptualizations', *International Marketing Review*, 27(3), 366–380.
List, F. (1841) *Das nationale System der politischen Ökonomie* (Stuttgart: Cotta'sche Verlag).
Little, I. M. D. (1982) *Economic Development: Theory, Policy, and International Relations* (New York: Basic Books).
Liu, G. S. and P. Sun (2005) 'The Class of Shareholdings and Its Impacts on Corporate Performance: A Case of State Shareholding Composition in Chinese Public Corporations'*Corporate Governance*, 13(1), 46–59.
Liuhto, K. (2007) 'A Future Role of Foreign Firms in Russia's Strategic Industries', *Electronic Publications of Pan-European Institute*, April 2007.

Liuhto, K. and P. Vahtra (2007) 'Foreign Operations of Russia's Largest Industrial Corporations – Building a Typology', *Transnational Corporations*, 16(1), 118–144.
Lu, J., X Liu and H. Wang (2010) 'Motives for Outward FDI of Chinese Private Firms: Firm Resources, Industry Dynamics, and Government Policies', *Management and Organization Review*, 7(2), 223–248.
Lucas, R. E. (1988) 'On the Mechanics of Economic Development', *Journal of Monetary Economics*, 22(1), 3–42.
Luo, Y. and R. L. Tung (2007) 'International expansion of emerging market enterprises: A springboard perspective', *Journal of International Business Studies*, 38, 481–498.
Mahoney, J. and K. Thelen (eds) (2010) *Explaining Institutional Change: Ambiguity, Agency and Power* (Cambridge: Cambridge University Press).
Makarkin, A. (2013) 'ĖkspansijaIgorjaSečina [Expansion of Igor Sechin]', *RBK Daily*, February 18, 2013.
Marshall, A. (1920) *Principles of Economics* (London: Macmillan).
Martin, M. F. (2012) *China's Banking System: Issues for Congress* (Washington, DC: Congressional Research Service).
Martínez-Nova, A. and E.García-Canal (2011) 'Technological Capabilities and the Decision to Outsource/Offshore R&D Services', *International Business Review*, 20(3), 264–277.
Marx, K. (1990) *Capital, Volume I* (London: Penguin).
Marzinotto, B. (2002) 'Book Review: Varieties of Capitalism: The Institutional Foundations of Comparative Advantage, *Review of International Affairs*, 78(3), 631–632.
Masiero, G. and L. Caseiro (2012) 'State Support for Emerging Market Multinationals: The Brazilian and Chinese Experiences', Documentos de trabajo UC-CIFF-IELAT, No. 10.
Mathews, J. A. (2002a) *Dragon Multinationals* (Oxford: Oxford University Press).
Mathews, J. A. (2002b) 'Competitive Advantages of the Latecomer Firm: A Resource-Based Account of Industrial Catch-Up Strategies', *Asia Pacific Journal of Management*, 19(4), 467–488.
Mathews, J. A. (2006a) 'Catch-up Strategies and the Latecomer Effect in Industrial Development', *New Political Economy*, 11(3), 313–335.
Mathews, J. A. (2006b) 'Dragon Multinationals: New Players in 21st Century Globalisation', *Asia Pacific Journal of Management*, 23(1), 5–27.
Mayer-Ahuja, N. (2006) 'Arbeitsverhältnisse unter Bedingungen globaler Wirtschaftsintegration. Eindrücke von Veränderungen des indischen Gesellschafts-undProduktionsmodells',*33.DGSConference:VarietiesofCapitalism? Zur globalen Diffusion von Gesellschafts-und Produktionsmodellen.* Kassel, October10, 2006.
Mccarthy, D., S. Puffer and O. Vikhansky (2009) 'RussianMultinationals: Natural Resource Champions', in R. Ramamurtiand J. V. Singh (eds) *Emerging Multinationals in Emerging Markets* (Cambridge: Cambridge University Press).
McNally, C. (2011) 'China's Changing Guanxi Capitalism: Private Entrepreneurs between Leninist Control and Relentless Accumulation', *Business and Politics*, 13(2), Article 5.
McNally, C. (2012) 'Sino-Capitalism: China's Reemergence and the International Political Economy', *World Politics*, 64(4), 741–76.

Mel'nikov, K. and A. Solodovnikova (2013) 'Èto"bol'šajapolitika"' [This is big politics], *Kommersant*, February 11, 2013.
Merco Press (2012) *Brazil Will Bring Up Europe Poultry-Meat Subsidies at Next Mercosur/EU Trade Round* (Montevideo: Merco Press).
Mikler, J. (2011) 'Sharing Sovereignty for Policy Outcomes', *Policy and Society*, 30(3), 151–160.
Mikler, J. (2012) 'The Illusion of the "Power of Markets"', *Journal of Australian Political Economy*, 68(Summer), 42–61.
Mikler, J. (2013) 'Global Companies as Actors in Global Policy and Governance', in J. Mikler (ed.) *The Handbook of Global Companies* (Oxford: Wiley-Blackwell).
Mirza, H., A. Giroud and K. H. Wee (2011) 'The Rise of TNCs from the South', in L. Brennan (ed.) *The Emergence of Southern Multinationals: Their Impact on Europe* (Houndmills and New York: Palgrave Macmillan).
Miyake, M. P., P. Guillotreau, C.-H. Sun and G. Ishimura (2010) *Recent Developments in the Tuna Industry: Stocks, Fisheries, Management, Processing, Trade and Markets* (Rome: FAO).
Moscow Times (2013) 'Zarubezhneft Gives Up Drilling Effort Off Cuba's Coast', http://www.themoscowtimes.com/business/article/zarubezhneft-gives-up-drilling-effort-off-cubas-coast/481027.html, date accessed June 16, 2013.
Motie and Mosf (2011) Main Issues of the Korea-US FTA and Our Answers, a website on the Korea-US FTA created by the Ministry of Trade, Industry &Energy(Motie) and Ministry of Strategy and Finance(Mosf) of the South Korean government, http://www.fta.go.kr/korus/issue/fta_point.asp, date accessed July 17, 2013.
Moura, F. and F. Marcelino (2009) 'Brazil Creating "Champions"with $58 Billion Loans: Week Ahead', *Bloomberg*, May 10, 2009.
Moura, F. and L. Kassai (2010) 'JBS May Scrap U.S. Unit IPO, Extend BNDES Debt Sale', *Bloomberg Businessweek*, December 26, 2010.
Myrdal, G. (1968) *Asian Drama: An Inquiry into the Poverty of Nations* (New York: Pantheon).
Neff, A. (2011) 'BP, Rosneft Announce Historic Share-Swap Deal, Joint Arctic Exploration Alliance', *Global Insight*, January 17, 2011.
Nestro (2012) 'RespublikaSerbskaja (BosnijaiGercegovina) [Serb Republic (Bosnia and Herzegovina)]', http://www.nestro.ru/www/webnew.nsf/index/devserb_rus, date accessed June 19, 2013.
Nestro (2013) 'JV LLC Rusvietpetro', http://www.nestro.ru/www/webnew.nsf/index/devrvp_Eng, date accessed June 16, 2013.
Newnham, R. (2011) 'Oil, Carrots, and Sticks: Russia's Energy Resources as a Foreign Policy Tool', *Journal of Eurasian Studies*, 2(2), 134–143.
Ning, L. and D. Sutherland (2012) 'Internationalization of China's Private-Sector MNEs: An Analysis of the Motivations for Foreign Affiliate Formation', *Thunderbird International Business Review*, 54(2), 169–182.
Nolan, P., J. Zhang and C. Liu (2008) 'The Global Business Revolution, the Cascade Effect, and the Challenge for Firms from Developing Countries', *Cambridge Journal of Economics*, 32(1), 29–47.
Nölke, A. (2004) ‚Transnationale Politiknetzwerke: Eine Analyse grenzüberschreitender politischer Entscheidungsprozesse jenseits des regierungszentrischen Modells', Habilitationsschrift, Universität Leipzig.
Nölke, A. (2010) 'A "BRIC"-Variety of Capitalism and Social Inequality: The Case of Brazil', *Revista de Estudos e Pesquisassobre as Américas*, 4(1), 1–14.

Nölke, A. (2011a) 'Transnational Economic Order and National Economic Institutions. Comparative Capitalism Meets International Political Economy', *Max Planck Institute for the Social Sciences, MPIfG Working Paper*, 11/3.

Nölke, A. (2011b) 'Non-Triad Multinational Enterprises and Global Economic Institutions', in D. Harald Claes and C. H. Knutsen (eds) *Governing the Global Economy: Politics, Institutions, and Economic Development* (London and New York: Routledge).

Nölke, A. (2012) 'The Rise of the "B(R)IC-Variety of Capitalism": Toward a New Phase of Organized Capitalism', in H. Overbeek and B. van Apeldoorn (eds) *Neoliberalism in Crisis* (Basingstoke and New York: Palgrave Macmillan).

Nölke, A. (2013) 'Der Aufstieg multinationaler Unternehmen aus Schwellenländern: Staatskapitalismus in besonderer Form', *Der Moderne Staat*, 6(1), 49–63.

Nölke, A. and A. Vliegenthart (2009) 'Enlarging the Varieties of Capitalism. The Emergence of Dependent Market Economies in East Central Europe', *World Politics*, 61(4), 670–702.

Nölke, A. and H. Taylor (2010), 'Non-Triad Multinationals and Global Governance: Still a North-South Conflict?', in M. Ougaard and A. Leander (eds) *Business and Global Governance* (London and New York: Routledge).

Nölke, A. and H. Taylor (2011) 'Indian Multinationals, Comparative Capitalism and the Implications for Global and Host Country Economic Institutions', in L. Brennan (ed.) *The Emergence of Southern Multinationals* (Hampshire and New York: Palgrave MacMillan).

North, D. (1990) *Institutions, Institutional Change and Economic Performance* (Cambridge: Cambridge University Press).

Nye, J. (1974) 'Multinational Corporations in World Politics', *Foreign Affairs*, 53, 153–175.

OECD (2002) *Foreign Direct Investment for Development. Maximising Benefits. Minimising Costs* (Paris: OECD).

OECD (2010a) 'Employment Protection Legislation: Strictness of Employment Protection Legislation: Overall', *OECD Employment and Labour Market Statistics* (database), doi: 10.1787/data-00317-en, date accessed April 1, 2012.

OECD (2010b) *Globalisation in Fisheries and Aquaculture: Opportunities and Challenges* (Paris: OECD).

OECD (2010c) *OECD.Stat*(database), doi: 10.1787/data-00285-en, date accessed April 1, 2012.

OECD (2010d) *Perspectives on Global Development 2010: Shifting Wealth* (Paris: OECD).

OECD (2012) *FDI Regulatory Restrictiveness Index*, http://www.oecd.org/document/45 /0,3746,en_2649_34529562_47216237_1_1_1_34529562,00.html (Paris: OECD).

OECD (2012) Statistical Profile: Brazil, http://www.oecd-ilibrary.org/economics/ country-statistical-profile-brazil_csp-bra-table-en, date accessed May 25, 2012.

OECD (2013) *OECD Factbook 2013 – Economic, Environmental and Social Statistics*, http://dx.doi.org/10.1787/factbook-2013-en, date accessed July 7, 2013.

OECD (no date a) *OECD Indicators of Employment Protection*, http://www.oecd.org/ document/11/0,3343,en_2649_33927_42695243_1_1_1_37457,00.html, date accessed October 29, 2010.

OECD (no date b) *Indicators of Product Market Regulation (PMR)*, http://www.oecd. org/document/36/0,3343,en_2649_34323_35790244_1_1_1_1,00.html, date accessed October 29, 2010.

Ohno, T. (1978) *Toyota SeisanHoshiki: Datsu-kibo no Keiei o Mezashite* [Toyota production formula: towards non-scale-based management] (Tokyo: Daiyamondo).
OIE (2011) *Terrestrial Animal Health Code* (Paris: World Organization for Animal Health).
Oliver, C. (1997) 'Sustainable Competitive Advantage: Combining Institutional and Resource-Based Views', *Strategic Management*, 18(9), 679–713.
Olsen, J. P. (2009) 'Change and Continuity: An Institutional Approach to Institutions of Democratic Government', *European Political Science Review*, 1(1), 3–32.
Olsen, Karsten Bjerring (2006), *Productivity impacts of offshoring and outsourcing: a review*, Working Paper 2006/1, OECD Directorate for Science, Technology and Industry, (Paris: OECD).
Ozawa, T. (1974) *Japan's Technological Challenge to the West, 1950–1974: Motivation and Accomplishment* (Cambridge: MIT Press).
Ozawa, T. (1979) *Multinationalism, Japanese Style: The Political Economy of Outward Dependency* (Princeton: Princeton University Press).
Ozawa, T. (1996) 'Japan', in J. Dunning (ed.) *Government, Globalization, and International Business* (Oxford: Oxford University Press).
Ozawa, T. (2005) *Institutions, Industrial Upgrading, and Economic Performance in Japan: The 'Flying-Geese' Paradigm of Catch-up Growth* (Cheltenham: Elgar).
Ozawa, T. (2009) *The Rise of Asia: The 'Flying-Geese' Theory of Tandem Growth and Regional Agglomeration* (Cheltenham: Elgar).
Ozawa, T. (2011) 'The (Japan-Born) "Flying-Geese" Theory of Economic Development – and Reformulated from a Structuralist Perspective', *Global Policy*, 2(3), 272–285.
Pathak, S., A. Laplume and E. Xavier-Oliveira (2012) 'Inward Foreign Direct Investment: Does it Enable or Constrain Domestic Technology Entrepreneurship?' *Columbia FDI Perspective*, No. 84.
Pederson, J. (ed.) (1999) *International Directory of Company Histories*, Volume 24 (London: St. James Press).
Pelto, E., P. Vahtra and K. Liuhto (2003) 'Cyp-Rus Investment Flows to Central and Eastern Europe', *Electronic Publications of Pan-European Institute*, February 2003.
Pena, A. (forthcoming) 'Explaining Brazil's Role in Private Governance: The Corporate Responsibility Movement, Party Politics and State-Business Relations', *Critical Perspectives on International Business*, 10.
Peng, M. W., D. Y. L. Wang and Y. Jiang (2008) 'An Institution-based View of International Business Strategy: A Focus on Emerging Economies', *Journal of International Business Studies*, 39(8), 920–936.
Pettigrew, A. M. (1987) 'Context and Action in the Transformation of the Firm', *Journal of Management Studies*, 24(6), 649–670.
Phillips, N. (2004) *The Southern Cone Model: The Political Economy of Regional Capitalist Development in Latin America* (London and New York: Routledge).
Porter, P. E. (1990) *The Competitive Advantage of Nations* (New York: Free Press).
Poussenkova, N. (2010) 'The Global Expansion of Russia's Energy Giants', *Journal of International Affairs*, 63(2), 103–124.
PR Newswire (2000) 'Popular Brand Will Be Wholly Owned by Thai Union: Tri-Marine/Edmund Gann Agree to Sell Investment in Chicken of the Sea', *PR Newswire*, December 26, 2000.

Pradhan, J. P. (2008) *Indian Multinationals in the World Economy* (Delhi: Hudson).
Pradhan, J. P. (2003) 'Liberalization, Firm Size and R&D Performance: A Firm Level Study of Indian Pharmaceutical Industry', *Research and Information System for Developing Countries, RIS Discussion Papers*, 40.
Pradhan, J. P. (2007) 'Growth of Indian Multinationals in the World Economy: Implications for Development', *Institute for Studies in Industrial Development, ISID Working Paper*, 2007/04.
Puffer, S. and D. McCarthy (2007) 'Can Russia's State-Managed Network Capitalism be Competitive? Institutional Pull versus Institutional Push', *Journal of World Business*, 42(1), 1–13.
Putin, V. (1999) 'Mineral'no-Syrevyeresursy v strategiirazvitijarossijskojékono miki' [Mineral resources in the strategy of Russianeconomicdevelopment], *ZapiskiGornogoInstituta, St. Peterburg*, 144(1), 3–9.
Quah, D. (2011) 'The Global Economy's Shifting Centre of Gravity', *Global Policy*, 2(1), 3–9.
Ramamurti, R. (2008) 'What Have We Learned about Emerging-Market MNEs?', *Copenhagen Business School Conference on Emerging Market Multinationals: Outward FDI from Emerging and Developing Economies*, Copenhagen, October 9–10, 2008.
Ramamurti, R. and J. Singh (2009) *Emerging Multinationals in Emerging Markets* (Cambridge: Cambridge University Press).
Ramasamy, B. and M. Yeung (2010) 'The determinants of foreign direct investment in services', *The World Economy*, 33(4), 573–596.
Randall, S. J. (2009) 'Boosting Productivity in Korea's Service Sector', *OECD Economics Department Working Papers*, No. 673.
Randall, S. J. and S. Urasawa (2012) 'Sustaining Korea's Convergence to the Highest-Income Countries', *Economics Department Working Papers*, No. 965.
Ren, B., H. Liang and Y. Zheng (2010) 'Chinese Multinationals' Outward Foreign Direct Investment: An Institutional Perspective and the Role of the State', *4th China Goes Global Conference*. October4–6, 2010, Harvard University.
Rodrik, D. (2013) 'The New Mercantilist Challenge', *Project Syndicate*, January 9, 2013.
Romer, P. M. (1994) 'The Origins of Endogenous Growth', *The Journal of Economic Perspectives*, 8(1), 3–22.
Rosstat (2010a) 'Russia in Figures 2009', http://www.gks.ru/bgd/regl/b09_12/Main.htm, date accessed February 13, 2011.
Rosstat (2010b) 'Rossijskijstatističeskiježegodnik 2009' [Russian Statistical Yearbook 2009], http://www.gks.ru/bgd/regl/b09_13/Main.htm, date accessed February 13, 2011.
Rosstat (2013) 'Ob inostrannychinvesticijach v I kvartale 2013 goda' [About the foreign investments in the first quarter of 2013], http://www.gks.ru/bgd/free/b04_03/IssWWW.exe/Stg/d01/106inv24.htm, date accessedJune10, 2013.
Rostow, W. W. (1960) *The Stages of Economic Growth: A Non-Communist Manifesto* (Cambridge: Cambridge University Press).
Rugman, A. (2000) *The End of Globalization* (London: Random House Business Books).
Rugman, A. (2005) *The Regional Multinationals: MNEs and 'Global' Strategic Management* (Cambridge: Cambridge University Press).

Rugman, A. and S. Collinson (2004) 'The Regional Nature of the World's Automotive Sector', *European Management Journal*, 22(5), 471–482.

Rugman, A. and S. Girod (2003) 'Retail Multinationals and Globalization: The Evidence Is Regional,'*European Management Journal*, 21(1), 24–37.

Rugman, A., A. Kudina and G. Yip (2007) 'The Regional Dimension of UK Multinationals', in A. Rugman (ed.) *Regional Aspects of Multinationality and Performance*, Volume 13(*Research in Global Strategic Management*)(Oxford: Emerald Group Publishing Limited).

Rural Payment Agency (2011) *Poultry – ET7 Leaflet* (London: Department of Environment Food and Rural Affairs).

Russian Federation (1997) 'Koncepcijanacional'nojbezopasnostiRossijskojFedera cii' [National security conception of the Russian Federation], *Krasnajazvezda*, December 27, 1997.

Russian Federation (2000a) 'National Security Conception of the Russian Federation, reprinted', in A. Melville and T. Shakleina (eds) *Russian Foreign Policy in Transition. Concepts and Realities* (Budapest, 2005: Central European University Press).

Russian Federation (2000b) 'Foreign Policy Conception of the Russian Federation, reprinted', in A. Melville and T. Shakleina (eds) *Russian Foreign Policy in Transition. Concepts and Realities* (Budapest, 2005: Central European University Press).

Russian Federation (2008a) 'Strategijanacional'nojbezopasnostiRossijskojFederaci i do 2020 goda' [National security strategy of the Russian Federation till 2020], http://www.scrf.gov.ru/documents/1/99.html, date accessed June 3, 2011.

Russian Federation (2008b) 'The Foreign Policy Concept of the Russian Federation', http://archive.kremlin.ru/eng/text/docs/2008/07/204750.shtml, accessedJune 3, 2011.

Samora, R. (2009) 'Brazil Merger to Create Major World Poultry Giant', *Reuters*, May 19, 2009.

Sampath, P. G. (2006) 'India's Product Patent Protection Regime: Less or More of "Pills for the Poor"?', *The Journal of World Intellectual Property*, 9(6), 694–726.

Sarathy, R. (2006) 'Strategic Evolution and Partnering in the Indian Pharmaceutical Industry', in S. C. Jain (ed.) *Emerging Economies and the Transformation of International Business: Brazil, Russia, India and China* (Cheltenham: Edward Elgar).

Sauvant, K. P. (2005) 'New Sources of FDI: The BRICs', *Journal of World Investment & Trade*, 6(5), 639–709.

Sauvant, K. P. and J. Strauss (2012) 'State-Controlled Entities Control Nearly US$ 2 Trillion in Foreign Assets', *Columbia FDI Perspectives*, No. 64.

Sauvant, K. P., G. McAllister and M. Maschek (2010) *Foreign Direct Investments from Emerging Markets* (London and New York: Palgrave Macmillan).

Schaumburg-Müller, H. (2001) 'Firms in the South: Interactions between National Business Systems and the Global Economy', in G. Jakobsen and J. E. Torp (eds) *Understanding Business Systems in Developing Countries* (London: Sage).

Schmitz, C. J. (1993) *The Growth of Big Business in the United States and Western Europe1850–1939* (Cambridge: Cambridge University Press).

Schneider, B. (2009) 'Big Business in Brazil: Leveraging Natural Endowments and State Support for International Expansion', in L. Brainard and L. Martinez-Diaz (eds) *Brazil as an Economic Superpower* (Washington, DC: Brooking Institution Press).

Scholvin, S. and G. Strüver (2013) 'Infrastrukturprojekte in der SADC Region: die Rolle Chinas', *German Institute of Global and Area Studies GIGA Focus*, No.2.

Schuman, M. (2011) 'State Capitalism vs. the Free Market: Which Performs Better?', *Time Magazine*, September 30, 2011.

Schumpeter, J. A. (1934) *The Theory of Economic Development* (New York: Oxford University Press).

Schumpter, J. (1950) *Capitalism, Socialism and Democracy* (New York: Harper and Brothers).

Scott, W. R. (1995) *Institutions and Organizations* (Thousand Oaks: Sage).

Seiser, M. (2012) 'Europa droht bei Patenten die Schlusslaterne', *Frankfurter Allgemeine Zeitung*, September 4, 2012, 15.

Sennes, R. and R. Mendes (2009) 'Public Policies and Brazilian Multinationals', in J. Ramsey and A. Almeida (eds) *The Rise of Brazilian Multinationals* (Rio de Janeiro: Elsevier).

Shambaugh, D. (2013) *China Goes Global: The Partial Power* (Oxford: Oxford University Press).

Shan, W. and S. Zhang (2011) 'The Treaty of Lisbon: Half Way toward a Common Investment Policy', *The European Journal of International Law*, 21(4), 1049–1073.

Sharma, R. (2013) 'How Emerging Markets Lost Their Mojo', *Wall Street Journal*, June 26, 2013, p.17.

Sharma, R., D. Nyange, G. Duteutre and N. Morgan (2005) 'The Impact of Import Surges: Country Case Study Results for Senegal and Tanzania', *FAO Commodity and Trade Policy Research Working Paper*, No. 11.

Shen, X. (2013) 'How the Private Sector is Changing Investment in Africa', *Columbia FDI Perspective*, No. 93.

Shin, I.-S. (ed.) (2000) *The Korean Crisis: Before and After* (Seoul: KDI).

Shin, J.-S, and H.-J. Chang (2003) *Restructuring Korea Inc.* (London: RoutledgeCurzon).

Solis, M., B. Stallings and S. Katada (eds) (2009) *Competitive Regionalism: FTA Diffusion in the Pacific Rim* (New York: Palgrave Macmillan).

Solodovnikova, A. (2013) 'RossijaiV'etnammenjajutsjanedrami' [Russia and Vietnam exchange soils], *Kommersant*, May 15, 2013.

Song, K.-H. (2012) *Handbook for Renegotiation of Korea-US FTA* (Seoul: Noksaekpyeongron).

Spector, M., L. Etter and A. Steward (2009) 'Brazilian Giant JBS Agrees to Buy Pilgrim's Pride', *The Wall Street Journal*, July 19, 2009.

Stal, E. and A. Cuervo-Cazurra (2011) 'The Investment Development Path and FDI From Developing Countries: The Role of Pro-Market Reforms and Institutional Voids', *Latin American Business Review*, 12(3), 209–231.

Starmer, E., A. Witteman and T. A. Wise (2006) 'Feeding the Factory Farm: Implicit Subsidies to the Broiler Chicken Industry', *Global Development and Environment Institute Working Paper*, No. 06–03.

Statistics Korea (2012) Household Finance and Welfare Survey, http://www.kostat.go.kr/, date accessed July 7, 2013.

Stiglitz, J. E. (2003) 'Towards a New Paradigm of Development', in J. Dunning (ed.) *Making Globalization Good: The Moral Challenges of Global Capitalism* (Oxford: Oxford University Press).

Stiglitz, J. E. (2012) 'Comments', in J. Y. Lin (ed.) *New Structural Economics* (Washington DC: World Bank).
Strange, S. (1997) 'The Future of Global Capitalism; or Will Divergence Persist Forever?', in C. Crouch and W. Streeck (eds) *Political Economy of Modern Capitalism: Mapping Convergence and Diversity* (London: Sage Publications).
Strategy (2012) 'Itogovyjdoklad o rezul'tatachėkspertnojrabotypoaktual'nymprobl emamsocial'no-ėkonomičeskojstrategiiRossiina period do 2020 goda"Strategija-2020: Novaja model'rosta – novajasocial'najapolitika"' [Final report on the results of the expert work on current problems of the social-economic strategy of Russia in the period up to the year 2020 'Strategy 2020: New Growth Model – New Social Policy'], http://2020strategy.ru/data/2012/03/14/1214585998/1itog.pdf, date accessed June 16, 2013.
Streeck, W. (2009) *Re-forming Capitalism: Institutional Change in the German Political Economy* (Oxford: Oxford University Press).
Stulberg, A. (2007) *Well-Oiled Diplomacy: Strategic Manipulation and Russia's Energy Statecraft in Eurasia* (Albany: SUNY Press).
Sutela, P. (2012) *The Political Economy of Putin's Russia* (Abingdon: Routledge).
Syrbe, T., I. Pavlovich and S. Nogovitsyna (2012) 'A Legal Overview of Foreign Investment in Russia's Strategic Sectors', http://www.cliffordchance.com/publicationviews/publications/2012/10/a_legal_overviewofforeigninvestmenti.html, date accessed June 19, 2013.
Tatur, M. (1998) 'Ökonomische Transformation, Staat und moralischeRessourcen in den post-sozialistischenGesellschaften' [Economic transformation, state and moral resources in post-socialist societies], *Prokla*, 112(28), 339–374.
Taylor, H. and A. Nölke (2009) 'Indian Multinationals and Their Institutional Environment: A Varieties of Capitalism Perspective', in C. Esser and H. Egbert (eds) *Varieties of Capitalism: Dynamics, Economic Crisis and New Players* (Saarbrücken: Lambert Academic Publishing).
Taylor, H. and A. Nölke (2010) 'Global Players from India: A Political Economy Perspective', in K. Sauvant, G. McAllister and W. Mascek (eds) *Foreign Direct Investments from Emerging Markets: The Challenges Ahead* (London: Palgrave Macmillan).
Teece, D. J., G. Pisano and A. Shuen. (1997) 'Dynamic Capabilities and Strategic Management', *Strategic Management*, 18(7), 509–534.
ten Brink, T. (2011) 'Kooperation oder Konfrontation? Der Aufstieg Chinas in der globalen politische Ökonomie',*Max Planck Institute fortheSocialSciencesMPIfG Working Paper*, 11/7.
ten Brink, T. (2013) *Chinas Kapitalismus: Entstehung, Verlauf, Paradoxien* (Frankfurt: Campus).
ten Brink, T. and A. Nölke (2013) 'Staatskapitalismus', *Der Moderne Staat*, 6(1).
Thelen, K. (2001) 'Varieties of Labour Politics in the Developed Democracies', in P.A. Hall and D. Soskice (eds) *Varieties of Capitalism: The Institutional Foundations of Comparative Advantage* (Oxford: Oxford University Press).
TSO (2012) 'Intelligence and Security Committee Annual Report 2011–2012', The Stationery Office, https://www.gov.uk/government/uploads/system/uploads/attachment_data/file/61292/21937_CM8403_ISC_Proof_V0_6_05-7.pdf, date accessed June 16, 2013.
Tulder, R. V. (2010) 'Toward a Renewed Stages Theory for BRIC Multinational Enterprises? A Home Country Bargaining Approach', in K. P. Sauvant, G.

McAllister and W. A. Maschek (eds) *Foreign Direct Investments from the Emerging Markets* (Basingstoke: Palgrave Macmillan).

UN COMTRADE (2011) 'United Nations Commodity Trade Statistics Database', http://comtrade.un.org/db/default.aspx, date accessed July 20, 2011.

UNCTAD (1991) *World Investment Report: The Triad in Foreign Direct Investment* (Geneva: United Nations-UNCTAD).

UNCTAD (2008) *World Investment Report: Transnational Corporations and the Infrastructure Challenge* (New York: United Nations Conference on Trade and Development).

UNCTAD (2011a) 'The World's Top 100 Non-Financial TNCs, Ranked by Foreign Assets, 2008', *Largest Transnational Corporations*, UNCTAD/ Erasmus University database, http://www.unctad.org/Templates/Page.asp?intItemID=2443&lang=1, date accessed April 5, 2011.

UNCTAD (2011b) *World Investment Report 2011: Non-Equity Modes of International Production and Development* (New York and Geneva: United Nations Conference on Trade and Investment).

UNCTAD (2012) *World Investment Report 2012* (New York: United Nations Conference on Trade and Development).

UNCTAD (2013) Statistical Database, http://unctadstat.org, date accessed June 10, 2013.

USDA (2008) *2008 Farm Bill Side-By-Side* (Washington, DC: United States Department of Agricultures).

USDA (2011a) *Countries/Products Eligible for Export to the United States* (Washington, DC: United States Department of Agricultures).

USDA (2011b) *Export Requirements for the European Union (EU-131)* (Washington, DC: United States Department of Agricultures).

Vahtra, P. and K. Liuhto (2004) 'Expansion or Exodus? – Foreign Operations of Russia's Largest Corporations', *Electronic Publications of Pan-European Institute*, 8/2004.

Valdez, R. (2011) 'A internacionalização do BNDES no Governo Lula', Master's Thesis. (Porto Alegre: Universidade Federal do Rio Grande do Sul – Instituto de Filosofia e Ciências Humanas).

Van Apeldoorn, B., N. de Graaff and H. Overbeek (2012) 'The Rebound of the Capitalist State: The Rearticulation of the State-Capital Nexus in the Global Crisis', *Globalizations*, 9(4), 467–470.

van der Pijl, K. (1998) *Transnational Classes and International Relations* (London: Routledge).

van Tulder, R. (2010) 'Toward a Renewed Stages Theory for BRIC Multinational Enterprises? A Home Country Bargaining Approach', in K. Sauvant, G. McAllister with M. Maschek (eds) *Foreign Direct Investments from Emerging Markets* (Houndmills and New York: Palgrave Macmillan).

Verbeke, A. (2009) *International Business Strategy: Rethinking the Foundations of Global Corporate Success* (Cambridge: Cambridge University Press).

Vernikov, A. (2012) 'The Impact of State-Controlled Banks on the Russian Banking Sector', *Eurasian Geography and Economics*, 53(2), 250–266.

Vernon, R. (1972) *The Economic and Political Consequences of Multinational Enterprise: An Anthology* (Boston: Harvard University).

Vernon, R. (1966). 'International Investment and InternationalTrade in the Product Cycle.'*The Quarterly Journal of Economics*, 80 (2), 190–207.

Vitols, S. (2001) 'Varieties of Corporate Governance: Comparing Germany and the UK', in P. A. Hall and D. Soskice (eds) *Varieties of Capitalism: The Institutional Foundations of Comparative Advantage* (Oxford: Oxford University Press).

Vnešĕkonombank (2010) 'Učastie v refinansirovaniiobjazatel'stvkompanij' [Participation in refinancing of companies'debts], http://veb.ru/sup/supref/, date accessed June 16, 2013.

Vogel, D. (1995) *Trading Up: Consumer and Environmental Regulation in a Global Economy* (Cambridge: Harvard University Press).

Vogel, S. (1996) *Freer Markets More Rules: Regulatory Reform in Advanced Industrialized Countries* (Ithaca: Cornell University Press).

Vogel, S. (2001) 'The Crisis of German and Japanese Capitalism: Stalled on the Road to the Liberal Market Model?', *Comparative Political Studies*, 34(10), 1103–1133.

Voss, H. (2013) 'The Global Company', in J. Mikler (ed.) *The Handbook of Global Companies* (Oxford: Wiley-Blackwell).

Wade, R. H. (2003) 'What Strategies Are Viable for Developing Countries Today? The World Trade Organization and the Shrinking of "Development Space"', *Review of International Political Economy*, 10(4), 621–644.

Wade, R. H. (2004) *Governing the Market: Economic Theory and the Role of Government in East Asian Industrialization* (Oxfordshire: Princeton University Press).

Wade, R. H. (2010) 'Is the Globalization Consensus Dead?', *Antipode*, 41(S1), 141–165.

Watson, M. (2003) 'Ricardian Political Economy and the "Varieties of Capitalism" Approach: Specialization, Trade and Comparative Institutional Advantage', *Comparative European Politics*, 1(2), 227–240.

Weikert, J. (2011) 'Chinese Companies' Response to Corporate Social Responsibility', in C. Scherrer (ed.) *China's Labour Question* (Munich: Hampp).

Weiss, L. (2003) 'Introduction: Bringing Domestic Institutions Back In', in L. Weiss (ed.) *States in the Global Economy: Bringing Domestic Institutions Back In* (Cambridge: Cambridge University Press).

Weiss, L. (2010) 'The State in the Economy: Neoliberal or Neoactivist?', in G. Morgan, J. L. Campbell, C. Crouch, O. K. Pedersen and R. Whitley (eds) *Oxford Handbook of Comparative Institutional Analysis* (New York: Oxford University Press).

Wells, L. T. (1983) *Third World Multinationals: The Rise of Foreign Investment from Developing Countries* (Cambridge: The MIT Press).

Whitley, R. (1992) *Business Systems in East Asia: Firms, Markets and Societies* (London: Sage Publication).

Whitley, R. (1999) *Divergent Capitalisms: The Social Structuring and Change of Business Systems* (Oxford: Oxford University Press).

Whitley, R. (2001) 'Developing Capitalisms: The Comparative Analysis of Emerging Business Systems in the South', in G. Jakobsen and J. E. Torp (eds) *Understanding Business Systems in Developing Countries* (London: Sage).

Whitley, R. (ed.) (2002) *Competing Capitalisms: Institutions and Economies* (Cheltenham: Edward Elgar).

Whitley, R. (2007) *Business Systems and Organizational Capabilities: The Institutional Structuring of Competitive Competences* (Oxford: Oxford University Press).

Whitley, R. (2009) 'The Multinational Company as a Distinct Organizational Form', in D. Collinson and G. Morgan (eds) *Images of the Multinational Firm* (Chichester: Wiley and Sons).
Wilks, S. (2013) 'The National Identity of Global Companies', in J. Mikler (ed.) *The Handbook of Global Companies* (Oxford: Wiley-Blackwell).
Williamson, J. (2003) 'The Washington Consensus and Beyond', *Economic and Political Weekly*, 38(15), 1475–1481.
Wolf, M. (2004) *Why Globalization Works* (New Haven and London: Yale University Press).
Womack, J. P., D. T. Jones and D. Roos (1990) *The Machine That Changed the World* (New York: Macmillan).
Wong, S. (2013) 'Varieties of the Regulatory State and Global Companies', *Global Policy*, 4(1), 173–183.
Wooldridge, A. (2012) 'The Visible Hand', *The Economist*, January 21, 2012.
World Bank (1993) *The East Asian Miracle: Economic Growth and Public Policy* (Oxford: Oxford University Press).
World Bank (2013) *World Development Indicators Online*, http://data.worldbank.org/data-catalog/world-development-indicators (Washington: World Bank).
Wright, M., Filatotchev, I., Hoskisson, R. E. and Peng, M. W. (2005).'Strategy research in emerging economies: challenging the conventionalwisdom'. *Journal of Management Studies*, 42 (1), 1–33.
WTO (1991) 'Mexico etc. versus US: "Tuna-Dolphin"', .http://www.wto.org/english/tratop_E/envir_E/edis04_E.htm, date accessed April 20, 2012.
WTO (2009) *WORLD TRADE REPORT 2009 – Trade Policy Commitments and Contingency Measures Trade Policy Commitments and Contingency Measures* (Geneva: World Trade Organization).
WTO (2010) *Understanding the WTO*, 5th ed. (Geneva: World Trade Organisation).
WTO (2011) 'Statistics database: Tariff Analysis Online facility World Trade Organisation', https://tariffanalysis.wto.org/welcome.aspx?ReturnUrl=%2fQueryEdit.aspx, date accessed August 20, 2011.
WTO (2012a) 'Chronological List of Disputes Cases', http://www.wto.org/english/tratop_E/dispu_E/dispu_status_E.htm, date accessed April 20, 2012.
WTO (2012b) 'United States – Measures Concerning the Importation, Marketing and Sale of Tuna and Tuna Products', http://www.wto.org/english/tratop_E/dispu_E/cases_E/ds381_E.htm, date accessed July 12, 2012.
Xing, L. and T. Shaw (2013) 'The Political Economy of Chinese State Capitalism', *Journal of China and International Relations*, 1(1), 88–113.
Xue, Q. and B. Han (2010) 'The Role of Government Policies in Promoting Outward Foreign Direct Investment from Emerging Markets: China's Experience', in K. P. Savant, G. McAllister with M. Maschek (eds) *Foreign Direct Investments from Emerging Markets: The Challenges Ahead* (London and New York: Palgrave Macmillan).
Yang, X. and C. Stoltenberg (2013) 'Chinese Multinationals and the State: An Institutional Perspective', in J. Farrar and D. Mayes (eds) *Globalisation, The Global Financial Crisis and The State* (Cheltenham: Edward Elgar).
Yi-Chong, X. (ed) (2012) *The Political Economy of State-owned Enterprises in China and India* (London and New York: Palgrave Macmillan).

Yoo, S.-M. (1999) 'Corporate Restructuring in Korea: Policy Issues before and during the Crisis', *KDI working paper*, No. 9903.

Žiznin, S. (2005) *ÈnergetičeskajadiplomatijaRossii: teorija, politika, praktika* [Energy diplomacy of Russia: theory, politics, practice] (Moskva: OOO "IstBruk").

Zutshi, R. and P. Gibbons (1998) 'The International Process of Singapore Government-Linked Companies: A Contextual View', *Asia Pacific Journal of Management*, 15(2), 219–246.

Index

Acer, 170
Africa, 20, 38, 49, 86–8, 142, 151, 180
Agricultural Market Access Database (AMAD), 171, 174
Argentina, 138, 144–5, 152, 160–5, 177, 179
Asia Pacific Group (formerly Pacific Asian Group), 88
Asian financial crisis, 8, 55–7, 60, 62, 75
Australia, 6, 23, 29, 144–5, 165, 176
Austria, 23, 143, 161, 165

Banco do Brasil, 133, 146, 148
Bangladesh, 49
Bank of Korea, 56, 61, 64
Bank of Russia, 97
bank-based finance, 57
banks, 4, 21, 38, 59–64, 70, 83, 125, 133, 136, 148–52, 169, 188
Belgium, 20, 23, 147, 161, 164–5
Bermuda Islands, 83, 97
bilateral agreements, 12, 156, 160, 188
bilateral investment agreements, 12, 160, 196
bilateral trade agreements, 12, 196
BNDES, 10, 52, 130–52, 182, 187, 189, 196
Bosnia and Herzegovina, 105
Bradesco, 144, 146, 148, 152
Brasil Foods, 11, 140, 171, 181–2, 185–6
Braskem, 135, 140, 144, 146
Brazil, 1, 3, 4, 6, 10, 16, 37, 73, 80, 85, 89, 130–52, 157, 160–1, 163, 164–5, 169, 172, 177, 181–2
Brazilian economy, 132, 137, 149
Brazilian government, 12, 132, 149–10, 172, 182
Brazilian multinationals, 10–11, 52, 130, 132–52, 182, 187, 189, 194–5

Brazilian National Treasury, 149
Brazilian public banks, 133, 136, 149
BRIC, 1, 5, 9–10, 16–17, 19, 28, 37, 80, 132–3, 135–6, 150, 152, 191, 195
Bulgaria, 104
business groups, 57, 69
business-government / state-business relations, 5, 24, 41, 69, 78–82, 172, 187, 189

Caloi, 143
Camargo, 10, 146, 151
Cambodia, 49
Canada, 23, 144, 160–1, 163, 165, 176–7, 196
capitalist class, 79, 88–9
capitalist relations of production, 22–3, 28–9, 38, 82
cartels, 32, 35, 69
catch-up, 4, 7–8, 31–51, 55, 76, 190
Central American Free Trade Agreement (CAFTA), 173
Central Bank of Brazil, 133, 138, 142
chaebol, 57, 59–76
  CJ Group, 68, 71
  Daelim, 68
  Dongbu, 68
  Doosan, 68
  DSME, 68
  GS, 68, 71, 74
  Hanjin, 68
  Hyundai, 57, 62–6, 68, 70, 72–3, 76
  Kumho-Asiana, 68
  Lotte Group, 68, 74
  Shinsegae Group, 68, 71, 74
  STX, 68
Cheil Bank, 60–1
Chile, 145, 161–5, 176–7
China, 1, 3–5, 8, 16–17, 19, 29, 34–41, 49–51, 77–81, 84–9, 95, 108, 132, 135–7, 152, 160–2, 165, 177, 189, 191–3, 197

Index

China FAW Group, 45
Chinese Communist Party, 36–7
Chinese economy, 37, 49
Chinese multinationals, 8, 9, 17, 37, 50, 77–9, 81–9, 99, 151, 193
Chinese state, 8, 37, 45, 50, 77–8, 83, 85–9, 137, 175, 193
Colombia, 133, 145, 160–4, 166
commodities, 92, 142, 151, 174
Common Agricultural Policy (CAP), 174
Commonwealth of Independent States (CIS), 91, 101, 104–5
comparative capitalism, 22–3, 29, 78–9, 82–3, 113, 188, 191–2, 197
competition, 3, 22–3, 27, 40, 86, 91–2, 94, 98, 102, 104–5, 108, 115, 127–8, 151, 196–7
competition policy, 12, 82, 84, 112, 190
competition regulation, 10
Confederation of Indian Industry, 126
coordinated market economies (CMEs), 22–8, 30, 79, 113–14
coordination, 21–3, 28, 79, 82, 98, 113–15, 184, 188
Corporate Finance, 79–80, 82, 125, 188
Corporate Governance, 5, 25–6, 57, 63–4, 79–80, 82, 112, 114, 125, 188–9, 195
Corporate Social Responsibility, 87, 195
Correa, 10, 144, 146, 151
corruption, 34, 69
CSN, 135, 146
Cuba, 37, 105
Cyprus, 97
Czech Republic, 79, 161, 165

Daewoo, 62–3, 66, 76
Denmark, 23, 136, 146, 161, 164–5
dependent market economies (DME), 79
deregulation, 8, 19, 24, 26, 33, 68–71, 74–5, 163
development banks, 5, 83, 130–3, 137–8, 140–2, 148–50, 155, 196

Brazilian development bank, *see* BNDES
developmental state, 3, 5, 7–8, 34–7, 45, 51, 58, 60–2, 65, 76, 85, 89, 108, 197
developmentalism, 33
dispute settlement, 171, 175, 179–80
Doha Round, 195
Dongwon, 181
double taxation, 185
Dr. Reddy's Laboratories, 122–3, 129
Dunning, John H., 1, 130–1, 165, 197

ECLAC, 142, 154
economic diplomacy, 32, 96, 193
education and training, 21, 23, 33, 68, 72, 74, 79, 114, 119, 177–8, 188, 190
Egypt, 160, 166
elites, 20, 34, 73–5, 91–2, 96, 98, 104, 196
embedded liberalism, 3, 22
Embraer, 10, 135, 146, 148, 151, 196
Empress International, 183
EU Food and Veterinary Office, 177
European Union (EU), 3, 6, 8, 10, 12, 17, 22, 29, 56–7, 62, 75–6, 96, 101–2, 106, 121, 130–52, 155–68, 172–81, 184–6, 191, 194–5
EUROTHON, 184
Evraz, 100
Ex-Im Bank, 47–8

families, 4, 9, 57, 82, 91, 99, 106, 125–6, 189
FDI promotion, 12, 82, 85, 132, 141, 151, 156, 158, 160, 189, 192
FDI regulation, 5, 11, 157, 165, 167, 187
FDI Regulatory Restrictiveness Index, 160–1, 165–7
FESCO, 99–100
financial institutions, 62, 74, 83–4, 125, 134, 152
financial markets, 2, 5, 7, 56–7, 68–71, 79, 96, 133, 137, 151
financial support, 5, 10, 47, 52, 83, 85, 93, 95, 105, 131–2, 141, 148, 150, 162, 182, 186–7

financial system, 23, 33, 63, 114, 116
Finland, 23, 161, 165
firm-specific advantages, 42–3
Food and Drug Administration (FDA), 177
Fortune Global 500, 1, 17, 19, 77, 82–3
FT Global 500, 1, 17, 77
FTAs, 8, 56, 62, 71–6

G20, 160
GATS, 156
GATT, 172, 179
Gazprom, 1, 95, 100–2, 107
General Electrics, 170
Gerdau, 10, 135, 144, 146
Germany, 3–4, 18, 20, 23–7, 79, 81, 96, 103, 135, 143–4, 146–8, 161, 163–5, 170, 190
Gerschenkron, Alexander, 4, 42, 44
Ghana, 184
Glenmark, 122–3, 129
global financial and economic crisis, 11, 20, 25, 29, 38, 55, 58, 62, 71, 76, 85, 95, 99, 106, 136, 159, 161–2, 188
globalization, 15, 19, 202, 28, 39, 70, 94, 136–7, 196
Gradiente, 134
gross domestic product (GDP), 9, 20, 49, 55, 61, 64, 79–80, 92, 95, 150, 165–8, 175
GRU (Russian military foreign intelligence service), 96
Guanxi, 9, 78, 82, 187

Haetae, 62
Halla Group, 62
Hanmi Bank, 60–1
home country, 21, 31, 36, 40, 45, 77, 90, 118, 165, 167, 193
home country government, 11, 131
home country policies, 131
home country-specific advantages, 93
Hong Kong, 19, 47, 51, 59, 77, 83–4, 152
host country, 9, 11, 37, 39–40, 77, 107, 113, 143, 155–8, 165–8
host country governments, 2, 107, 193

Huawei, 36, 50, 77–8, 83
hukou system, 84
Hungary, 102, 143, 161, 165

IBM, 77, 84
import substitution, 33, 40
India, 1, 3–4, 10, 16, 29, 37, 45, 79–80, 86, 89, 109–29, 132, 135–6, 144, 160–1, 166, 190, 192–3
Indian economy, 111, 117–18, 193
Indian MNCs, 9, 86, 109–13, 116–17, 121, 125–9
Indian pharmaceuticals, 9, 109–29, 190
Indian state, 9, 110, 117–18, 120–1, 126
Indonesia, 160, 166
industrial policy, 8, 34–5, 62, 65, 67, 70, 73, 124, 136–7, 159, 170, 191
industrial relations, 23, 82, 112, 114, 188, 190
industrialization, 4, 7–8, 31–51, 55, 57, 60, 69, 85
Information and Communication technology (IT), 43, 50, 62, 111, 138, 141, 178
institutional advantages, 110, 114, 116–17
institutional complementarities, 22, 25, 80, 111–12, 115, 125, 188
intellectual property rights, 12, 73, 93, 111, 127, 190–1, 294
International Accounting Standards Board (IASB), 196
international business, 1–2, 82, 88, 112, 114, 116–17, 128, 130, 132, 155, 172, 192, 197
International Labour Organisation (ILO), 194
International Monetary Fund (IMF), 15, 19–20, 56–8
international political economy (IPE), 2, 34, 78, 192, 197
international trade, 11–12, 16–17, 26–8, 89, 156, 169, 185–6
interventionism, 52, 57, 67, 70, 73, 149
investment development path, 165

Iraq, 104–5, 133
Ireland, 23, 145, 161, 165
Italy, 104, 143–4, 146–7, 161, 164–5
Itautec, 138
Itaú-Unibanco, 146, 148, 152

Japan, 3–4, 17–18, 20–9, 34–6, 38, 45–9, 52, 56–7, 79, 81, 88–9, 142, 152, 160, 162, 166, 170, 182–3, 191
Japan International Cooperation Agency, 47
JBS (formerly Sadia / Perdigao), 138–40, 144, 146, 181–2
Johnson, Chalmer, 34
Jordan, 25, 60

Kazakhstan, 101, 104, 160, 166
keiretsu, 47, 52
Kia Motors, 64–6
Korea Exchange Bank, 60–1
KT, 59, 66, 68, 76
KT&G, 59
Kyrgyz Republic, 160

labour unions, 21, 86, 190
latecomers to industrialization, 4, 7, 44
Latin America, 10–11, 20, 33, 38, 41, 73, 103, 105, 130, 138, 141–2, 151–68, 191–2, 194
Latvia, 160, 165
Lenovo, 36, 84
LG, 62–6, 73, 76
liberal market economies (LME), 22–8, 30, 79, 113–14
liberalization, 10–11, 26, 74, 85, 117, 121, 124, 126, 128, 134, 151, 157–9, 161, 165–8, 180–1, 193–5
linkage, leverage and learning (LLL) approach, 1, 130, 141, 197
Lisbon Treaty, 11, 156–7, 160
List, Friedrich, 3–4
Lithuania, 160
lobbying, 24, 59, 81–2, 184, 195
LUKoil, 100, 103–4
Luxembourg, 20, 97, 152, 165

Madagascar, 133

Marketing, 45, 122–4, 148
Mechel, 100
MERCUSOR, 134, 152, 194
mergers and acquisitions (M&A), 12, 49, 59, 133, 137–8, 143, 148, 178, 181–3
Middle East, 38, 40
MMK, 100
modernization theory, 4
Mongolia, 160
Morocco, 160, 166
MW Brands, 181, 183–4

NAFTA, 72–3, 156
national business systems, 21–2, 79, 110–11, 113, 115–17, 125
national champions, 12, 36, 39, 41, 83, 90, 93, 107, 158–9, 169, 182, 186, 191, 196
National Monetary Council (Britain), 137
Natura, 143, 147
neoliberalism, 3, 8, 15, 19, 26, 67, 69, 71–2
Netherlands, 23, 97, 104, 161, 163–4
New Zealand, 23, 166, 176
NGO, 59, 87, 195
Nippon Steel, 170
Nissan, 45, 66
NLMK, 100
NordGold, 100
Norilsk Nikel, 100
Norway, 23, 36, 166

Odebrecht, 10, 147, 151
OECD, 17, 26–7, 55, 58, 61, 70, 74, 156, 159–61, 195–6
offshoring, 158
OPEC, 32, 40
Original Equipment Manufacturers (OEM), 183, 185
Ownership, Location and Internationalization (OLI), 130
Oxiteno, 135, 147

patent laws, 10, 73–5, 119, 120–1, 124, 127–8, 191
Peru, 145, 160–2, 166
Petrobras, 1, 10, 133

Index 231

political networks, 5, 82, 86–8, 90–4, 98, 100–1, 106–8, 188–9
Portugal, 136, 138, 143–7, 161, 164–5, 184
POSCO, 59, 63–6, 68, 76
Post-Washington consensus, 15
preferential trade agreements, 175
private equity, 66, 76, 183
privatization, 8, 19, 26, 33, 37–8, 58–60, 62–4, 69, 72, 74–5, 91, 104, 134–5, 151, 191–2
product cycle theory, 1, 130, 197
property rights, 12, 73, 93, 111, 123, 127, 190–1, 194
protectionism, 3, 11, 43, 48, 157, 159, 160–1, 165, 168

Randon, 143
Renova, 99, 100
rent-seeking, 8, 68–71, 74
research and development (R&D), 7–8, 45–6, 48, 59, 65–9, 73–6, 122, 124–6, 143
resource extraction, 7, 38, 43, 49
resource-seeking, 47
reverse engineering, 81, 19, 127, 191
Romania, 104, 160, 165
Romi, 143, 147
Rosneft, 99–100, 102–3, 105, 107
round tripping, 97
Rusal, 100
Russia, 1, 9, 16, 37–8, 80, 90–108, 132, 135, 160–1, 166, 189, 194
Russian economy, 91–2, 96, 99
Russian government, 93, 94, 96
Russian MNCs, 9, 90–108

Sabó, 143, 147
Samsung, 1, 57, 62–6, 69, 70–3, 76, 170
SASAC, 83
Saudi Arabia, 160, 166
Sberbank, 95
Schumpeter, Joseph, 7, 43, 51, 170
Serb Republic, 105
Severstal, 100
Seychelles, 184
shareholder value, 8, 22, 25, 57–60, 62–3, 69, 71, 75–6, 188

Singapore, 20, 34, 36, 47, 49
Sinopec, 1
Sistema, 100
SK Group, 62, 64, 73, 76
Slovakia, 79, 165
small and medium sizes enterprises, 60–2, 72–3
South Africa, 160, 166
South Korea, 1, 3–6, 8, 29, 34, 40, 47–9, 55–76, 166, 170
South-South cooperation, 194
Sovcomflot, 99–100
sovereign wealth funds (SWF), 36, 38
Soviet Union (USSR), 3, 37–8, 96, 101, 103, 105
Spain, 135–6, 143–4, 146, 157, 161, 163–5, 168
Ssangyong, 62, 76
Starkist, 181
state capitalism, 1–12, 34–9, 41, 50–1, 55, 78–9, 85, 89, 90–108, 149, 156, 168, 187, 196–7
state-owned banks, 72, 78, 84, 95, 99, 149, 182, 186, 189
state-owned/-controlled enterprises (SOE), 4, 5, 8–9, 27, 36–9, 50, 62, 77–8, 81–5, 88, 91, 95, 102–7, 119, 131–4, 189
state-permeated market economy (SME), 78–81, 89
Sun Pharmaneuticals, 122
SVR (Russian foreign intelligence service), 96
Switzerland, 23, 100, 147, 166

Taiwan, 19, 29, 34, 36, 47–9, 56–7, 77, 170
Tallard, 138
Tamil Nadu Technology Development & Promotion Center, 126
tariffs, 3, 72–3, 89, 171–5, 178, 180
Tata Motor, 1, 45
taxation, 40, 72, 82–3, 85, 97–9, 124, 127, 141, 149–50, 158, 169, 184–5, 188, 193–4
Thai Ruamsin Pattana, 183
Thai Union Frozen (TUF), 12, 171–2, 181, 183–6

Thailand, 1, 6, 12, 29, 169–86
TNK-BP, 99–100, 103
Toyota, 48, 170
Transatlantic Trade and Investment Partnership (TTIP), 195
transition economies, 98, 162–3
Trans-Pacific Partnership Agreement (TPP), 195
Treaty of Lisbon, 11, 156–7, 160
Treaty of Rome, 160
Trilateral Commission, 88
TRIMS, 156
TRIPS, 127, 194–5
Tunisia, 160, 166
Tupy, 140, 143, 147–8

Ukraine, 101–2, 160, 166
UNCTAD, 1, 38 156, 159, 162
UNCTAD transnationality index (TNI), 19–21, 29
United Kingdom, 3–4, 7, 24, 25, 27–8, 79, 118–19, 143, 146–7
United States, 1, 3–6, 8, 12, 17–18, 37–8, 48–9, 62, 72–5, 104–6, 138, 142, 151–2, 156, 160–6, 170–6, 191, 194–5
Uppsala model, 130
Uruguay, 164, 177

Uzbekistan, 104

Vale, 10, 140, 145, 147
varieties of capitalism (VoC), 16, 19, 22–3, 25, 28–9, 113–17, 125, 188
Venezuala, 102–3, 105, 164, 179
Vietnam, 37–8, 49, 105
Virgin Islands, 95
Vneshekonombank (VEB), 95, 105
Vneshtorgbank, 95
Voluntary Export Restraint (VER), 48
Votorantim, 10, 145, 147

Washington Consensus, 15, 19, 20, 33, 156, 161
WEF (World Economic Forum), 88
WEG, 138, 147
Western MNCs, 2, 81, 87, 192–3
Woori Bank, 60
World Bank, 15, 19, 56, 166
World Organisation for Animal Health (OIE), 175, 178
WTO, 127, 137, 171–5, 178, 180, 194, 196

Zarubezhneft, 100, 104–5, 107
ZTE, 50
Zydus Cadila, 122–4, 129

Printed and bound by CPI Group (UK) Ltd, Croydon, CR0 4YY